TOBAGO

THE UNION WITH TRINIDAD 1889–1899

TOBAGO

THE UNION WITH TRINIDAD 1889–1899

Myth and Reality

LENNIE M. NIMBLETT

authorHOUSE®

AuthorHouse™ UK
1663 Liberty Drive
Bloomington, IN 47403 USA
www.authorhouse.co.uk
Phone: 0800.197.4150

Published by AuthorHouse   04/21/2016

ISBN: 978-1-4772-3450-1 (sc)
ISBN: 978-1-4772-3449-5 (hc)
ISBN: 978-1-4772-3451-8 (e)

Library of Congress and Control Number: 2012919201

**To my colleagues
of the**
Tapia House Movement

CONTENTS

List of Illustrations

LIST OF MAPS

PROLOGUE

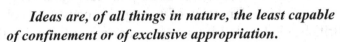

Ideas are, of all things in nature, the least capable of confinement or of exclusive appropriation.
Thomas Jefferson[1]

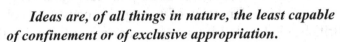

THE IDEA IS LEGENDARY among residents of Tobago that at some time in its past, the island enjoyed great political independence administered through great political institutions. That this independence was lost and its institutions destroyed in 1889, when the island was annexed to Trinidad, is also part of the folklore. Indeed, much of what is believed about the union continues to be shrouded in myth, and to some extent the legal status of the island during the seventeenth century remains a mystery. With this mindset most people balk at the idea that the government of Tobago was subordinate to that of Grenada in the period prior to the union. Despite the availability of a handful of historical accounts by local and foreign authors, the ignorance about this and other important historical facts about Trinidad and Tobago point to a problem of inadequate political education. In some respects the historical accounts themselves fall short, and to that extent they contribute to the ongoing woolly ideas about the union.

---

[1] Cited in Peterson, Merrill D., *Thomas Jefferson and the New Nation: A Biography*, Oxford: Oxford University Press, 1970, p. 90.

THE NEED FOR A NEW SOLUTION

In the 1880s, after almost 120 years of British colonialism, Tobago was recognised as a failed colony, and so the need arose for a fresh constitutional solution. While the colony continued to enjoy great security, particularly when compared with its status during the seventeenth and eighteenth centuries, the majority of the people suffered from the general absence of welfare, resulting in unrest and steady emigration; moreover, the elaborate constitutional structure left the same majority bereft of basic political rights. The failure did not come about for want of trying. Its constitutional status under British rule had left it with headquarters in Grenada, then in Barbados, then in Grenada again, while its status changed from a self-governing entity to a Crown colony. There was a brief period of French rule, but this did not significantly alter the constitution or laws of the colony.

Throughout this period, more so before 1834, Tobago was virtually a slave society, and the majority of the people had almost no rights. The concept of welfare existed only spasmodically at the initiative of a few persons with religious motives. Following emancipation, the civil rights of the people improved but only with great resistance from the leaders. At the same time the decline of the economy resulted in a deterioration of general welfare. When the economy finally ground to a halt in 1882, the time had come for firm decisions to be taken about the future of the colony.

THE OBSCURE ORIGIN OF THE UNION

The change came in the form of a union with the neighbouring British colony of Trinidad. The idea of a union between Trinidad and Tobago did not come about whimsically in 1888 nor, as has been suggested, because the British government was seeking to rid itself of the economic situation in Tobago. As long ago as 1666, Dutch explorers foresaw the possibility of trade between the two neighbouring islands. Nevertheless, while the Colonial Office[2] played a major part in the executive action that established the union, the idea of the union had a somewhat prolonged gestation. The notion that the political institution in Tobago was unviable was first brought to the attention of the Colonial Office by Lieutenant Governor H. T. Ussher in 1872. Lieutenant Governor Augustus Frederick Gore confirmed in 1877 the lack of viability and went further to suggest the union with Trinidad. The Crossman Commission of 1882 sought to mitigate the problems of Tobago in constitutional change within the Windward Islands Group that then included Tobago. Sir William Robinson suggested the depopulation of Tobago, and finally Mr Walter J. Sendall, the governor of Tobago, then based in Grenada, proposed annexation. These administrators displayed a sense of altruism that is peculiarly absent from modern commentators on the union. If the Colonial Office is to be faulted in this matter it is not for ramming the union down the throats of the natives but for being unduly prolix in bringing about the change that was so necessary. The actions of these bold men resulted in 1888 in an Order in Council from the Colonial Office that brought the two islands together under a common governor with common laws, but with Tobago maintaining its own treasury. The near disaster that followed this somewhat hasty arrangement gave birth to a second idea: that Tobago should be a ward of the colony of Trinidad and Tobago.

The origin of the latter idea remains as obscure as the origin of the idea of the union. That Tobago should be governed as an administrative district of Trinidad and Tobago is at the root of the constitutional arrangements that have legally bound the two islands since 1898. One would have expected the notion to arise from a resolution of the Legislative Council of Trinidad and Tobago, the Financial Board of Tobago, the Colonial Office, or the British Parliament which were the law-making bodies for Trinidad and Tobago in 1894. Instead, the

---

[2] "The initiative for the union of Trinidad and Tobago came neither from Tobago nor from Trinidad but from the Secretary of State for the Colonies." Williams, Dr. E. E., *History of the People of Trinidad and Tobago*, Brooklyn, New York: A & B Publishing, 1993, p. 169.

idea came from the pen of Mr William Gordon-Gordon as a footnote to a report of a committee of which he was a member.

Mr Gordon-Gordon was one of six members of a select committee of the Legislative Council of Trinidad and Tobago appointed to determine the loss of customs duties in Tobago that ensued from the rules of the Order in Council of 1888. The Select Committee submitted its report on January 1894, and Mr Gordon-Gordon, in signifying his agreement with the contents of the report, appended the following note:

> *"I approve the foregoing Report with the addition of the following words: That if Tobago could be made a ward of Trinidad and its affairs managed economically its position and prospects would be materially altered in a few years and it would become a valuable adjunct to Trinidad."*[3]

Thereafter the snowflake that was the idea grew into an avalanche, and it was little surprise that in the autumn of 1898, the Colonial Office issued an Order in Council that made Tobago a ward of Trinidad and Tobago and ended a decade of political uncertainty for the people of Tobago.

THE REASONS FOR AND NATURE OF THE UNION REMAIN MYSTERIOUS

Whenever the nation discusses constitution reform, the relationship between the two islands naturally comes into question. When one enters into a discussion on the subject one realises the vast chasm that exists about the knowledge of the subject of Tobago and its union with Trinidad. So casually is the topic regarded that A. N. R. Robinson, who went on to become in turn prime minister and president of Trinidad and Tobago, wrote a book in which he got the

---

[3] **Council Paper No. 22, 1894,** of the Legislative Council of Trinidad and Tobago.

date of the union wrong, not once but twice.[4] And if few persons can quote the date of the union correctly, fewer still would be aware of the origin of the idea. The basis for the constitutional arrangement between the two islands is not generally known; the circumstances that propelled Tobago into forming a union with Trinidad is often lost in the romanticism of an era of Caribbean splendour, Spanish gold, buccaneers, and the mythical wealth of London sugar barons.

> "Tobago *had considerable economic and strategic importance for most European powers. After 1802, when Tobago, together with Trinidad, became a British possession, it proved to be one of the most prosperous sugar islands and assumed greater importance in British colonial policy than Trinidad. The Governor of Trinidad considered his transfer to Tobago a promotion.*"[5]

While the statement may not be entirely accurate or at best merely reflect the poor judgement of the governor, it does embody an idyllic but popular view of what Tobago was.[6] But Premdas has no explanation and offers none as to why Tobago, despite its great prosperity and greater importance, had to be annexed to Trinidad which, like Tobago, produced sugar and was subject to the same constraints.

Some doubts remain about the nature of the union. Was the union intended to be federal or unitary? Did Tobago lose a superior constitution for something that was inferior? To dispel the mystery that surrounds the union of Tobago with Trinidad, therefore, it is

---

[4]   Robinson, A. N. R., *The Mechanics of Independence*, Cambridge, MA and London: MIT Press, 1971, pp. 22-23.

[5]   Premdas, Ralph R., *Secession and Self-Determination in the Caribbean: Nevis and Tobago,* Port-of-Spain, Trinidad: UWI School of Continuing Studies, 1998, p. 103.

[6]   "The island of Tobago is a small island situated some forty [sic] miles north-east of Trinidad. Thanks to Daniel Defoe who placed his famous Robinson Crusoe on its shores, it has enjoyed renown far out of proportion to its importance." Crouse, Nellis M., *French Struggle for the West Indies (1665-1713)*, New York, NY: Columbia University Press, 1966, p. 116.

worthwhile to trace the origin of the idea for producing this book. It is only when we look at the background of the decision making process that we begin to understand the economic, social, and political problems that propelled Tobago towards the union with Trinidad.

The world in which Tobago found itself in 1888 was vastly different from when the country was ceded to Britain in 1763. At the end of the Seven Years War, Britain was the unchallenged ruler of the seas and controlled a great part of the growing international trade that made her the workshop to the world in the heyday of the first British Empire. By 1888 Britain had lost the American Colonies (1776), and the Congress of Vienna (1815) had secured a long period of peace for the warring countries of Europe. The sugar industry,[7] that was a source of so much wealth that Britain enjoyed during the seventeenth century, had declined to the point where it became problematic in the West Indies by the end of the nineteenth century.

Economically, by 1888, the thrust of the empire had shifted from the Atlantic to the Pacific; the American colonies were lost, the Suez Canal was opened (providing quicker access to the Far East), and both Germany and the United States of America were beginning to challenge the economic power of Britain. In fact a second empire had emerged, embracing people scattered over the globe and presenting fresh challenges. In international law, the trading in Negro slaves was abolished and slavery itself was abolished in keeping with the new humanitarianism generated by the American Declaration of Independence, the French Revolution, and the revolution in Haiti.

Politically, the Parliament and the Cabinet in Britain continued to encroach upon the authority of the Royal prerogative exercised over the colonies. Moreover, the political independence of these colonies

---

[7]   "The profits of a sugar plantation in any of our West Indian colonies are generally much greater than those of any other cultivation that is known either in Europe or in America." Smith, Adam, cited by Williams, Dr. E. E., in *Britain and the West Indies*, the University of Essex Noel Buxton Lecture, London: Longmans, 1969, p. 4.

presented fresh problems for the government of the empire. In the slave colonies that had self-governing assemblies, there was great resistance to the abolition of slavery, as there was to earlier attempts at amelioration of the condition of the slaves. When matters came to a head in Jamaica with the Morant Bay riots (1868), the British government moved swiftly to impose Crown colony government throughout the Caribbean region.

And if the economics and the politics had changed so too did political economy. At the end of the nineteenth century we see Britain moving to adopt a more responsible role for the development of the colonies in recognition of the roles of education and the development of physical infrastructure in economic development. All of these changing trends brought pressure to bear on the governance of Tobago, and when eventually the crunch came, union was the best option available.

THE ISSUE OF POLITICAL EDUCATION

The uncertainty that surrounds the history of Tobago is one of the motives for producing this book. Not only is the history uncertain, but only a minority of the citizenry is aware of this fundamental facet of the constitution of the unitary state. It is hoped, therefore, that the material here would assist in the political education of the people of Trinidad and Tobago.

Because of its late start, Trinidad has always lagged the rest of the West Indies in political education. The evidence for this need is both ancient and legion. In his report on the inquiry into the state of public education in Trinidad in 1869, Patrick Keenan, Chief of Inspection of the Board of National Education, Ireland, had this to say:

> "The books which I found in use ... no set of primary school books ever previously published in the English language could surpass or even equal them. But notwithstanding their recognized excellence and reputation, I should desire to see them superseded by a set of books whose lessons would be racy of the colony—descriptive of

> its **history**, of its resources, of its trade, of its natural
> phenomena, of its trees, plants, flowers, fruits, birds,
> fishes, etc."[8]

The inadequacy of the curriculum of the education system did not require the independent opinion of Patrick Keenan but was well articulated earlier in 1858 by local sage Dr L. A. A. de Verteuil:

> "It is really surprising how uninformed even Trinidadians
> are regarding their own country. Our best school boys are
> able to give the names of the chief rivers and the position
> of the principal towns of Great Britain, France, and even
> in Russia and China; but they are ignorant, perhaps,
> of the manes of the Guatero and Oropuche, or through
> what country the Caroni has its course . . . Not only is
> such ignorance discreditable, but its effects cannot but be
> prejudicial to the best interests, and consequently to the
> advancement of the colony."[9]

While Keenan's advice was directed to Trinidad in 1869 it clearly applied to Trinidad and Tobago after the union of 1889. In terms of political education, the people of Tobago were marginally better off, benefiting as they did from the presence of a relatively larger number of immigrants from Barbados which had an unquestionably longer tradition of parliamentary proceedings.

The parlous state of political education in Trinidad may be gleaned from a reading of the reports of the Royal Franchise Commission of 1889 at about the same time that the union of Trinidad and Tobago was born. This Commission is of historical importance as it is among the earliest of a long sequence of political moves that sought to alter the Constitution of Trinidad from the Crown colony as it then was. The commission was established pursuant to a petition sent to the

---

[8]   Cited in Williams, Dr. E. E., *History of the People of Trinidad and Tobago*, New York, NY: A & B Publishing, 1993, pp. 200-201.

[9]   De Verteuil, Dr. L. A. A., *Trinidad*, cited in Cudjoe, Dr. Selwyn R., *Beyond Boundaries*, Wellesley, MA: Calaloux Publications, 2009, p. 156.

Crown from a relatively few citizens, the bulk of whom it was felt did not understand its contents. The main report from which the chairman, Stephen H. Gatty, the attorney general, dissented, was rejected by the Colonial Office. In his minority report Mr Gatty noted the following:

> *"In my opinion the Franchise suggested by the majority of the Commissioners would not constitute an intelligent judgment on public affairs and would not ensure the fair representation of all the interests in the island. I therefore dissent from the recommendations of the majority.*
>
> *"I have further humbly to report that in the present circumstances of Trinidad an electorate to consist of persons qualified by knowledge and education and at the same time represent all interests in the island cannot be found. An electorate based upon the representatives of all interests would necessarily include a very large number of ignorant and illiterate persons."[10]*

The deputy chairman of the Commission was the illustrious and long serving Dr L. A. A de Verteuil. He was virtually the author of the report since the chairman had dissented and elected to submit a minority report. Dr de Verteuil was naturally disappointed with the rejection of the majority report and had this to say to his fellow commissioners at a meeting after the governor had disclosed the decision given by the secretary of state:

> *"Gentlemen, I beg to say a few words before we close this meeting. You have heard the decision of the Secretary of State and the reasons why he came to that decision. I say this: His decision will be received by a large number of persons in this Colony, with indifference, by some with satisfaction and by others and by us—I mean the majority of the Commission—with regret that we have not been granted what we considered ought to have been, or rather*

---

[10] Minority Report of the Royal Franchise Commission (Trinidad) of 1889.

*might have been of benefit to this Colony. But those who will come after us will doubtless be granted what has now been refused to us and what I advise you to do, if I can offer you advice at this table, is that you should prepare yourselves by education and industry to really become worthy of the boon which you desire should be given to you. I believe the time must come when the people of Trinidad will be called upon to take an interest in their own affairs. There may be now some reason for which this boon is deferred for the present moment, but I am sure that eventually, **if the people are educated, they will receive it but until they become more or less educated and fit for the Franchise, the time will be postponed** [my emphasis]. These are the words which I wish to address to you before closing the business of this meeting."[11]*

Dr L. A. A. de Verteuil

---

[11]   The source for this quotation is lost: most probable source is *Public Opinion*, extant Trinidad newspaper, 1888.

The political indifference to a franchise in 1889 was in keeping with the lukewarm reception that the union met in Trinidad in 1887 and, if anything, confirmed the low level of political awareness that prevailed at that time. Indeed it is curious how cursorily this matter of such constitutional significance is treated in most of the books about the history of Trinidad and Tobago which came about in 1889. The centenary of the historic event passed without much public notice.

As we travel throughout the Caribbean, we are struck by a political sense of self-awareness that is absent from Trinidad and Tobago.

The weak political education and lagging political development has been the downside to the strong executive enjoyed in Trinidad since the advent of the Europeans. Particularly since the Cedula of Population in the 1770s and under the British after the conquest in 1797, the country has thrived on strong executive government. The evidence of this may be seen by comparing the progress of Trinidad with that of the other countries of the Caribbean since 1800. In the period that preceded the conquest, the historian James Millette describes Trinidad as a Spanish colonial slum. By 1889, however, its export trade had surpassed the older and larger colony of Jamaica. The strong executive government, which was characteristic of the Crown colony system, was no doubt a contributing factor to the country's rapid development. The strong executive of the colonial days was maintained despite the change of political status from colony to independent republic.

Dr Williams with an epoch changing effort, achieved tremendous success in getting rid of the legacy of political backwardness especially in party political education. Fifty years after his political lectures at Woodford Square, that venue is still referred to as the University of Woodford Square. Despite his Herculean effort, Dr Williams failed the test as proposed by Aristotle, for whom the main goal of education was good citizenship or proper participation in the affairs of the State. Williams's shortcoming, in my opinion, was his failure to include and integrate political education into the broader state education programme. Nevertheless, in the intervening period much progress has been made with social studies, compulsory courses on Caribbean studies at the University of the West Indies, mock parliaments, and so on. But if one is to judge from the comments made on current political discourse by many experts, we must conclude that the political education falls short in two areas in particular: in knowledge of the constitution and in the historical knowledge of the Union of Trinidad and Tobago.

CONCLUSION

To put it simply, the purpose of the book is threefold: *to show precisely* the events, circumstances, and persons that led to the formation of the Union of Trinidad and Tobago; *to remove some of the wool* in which the decision to form the union has been shrouded by historians; and in so doing *to highlight the need pointed out by Keenan in the middle of the nineteenth century for relevant content in our education programme.* The book therefore should be seen as a timely effort to enhance our understanding the background to the constitutional problem of Tobago as we contemplate reform of the constitution. The purpose of the work is not so much to cast new light on the history of Tobago as it is to illuminate dark areas of the decision making process that went into making the union; to illuminate the early problems generated by the union and how they were resolved; and to illuminate the peculiar nature of the union and the early growing pains experienced so as to better understand the reasons for the existence of the ties that bind together these two former British colonies situated at the edge of the hurricane belt in the south of the Caribbean.

The most effective way of presenting the historical information is to let the facts speak for themselves. Chapter I deals with the chronology of events before the union; chapter II outlines the constitution and the society. Chapter III documents the growth in relations between the two colonies and the decision making processes in the Caribbean while chapter IV does likewise in England. Chapters V and VI describe the new colony and the teething problems experienced in the first decade that threatened to disrupt its unity. Chapters VII and IX deal with matters of the historiography by examining some views of the historians on the union, and their judgements on the decision are examined briefly. Chapter VIII deals with a political analysis of the political institutions of Tobago.

In covering those topics the following historical documents were included: Resolution of the Tobago Legislative Council; the Resolution of the Trinidad Legislative Council; the Trinidad and Tobago Act passed by the British Parliament; the Order in Council of 1888; the Proclamation in Port-of-Spain of the governor's authority over Tobago; the Order in Council of 1898. The book could have ended with the Order in Council of 1888 were it not for the fact that it turned out to be a false start. Amid this turmoil came the Gordon-Gordon suggestion that resulted in the issue of a second Order in Council of 1898 that settled the matter decisively. The idea was not original since it could be found in the recommendations of several administrators that preceded him. It was, however, the right idea at the right time and led ultimately to the decision that created the cornerstone of the Constitution of Trinidad and Tobago. Contemporary political opinion about the union is no doubt strongly influenced by the written history and to some extent by the oral history of the relationship between the two islands. Some of the many myths that persist about the union are dealt with to dispel widely held but erroneous views about the union. It is hoped that this will provide a factual basis for what brought about the union and dispel some of the myths that persist some 120 years after the event took place. Finally, in the Epilogue, I give my own judgement on the conditions that led to the union and to the process of arriving at the union.

The vision of the two islands living in harmony precedes the union by some 220 years as was expressed in a memorial prepared for the authorities of the United Provinces of Holland. Unfortunately the author of the vision remains unknown, and there, for now, rests the mystery of the origin of the Union of Trinidad and Tobago.

ACKNOWLEDGEMENTS

THE AUTHOR WISHES TO acknowledge the assistance rendered by the staffs of the Heritage Library, the National Archives, the Parliament Library, and the Law Library in retrieving some of material contained herein. I also wish to thank the Library of Congress, the Staff at AuthorHouse and the Author Learning Centre.

A profound debt of gratitude is owed to the following historians whose work provided the majority of the material of the nineteenth century Trinidad and Tobago on which the author relied: Dr James Millette, Dr E. E. Williams, Prof Bridget Brereton, Mr. C. R. Ottley, Dr Susan E. Craig-James, Mr A. N. R. Robinson, Dr Ralph Premdas, and Mr Rupert Douglas Archibald.

Thanks to Mr Justice Hamel Smith and Mr Bernard Shepherd, notary public, for assistance in accessing the Law Library at the Hall of Justice.

I also wish to thank Father De Verteuil for reading an early draft and for his comments thereon; he and Dr Beckles for reading the manuscript; Dr. Susan Craig-James for her incisive comments on Chapter VII;.

The images of *Pope Alexander VI* and *Christopher Columbus* are in the public domain and were copied from Wikipedia. The images of *Lord Glanville* and *The Catholic Kings* are in the public domain {{PD-1996}} were copied from Wikipedia. The image of *Sir Henry Wylie Norman* (1895) is by an unknown author and released by the

State Library of Queensland, Australia. The family photograph of *Si John Gorrie* is reproduced from *Law Justice and Empire: The Colonial Career of Sir John Gorrie 1829-1892* and published by University of the West Indies Press with the kind permission of Professor Bridget Brereton. The photographs of *Sir William Robinson, Sir F. Napier Broome, Sir H. R. H. Jerningham* and *Mr William Gordon Gordon* together with the image of *Lowlands Estate, Tobago 1838*, are reproduced with the kind courtesy of Mr Adrian Camps-Campins

The image of Mr C. R. Ottley is reproduced with the kind permission of his son Mr Ronald Ottley. The images of Dr E. E. Williams and Mr A. N. R. Robinson are reproduced with the kind permission of the Government Information Service Limited of Trinidad and Tobago, owners of the copyright.

The *Atlantic Map showing the Papal Donation* is reproduced with the permission of Encyclopaedia Britannica owners of the copyright. The portrait of William Murray, 1st Earl of Mansfield by the artist John Singleton Copley is licensed by the National Portrait Gallery of Britain.

While the valuable contribution of so many persons is readily recognized the errors that remain in the book are all of my own making.

Author's Note

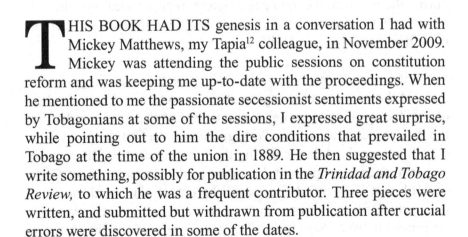

Neither acquiescence in scepticism nor acquiescence in dogma is what education should produce. What it should produce, is a belief that knowledge is attainable in a measure, though with difficulty; that much of what passes for knowledge at any given time is likely to be more or less mistaken, but that the mistakes can be rectified by care and industry.

Bertrand Russell, ***On Education.***

THIS BOOK HAD ITS genesis in a conversation I had with Mickey Matthews, my Tapia[12] colleague, in November 2009. Mickey was attending the public sessions on constitution reform and was keeping me up-to-date with the proceedings. When he mentioned to me the passionate secessionist sentiments expressed by Tobagonians at some of the sessions, I expressed great surprise, while pointing out to him the dire conditions that prevailed in Tobago at the time of the union in 1889. He then suggested that I write something, possibly for publication in the *Trinidad and Tobago Review,* to which he was a frequent contributor. Three pieces were written, and submitted but withdrawn from publication after crucial errors were discovered in some of the dates.

---

[12] The Tapia House Movement is a political organization akin to the Fabian Society. Founded by Lloyd Best, economist and publicist, it publishes the *Trinidad and Tobago Review.*

My original interest in the Tobago matter was sparked by Selwyn Cudjoe's memoir of 1999 of Michel Maxwell Phillip[13], who as acting attorney general had moved the motion for union in the Trinidad Legislature. In pursuing the matter at the National Archives I made copious notes of the debates and problems surrounding the union in the period 1889 to 1899.

The motivation for publishing the book came from another source: Dr Neave Beckles, an old colleague at St. Andrews University who in 2008 sent me a copy of his *Wasting Opportunities for Quality-of-Life in Trinidad and Tobago*. After trying for many years, Neave finally persuaded me that rather than embed the work in a larger book, as I was contemplating, I should take it to press in the form of a booklet. He also provided valuable information about ISBN, copyrights, paper size, printing, marketing, and so on.

Writing the book, nevertheless, had at least two unintended consequences. Firstly, it brought me face to face with the endemic problem of the West Indian assemblies, with the executive subordinate to the Legislature. This problem of constitutional conflict that dogged the West Indian assemblies and devastated Jamaica and Tobago during the nineteenth century is inherent in all political systems, as Montesquieu discerned, and can only be overcome with the deftest of political skill and good will.

Secondly, it made me aware of certain gaps that exist in pertinent areas of the history of the region: there is no translation in English of the Treaty of Medina del Campo that set the tone for sharing the discoveries made by the Portuguese and the Spaniards on their expeditions in the Atlantic during the fifteenth century; there is no access to such an important document as the Barbados Slave Code of 1661 that influenced the establishment of slavery throughout the early British Empire; and there was uncertainty over the agreement between Sir Thomas Warner of England and Sieur Belain

---

[13] Cudjoe, Selwyn R.,(Ed.), *Michel Maxwell Philip*, Wellesley, MA: Calaloux Publications, 1999

d'Esnambuc of France in 1627 regarding the neutrality of a number of islands in the Caribbean.

If this book succeeds in furthering the cause of political education in Trinidad and Tobago, it will be an added bonus if it generates research into these dark areas of our history.

Lennie M. Nimblett
St. Anns
Trinidad
2012-08-31.

CHAPTER I

Tobago in the Changing Atlantic World

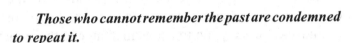

*Those who cannot remember the past are condemned
to repeat it.*
George Santayana, *The Life of Reason, Vol. I*

BACKGROUND TO THE COLONISATION OF TOBAGO

THE DISCOVERY OF TOBAGO by Columbus in 1498 had its genesis in an Iberian initiative taken more than sixty years before. Ferdinand V of Aragon and Isabella I of Castile, known as the Catholic Kings of Spain, had at their disposal in their negotiations between 1486 and 1492 with Christopher Columbus, the Treaty of Alcáçovas of 1479 with John II of Portugal.[14] The treaty was the basis for the allotment of the lands of the then undiscovered world to the two exploring countries of the Iberian Peninsula. The Spaniards were ecstatic over the offer by Columbus, who had earlier taken his proposition to the Portuguese. The latter, under the drive of

---

[14] This treaty confirmed the Treaty of Medina del Campo of 1431 between Juan I of Portugal and Juan II of Castile: a treaty of peace, it agreed to a division of islands known and to be discovered from navigation of the Atlantic Ocean.

1

Henry the Navigator and inspired by the *reconquista*, had discovered and settled both the Madeira (1420) and the Açores (1427) and had established successful trading posts for slaves and gold down the west coast of Africa. Moreover, by 1488 they had gone around the Cape of Africa and into what became known as the Indian Ocean. In contrast to the Portuguese, Columbus proposed to get to India by sailing west across the Atlantic. With the benefits anticipated from his proposed enterprise, the Catholic Kings acceded to the exorbitant requests of Columbus.

After the latter's first successful voyage in 1492, Pope Alexander VI, then resident in Spain, issued a Papal Bull, known to historians as the Papal Donation, that set up a line of demarcation from pole to pole at a hundred miles from the Cape Verde Islands, with the lands to the west of it going to Spain and those to the east of it to Portugal. It was not unusual for the pope to act as mediator in those matters: arising from differences over the Treaty of Medina del Campo in 1431, the pope in 1437 was asked to mediate between Portugal and Castile on matters concerning the status of the Canary Islands.

Christopher Columbus

The Catholic Kings

Pope Alexander VI

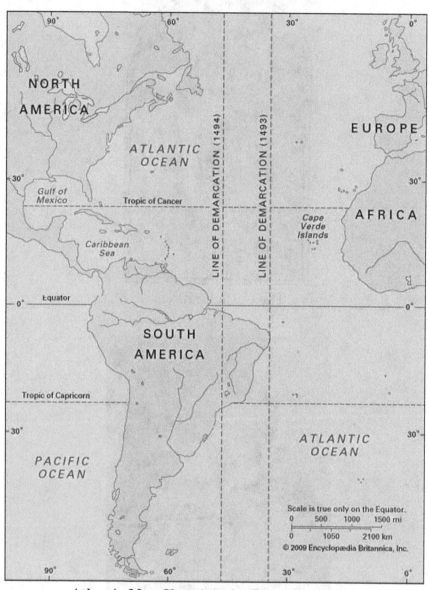

Atlantic Map Showing the Papal Donation

In 1452 and 1456, Papal Bulls granted to Portugal a monopoly of trade with newly discovered lands.

The Portuguese disputed the terms contained in the Bull issued after Columbus's initial discoveries, and at the Treaty of Tordesillas in 1494 a new line of demarcation was fixed and agreed at 370 leagues west of the Cape Verde Islands. As diplomats spread the news of this agreement, of the agreement of the Catholic Kings with Columbus, and of the latter's discoveries, a mad scramble ensued for the new territories in the Western World, resulting eventually in the separation of church from state, a new doctrine called the balance of power, and the rise of the modern European states.[15] It is remarkable how rapidly thereafter the stage was set for the conflict between the European countries that raged for the next three hundred years. In 1496 Columbus was wooed to England, only to be warned off by the Catholic Kings. In 1497 Henry VII of England, not unlike the Catholic Kings, in return for new lands to be discovered, issued Letters Patent to Henry Cabot and his sons, granting them a monopoly of trade with Bristol. In 1498 the Spanish ambassador again complained to England, and in 1526 Francis I of France stated in relation to the great bounty enjoyed by Spain with its discoveries in the New World:

> *"The sun shines on me as on all others. I should be happy to see the clause in Adam's will which excluded me from my share when the world was being divided."*[16]

In addition to formal warfare, Spanish galleons carrying bullion of gold and silver were the targets of numerous pirates on the high seas. In 1562 the English formally denounced the Papal Donation; in 1579 the Union of Utrecht empowered the Netherlands to join in the

---

[15] "The medieval concept of an united and stratified Christian Europe ruled from on high by the Pope and the Holy Roman Emperor gave way to the idea of a system of states based on the principle of equal rights." *Encyclopaedia Britannica*, p. 1082, *Macropaedia Vol. 6*, 1975.

[16] Williams, Dr. E. E., *Documents of West Indian History, Vol. I*, New York, NY: A & B Publishing, 1994, p. 201.

fray; and by 1648 at the Treaty of Munster the Papal Donation was brought to an end.[17]

Although Columbus, on his third voyage in August 1498, reportedly caught sight of the Island of Tobago to the northeast when he left Trinidad through the Gulf of Paria, he did not make landfall but merely named it Assumption, in accordance with the liturgical calendar. The name "Tobago" derives from "Tavaco," a form of long stemmed pipe used by Amerindians in a communal rite of inhaling the smoke of the native weed now known as tobacco. The discovery of the island, in accordance with the Treaty of Tordesillas, was sufficient to establish a claim by Spain. But because Columbus meticulously recorded in his diary the details of that voyage, it was a simple matter for mariners to follow the route that he took and to locate the islands. The stage was set for conflict in the Caribbean and South Atlantic by the terms of the Treaty of Cateau-Cambrésis of 1559.[18] Tobago thus became what we call today a political football[19] of the European nations in an age of war and piracy played out in the Caribbean.[20] The wars that were fought in Europe were simultaneously waged in the Caribbean, and the fluctuating fate of Tobago was shared with other islands that included Grenada, St. Lucia, and Martinique.

---

[17]   Ibid., p. 207.

[18]   "West of the prime meridian and south of the Tropic of Cancer—violence done by either party to the other side shall not be regarded as in contravention of the treaties." Cited in Williams, Dr. E. E., *History of the People of Trinidad and Tobago*, New York, NY: A & B Publishing, 1994, pp. 222.

[19]   "No island in the Caribbean has had a more tortuous history than Tobago." Robinson, A. N. R., *The Mechanics of Independence*, Cambridge, MA and London: MIT Press, 1971, p. 19.

[20]   "During the twenty years of the war with Spain, 1585-1604, there was 'no peace beyond the line' and the value of prize money brought to England from the Caribbean ranged from £100,000 to £200,000 per year. Privateering, linked directly to contraband trades, continued to be important well into the century." Beckles, Hilary McD., *The Hub of Empire: The Caribbean and Britain in the Seventeenth Century*. In Canny, Nicholas (Ed.), *The Oxford History of the British Empire, Vol. I*, Oxford: Oxford University Press, 1998, p. 216.

THE CLIMATE AND NATURAL HISTORY

Located approximately at Latitude 11° north and Longitude 61° west, the island in its pristine state was sparsely populated by two Amerindian tribes, the peaceful Arawaks to the north and the warlike Caribs to the south. Its location to the south of the Windward Islands endowed it with a relatively low frequency of hurricane disruptions that was endemic throughout the region. Its harbours apart from the difficulty of access posed by coral reefs, are generally secure. The island had a tropical climate with temperatures varying between 22.5°C and 31°C and experienced annual rainfall of 167 cm, with a shape that approximates a cigar and with dimensions of 42 km and 11 km. The total population has been estimated at the time of discovery to be no more than fifteen hundred.

The island was known to many of the early European explorers that followed Columbus across the Atlantic, particularly those in search of the legendary El Dorado. Their ships stopped at Tobago for wood and water, but there was no earnest attempt to claim the island nor to colonise it. There were two principal impediments: the first was the hostility of the native Amerindians and the second appears to have been the inclemency of the climate, probably due to the yellow fever- or malaria-carrying mosquitoes and numerous marine dangers in approaching the island. In 1639, the first Courlanders to have landed there soon perished from disease. In 1688 Colonel John Scott in his descriptions published:

> *"The Goodnesse of the Land hath occasioned several to attempt the settlement, but have either with ye Feavor and Ague or by hands of the Native Proprietors, found little other welcome than a Resting place for their bones."*[21]

The water at the mouth of the Great Courland River was thought to be very unhealthy. In February 1787, General Comte Arthur Dillon, the French governor, reported that around Scarborough was

---

[21] Douglas Archibald, Rupert, *Tobago: Melancholy Isle, Vol. I, 1498-1771*, Port-of-Spain, Trinidad: Westindiana, 1987, p. 10.

hotter and more humid than in other French islands, and that this encouraged the soldiers to habitually drink in excess. He referred, also, to the marshes of the lower town, formed by two small rivers, from which dangerous exhalations arose. He said that the drinking water was of bad quality. In 1801, a fever resulted, and there is testimony for this in the church register that indicates a high incidence of deaths among the whites.[22] A violent contagious disease made its appearance at Fort King George towards the end of 1820 and proved to be fatal to many of the officers and to other ranks. This concern over the salubrity of the climate in Tobago is not misplaced and may well have been a factor in the high mortality rates of the slave population.[23]

Apart from the uncertainty over its healthiness, the island was well endowed for sustaining life with fertile and arable land, a plentiful supply of fish and game, and adequate fresh water in its rivers, with some of the latter capable of providing power for water driven mills. In preparing some information for the governing bodies in the United Provinces during the reoccupation of Tobago by the Dutch in 1667 after the Treaty of Breda, an unknown writer wrote:

> "A very good and temperate climate, about 20 fresh rivers which ran into the sea, very fresh in fish; many of the rivers run with such force especially in times of the rains, that they turn mills for the grinding of sugar canes. Fruit trees; other trees for producing lumber; limestone; clay for making pots; very arable land; ginger; sugar cane; indigo; cassia fistula; cacao; roucou; coconuts; oranges; lemons; tobacco; rice; cabbage; potatoes; many peas

---

[22]   Douglas Archibald, Rupert, *Tobago: Melancholy Isle, Vol. II, 1775-1815,* Port-of-Spain, Trinidad: UWI School of Continuing Studies, 1995, p. 130.

[23]   "In a study performed of the slave population in Trinidad where a registry was established in 1812, high mortality rates of slaves and Europeans alike were attributed to the harsh frontier environment." c.f. John, A. Meredith, *The Plantation Slaves of Trinidad, 1783-1816,* Cambridge University Press, 1988, p. 161.

*and beans; Turkish wheat; wild hogs; goats and all kinds
of fish and fowl."*[24]

In the period before the European countries started warring for
possession, the island was used by explorers for water and timber.
A comprehensive catalogue of the latter was made by the English
explorer Captain John Poyntz and published in a pamphlet in 1683.[25]

THE COLONISATION

The discovery of the huge continent of America and the several
islands of the Caribbean presented an opportunity to Spain to
extend its realm by establishing colonies in these new territories
that included Tobago. After some initial planning the colonisation
process was commenced in earnest.

- 1511: Ferdinand II, the king of Spain, issued a Cedula
  permitting persons to wage war against and to enslave
  and sell the Caribs of Tobago. The purpose of this law of
  Burgos was twofold: firstly to stop the mass extinction of
  the Amerindians that was taking place at the hands of the
  conquistadores and secondly to rid the Spaniards of the
  menace of the hostile Caribs.[26]
- 1596: Spain considered colonisation of Tobago as a means of
  subduing the Caribs and abating their attacks on Trinidad.
- 1614: A failed attempt was made by Johannes Roderigo of
  Spain to establish trade with the Caribs of Tobago.
- April 1628: After Jan de Moor received an exclusive franchise
  from the Dutch West India Company, an expedition under
  the command of Jacob Maersz arrived in Tobago in the first

---

[24] Douglas Archibald, Rupert, *Tobago: Melancholy Isle, Vol. I, 1498-1771,*
Port-of-Spain, Trinidad: Westindiana, 1987, p. 42.

[25] "The Present Prospect of the Famous and Fertile Island of Tobago with a
Description of the Situation, Growth, Fertility and Manufacture of the said
Island. To which is added Proposals for the Encouragement of all those that
are minded to settle there." Ibid., p. 56.

[26] Ibid., p. 7.

successful attempt by a European power at colonisation. He renamed the island "New Walcheren."

- 1628: Charles I of England by Letters Patent granted the island among other things to the Earl of Montgomery. The island was one of several in the West Indies putatively claimed by Sir Thomas on behalf of the English Crown on a journey to the Guianas during the late sixteenth century.
- 1629: The Dutch were driven off the island by Don Luis de Monsalves, then governor of Trinidad.
- 1632: The Dutch under Jan de Moor again attempted to settle the island and were subsequently driven out in 1636 by Don Diego Lopez de Escobar, governor of Trinidad.
- 1637: Puritans led by Rev. Nicholas Leverton, trying to escape the licentious life in Barbados, on learning that the island was vacated by the Dutch tried to settle Tobago but were defeated and driven out by the Caribs.
- 1639: The Courlanders made their first attempt to settle the island, landing at a point that now bears their name. That same year it appeared that the settlers succumbed to some sort of illness with the result that the island was abandoned.
- 1639: The Earl of Warwick acquired the Letters Patent from the Earl of Pembroke (formerly the Earl of Montgomery) and renewed the English claim. An expedition headed by Captain Robert Marsham landed in Tobago in October and was defeated by Caribs in Tobago and by Don Lopez de Escobar in Trinidad.
- 1642: Warwick made a second attempt under the command of Captain Marshall of Barbados who after a year of ceaseless attacks from the Caribs abandoned the island.
- The Treaty of Munster of 1648 signalled the end of the Papal Donation in giving recognition to Dutch possessions in the West Indies.
- 1651: The Courlanders acquired the Letters Patent from the Earl of Warwick. They occupied the island in the middle of 1654 and over the next four years made shipments of pepper, indigo, sugar, and tobacco to Europe.
- 1654: Adriaen and Cornelis Lampsius of the States General of the United Provinces (the Netherlands) on receipt of

Letters Patent from Louis XIV, king of France, fitted out an expedition and landed on the island and established a settlement at Rockley Bay. Since the Courlanders remained in settlement at Jacobus Bay this placed the ownership of the island in dispute. However there were no hostilities on account of an existing treaty between the Netherlands and the Duke of Courland.

- 1658: Charles X of Sweden invaded Courland and captured the Duke. Possession of Tobago passed to the Swedes. In the meantime the Courlanders on the island sold their rights to the Dutch for 500 reichsthalers, and the latter arranged for their return to Europe.
- 1660: The Treaty of Oliva released the Duke of Courland, and his claims in respect of Tobago reverted to him. His attempt to recover from the Dutch was rejected.
- 1662: The Dutch claim was strengthened by a grant of the island by Letters Patent from Louis XIV, king of France, to the brothers Adriaen and Cornelis Lampsius together with a renunciation by the French West India Company of their claim to settle the island.
- 1664: The Duke of Courland, a godson of James I, was granted Tobago by Charles I to plant for his heirs and successors as compensation for the destruction of a fort at the mouth of the Gambia River possessed by the duke that was destroyed by the Royal African Company.
- 1665: Jamaican buccaneers drove off the Dutch.
- 1666: The English (Willoughby of Barbados) moved in and paid off the Jamaican privateers.
- 1666: The French (Le Sieur Vincent of Grenada) captured Tobago.
- 1667: After the Treaty of Breda, signed by England, France, the Netherlands, and Denmark, the Dutch reoccupied Tobago, appointed Pieter Constant governor, and rebuilt Dutch Fort.
- 1670: The Treaty of Madrid ceded Spanish territory held by Britain in the West Indies.
- 1672: England declared war against the Netherlands and captured Tobago.

11

- 1673: The Dutch defeated the English in the third Anglo/ Dutch war and occupied Tobago in May 1674 after the Peace of Westminster.
- Early in 1677: The French failed to take Tobago but left the Dutch devastated and exhausted.
- Late in 1677: The French returned and captured Tobago.
- 1678: By the Treaty of Nijmegen, Tobago was ceded to France by the Dutch.
- The French abandoned the island and paid visits twice a year to ensure that their rights were not violated. The island remained in dispute between Britain and France and was essentially a neutral island between 1679 and 1763.
- 1684: The Treaty of Ratisbon ended piracy (buccaneerism) in the West Indies and confirmed the status quo at the Treaty of Nijmegen.
- 1748: The Treaty of Aix-la-Chapelle brought an end to hostilities carried out simultaneously in Europe (the War of Austrian Succession) and the Caribbean (the War of Jenkins' Ear). Not much was achieved as the treaty restored the status quo ante bellum. Tobago, Dominica, St. Lucia, and St. Vincent were confirmed as neutral islands, and the British and the French undertook to remove all their subjects who might have settled there, leaving those islands solely to the native Amerindians.
- Tobago formally ceded by France to Britain at the Treaty of Paris 1763 after the Seven Years War.
- 1763: The government of Grenada created by George III, King of Great Britain; it included Dominica, St. Vincent, Grenada and the Grenadines, St. Vincent, and Tobago.
- 1770: Dominica was separated from the government of Grenada and erected into a district seignory under the command of Sir William Young as captain general and governor-in-chief (assumed office on 22 April 1771).
- 1779: The French captured Grenada, severing its link with Tobago.
- The French captured Tobago during the hostilities over the American War of Independence in 1781.
- Tobago ceded to France at the Treaty of Paris 1783.

- 1793: Britain captured Tobago during the French revolutionary war.
- 1802: Tobago ceded to France at the Treaty of Amiens.
- 1803: Britain captured Tobago during the Napoleonic war.
- 1814: Tobago ceded to Britain at the Treaty of Paris.

A BRIEF RESPITE

In the period to 1763 Tobago was used as a trading post rather than a settled colony. In the intervening period various treaties— Treaty of Munster; Treaty of Breda; Treaty of Nijmegen; Treaty of Ratisbon; Treaty of Aix-la-Chapelle; Treaty of Amiens—brought peace in the short term but left the region divided between the emergent European powers after decimating the native Amerindian population. Ironically for Tobago, the peace that brought stability and got rid of the buccaneers brought with it economic decline. Despite the earnest efforts and partial successes of the Courlanders and the Dutch there was no legacy to show that the early colonists had established any form of what we can properly call government. Private treaties between the French and the English colonists in the Caribbean established several neutral islands for the safety of the Amerindians. After 1684, the behaviour of the French who acquired the island at the Treaty of Nijmegen seemed to conform to the belief that Tobago was a neutral island. The Treaty of Madrid of 1670, with Spain already a broken country, sounded the death knell of buccaneerism.

Map of the West Indies

With a new hegemony in the Atlantic in 1684 at the Treaty of Ratisbon piracy was formally put to an end throughout the Caribbean. The merry-go-round had a formal stop with the Treaty of Aix-la-Chapelle in 1748 but further hostilities led to the Treaty of Paris 1763, when Tobago was formally ceded by France to the United Kingdom. In keeping with the prevailing doctrine in Britain, these conquered lands belonged to the king, and the cession was soon followed by a formal attempt by Britain to establish a colony through the sale of newly acquired Crown lands. In 1763 George III named Tobago part of the government of Grenada that included Grenada, the Grenadines, St. Vincent, and Dominica. The group was known informally as the South Charibee Islands. The seat of the government was in Grenada and was led by the Governor-General General Robert Melville. Alexander Brown was appointed the first lieutenant governor of Tobago. After a petition in 1767 for the establishment of a Council, in 1768 Melville granted to Tobago the beginnings of local government when he granted a Council in 1768.[27]

In June 1768 a Legislature established with two chambers: the upper chamber or Council comprising the lieutenant governor, eleven appointed members, and a secretary. The lower house or Assembly would comprise thirteen elected members from well-defined constituencies. In the American War of Independence, the French were allies of the Americans and in 1781 captured Tobago from the British.

THE FRENCH INTERLUDE

The turmoil that began with Tobago's discovery by Columbus came to a halt temporarily with the Treaty of Paris in 1763 and finally ended with the Congress of Vienna. Tobago's relationship with Grenada was severed when the French captured Grenada in 1779 and between that date and 1781 fell under the control of the imperial government. Under French occupation the Articles of Capitulation were such that the British institutions were preserved:

---

[27]   Douglas Archibald, Rupert, *Tobago: Melancholy Isle, Vol. I, 1498-1771*, Port-of-Spain, Trinidad: Westindiana, 1987, p. 119.

civil government, laws, customs, rights, privileges, ordinances, and justice. There was, however, one exception: the Court of Chancery was comprised of members of the Council.[28,29] When recaptured in 1793 Tobago was reduced to a British dependency because of the situation that existed in Grenada. Thus after 1777 Tobago had its own governor, at first British, from 1781 French and after 1793 British once more. This continued throughout the Revolutionary and Napoleonic wars and was the status at final settlement by the Treaty of Paris in 1814. Thus Tobago was either a neutral isle or in dispute among the Dutch, Courlanders, French, and British over a period that spanned almost two centuries. As a British colony after1763 its seat of government was in Grenada. However, between 1781 and 1814 because of the Revolutionary and Napoleonic wars, the status of the island was in dispute and had its own governor, at first French and from 1793 onwards British. As was the consensus at the Treaty in 1814, the following year most of the countries of Europe were represented at the Congress of Vienna and agreed to terms that brought peace until the First World War. Thus after 1814, Tobago and the rest of the Caribbean entered a period of relative calm that was not experienced for over two centuries.

PEACE WITHOUT STABILITY 1814-1888

The period between 1814 and 1888 left Tobago bogged down in a slew of problems, economic in nature on the one hand and constitutional on the other. The economic problem arose from the decline of the sugar industry, and the constitutional problem was evident in the landless peasantry, the poor social welfare, and the weak infrastructure and high cost of administration of a regime that was dysfunctional. And one problem tended to reinforce the other.

---

[28] Woodcock, Henry Isles, *A History of Tobago,* Frank Cass, Library of West Indian Studies, p. xx.

[29] Douglas Archibald, Rupert, *Tobago: Melancholy Isle, Vol. II, 1782-1805,* Port-of-Spain, Trinidad: UWI School of Continuing Studies, 1995, p. 56.

FOCUS ON ADMINISTRATION

The deflation that followed the Napoleonic wars left the island in economic ruin throughout the nineteenth century. In this period the administration was occupied with two major issues: the first was the matter of putting the economy of the sugar producing slave colony on a sound and sustainable footing, and the second was the reform of constitution by which the majority of the people had no civil rights in an age that was witness to rapid changes in what was acceptable as human rights. In this period as a member of the evolving British Empire, with a laissez-faire policy backed with property rights in the ownership of slaves, life in Tobago, as indeed, it was in the rest of the British West Indies, was no bed of roses. The state of human rights in the Caribbean during the eighteenth century was one of horrors throughout. The Barbados Slave Code embodied the despicable conditions under which the majority of the slaves lived, especially in the British colonies.

In the year before the abolition of slavery, Tobago lost its independence enjoyed during the wars with France. The island became a member of the Windward Islands group with a governor general based in Barbados and included Grenada and St. Vincent and the Grenadines. St. Lucia joined the group in 1838. That restructuring saw a downgrading of the governor to that of lieutenant governor. Shortly after the abolition of slavery, Merivale in lectures at Oxford had drawn to the attention of the Colonial Office the need for administrative reform in the colonies.[30] Merivale, while dealing with

---

[30] "Each little community, of a few thousands only, has its miniature King, Lords and Commons, its Governor, Council, and Assembly, together with a host of administrative and paid functionaries, most disproportionate to its importance. And each Assembly guards (or until very recently guarded) with the utmost jealousy, not only the right of taxation, but the anarchical prerogative of voting away at will, without initiative proposal of the Governor. All this overweighted system of local government is a relic of times past away. . . . The system has ceased; but many of the places remain; and the impoverished communities, which can scarcely afford to pay the salaries, seem, nevertheless, to entertain the strongest objection to reducing or consolidating offices which have become objects of local ambition."

the British Empire as a whole, suggested strongly that the colonies were over-governed. This was certainly true of Tobago with not more than two hundred persons entitled to vote in a constitutional system that was manifestly top heavy. Of course there were many initiatives to reduce the cost of administration. In January 1854 the garrison at Fort King George was withdrawn and relocated in Barbados.

An Act of 1855 created a Privy Council as an advisory council of the governor. The same act provided for the creation of an Executive Committee to assist the lieutenant governor in the execution of his duties. In 1865 the salary of the chief justice was reduced. In 1874 the structure of the Legislature was changed from two chambers to a single chamber, thus reducing the number of paid officials. Another initiative to reduce the cost was to abolish the post of lieutenant governor in 1880. But as the country entered the last quarter of the nineteenth century it became increasingly evident that Tobago required a much more fundamental change. This need was recognised by almost every administrator in the twenty-five years that preceded the proposal from Governor Sendall to the Secretary of State for the Colonies in 1886 to form the union. Frederick Augustus Gore was the last person to be appointed lieutenant governor of Tobago. When he left office in 1880 his replacement, Mr Edward Laborde, was designated administrator, a post considered to be equivalent to that of a colonial secretary.

COLONEL WILLIAM CROSSMAN, COMMISSIONER (1882-1883)

Late in 1882 a Royal Commission with Colonel William Crossman as chairman was appointed by the imperial government to enquire into the public debts, revenue, expenditure, and liabilities of Jamaica, Grenada, St. Vincent, St. Lucia, Tobago, and the Leeward Islands. The commission noted in respect of Tobago that the

---

Merivale, Herman, *Lectures on Colonization and Colonies, delivered before the University of Oxford in 1839, 1840, and 1841.* Cited by Robinson, A. N. R., in *The Mechanics of Independence*, Cambridge, MA and London: MIT Press, 1971, pp. 25, 26.

colony was in a state of financial ruin; people refused to labour in public roads and works, as they were forced to remain for months without remuneration; public officers also suffered financially owing to the empty coffers; and money lenders were numerous to deal with the situation. The commission recommended and the imperial government accepted that St. Vincent, St. Lucia, Grenada, and Tobago, which were all governed as Crown colonies, form a single colony led by Barbados with its ancient constitution. The Bajans rioted and opted out of such an arrangement to stand as an independent colony. These changes were effected by Letters Patent during the year, and the governor of the reformed Windward Island group was based in Grenada. Clearly the viability of Tobago as the most southerly of the Windward Islands became a pressing issue for the government and after the governor-in-chief of the Windward Islands, with the concurrence of the administrator of Tobago, suggested it, Lord Glanville, Secretary of State for the Colonies, proposed that the Legislative Councils of Tobago and Trinidad consider the feasibility of forming an united colony.

H. T. USSHER, LIEUTENANT GOVERNOR OF TOBAGO (1872-1875)

There can be no doubt that Lieutenant Governor H. T. Ussher was reform minded. It was under his watch that the Single Chamber Act was passed and the composition of the Privy Council reduced. The island, not unlike many of the British colonies of the time, was thought to be over governed with a multiplicity of petty offices. In the opinion of the lieutenant governor:

> *"One of the principal obstructions of the progress in the island is the present form of government. Its machinery may well be adapted to a country like Victoria or the Cape, but its adaptations to a country like Tobago, an island of 90 square miles in extent, numbering a population of little over seventeen thousand souls is doubtful in the extreme. One of the results has been the creation of a multiplicity of petty offices with salaries attached of the lowest class, rendering it next to impossible to obtain*

for the performance of the duties thereof qualified and responsible officers, but at the same time sufficing to induce a certain class to look forward to obtaining them, and to avoid being obliged to betake themselves to more profitable but more undignified pursuits entailing upon them the necessity of hard work."[31]

AUGUSTUS F. GORE, LIEUTENANT GOVERNOR OF TOBAGO (1877-1880)

Gore, a committed West Indian who had married a Bajan Creole and served governments in British Guiana and Barbados before his appointment as lieutenant governor in Tobago, was somewhat altruistic of the conditions that prevailed in Tobago and of what was required.

"I am of opinion that there is no necessity for maintaining the Colony as a separate government. The distance from Trinidad to Tobago is only 18 miles from land to land, and if a good road were made from Port-of-Spain to Toco, and a steam launch was employed, daily communication might be established between Port-of-Spain and Scarborough. The Savings that would be effected by the move would be £3,373. This would be the immediate saving that would be made were Her Majesty's Government to adopt my suggestion; but I have no doubt others would follow as soon as the Government of Trinidad had had a little experience in the wants of Tobago. I have come to the conclusion from seeing the small amount of work to be done by the officials whose salaries I propose to abolish. I have not alluded to the Colonial Secretary's salary as someone would still be required to keep the local records and to be the mouthpiece of the Governor of Trinidad. I make this suggestion at the present time because I am aware that at the present moment most of the sugar

---

[31] Williams, Dr. E. E., *History of the People of Trinidad and Tobago*, New York, NY: A & B Publishing, 1993, pp. 132, 133.

estates are in a depressed condition and that next year's crop will be even a shorter one than this year's, and because planters are not able to find employment for the labourers actually in the colony, much less to be able to pay the export tax on produce which was imposed for the purpose of immigration. There are large tracts of land in Tobago which would produce cocoa, but which for want of capital are now lying idle, but which were this little island incorporated with Trinidad, will soon I am convinced be taken up by speculators from Trinidad, as these would be sold at a low rate, and wages here are much lower than in the neighbouring colony. I am aware than in making these proposals, I am so to speak cutting my own throat, but I have no fear that if I do my duty in this, calling attention to the saving that could be affected, Her Majesty's government would not make me suffer."[32]

In the spirit of administrative reform taking place, Gore was the last lieutenant governor of Tobago. The most senior official after Gore was known as the administrator, with pay, if not responsibilities, much reduced from that of a lieutenant governor. It was thought that the post was equivalent to that of a colonial secretary in other established governments.

EDWARD LABORDE,
ADMINISTRATOR OF TOBAGO (1880-1883)

The status of the island was a Crown colony, by the Constitution Act of 1876. Money was scarce and had been scarce for some time.

As administrator, Edward Laborde understood very well the economic problem in Tobago: chronic underemployment of the labour force; a dire shortage of working capital; and outmoded manufacturing technology. In addition he felt that the land resources could support a larger labour force to be augmented by immigration. But he also

---

[32] Cited in Ottley, C. R., *The Story of Tobago*, Port-of-Spain, Trinidad: Longmans Caribbean 1973, p. 90 ff.

sensed that those who had the capital had neither the will nor the inclination to invest for the betterment of the colony.

> *"Much of the depression that weighs on the Colony is owing to the scant means given to the cultivation of the soil. The land is fertile and seems well adapted to the sugar cane. The yield per acre from a well-cultivated field is large and the quality of it is good. As now conducted the estates do not give good continuous employment to the labourers, who, were matters different, would be found to be few in number for the work to be done. Capital, immigrant labour, and an improved system of manufacture are needed with these, and if possible more proprietors resident in the island, who would have the well-being and advancement of the people at heart, and the general development of its resources. Tobago would soon again become a thriving Colony. I much fear, however, that so long as cane cultivation is relied upon as the sole source of profit from the fertile soil of the island so long will the present struggle for existence continue on the part of the planter or the lessee of estates."[33]*

SIR WILLIAM ROBINSON, GOVERNOR OF TRINIDAD (1886)

Sir William Robinson was a well-seasoned colonial administrator when he became governor of Trinidad in 1885. He was a member of the Slave Trade Commission in 1869, was governor of the Bahama Isles from 1874 to 1880, governor of the Windward Islands that included Tobago from 1881 to 1884, and governor of Barbados 1884 to 1885. While governor-in-chief of the Windward Islands, he had responsibility for the welfare of Tobago, particularly so after 1885 when the post of lieutenant governor of the island was abolished. In 1886 as governor of Trinidad he made the following proposal to the Colonial Office:

---

[33]   Douglas Archibald, Rupert, *Tobago: Melancholy Isle, Vol. III, 1807-1898,* Port-of-Spain, Trinidad: Westindiana, 2003, p. 201.

"Tobago should in my opinion be incorporated with Trinidad and become part and parcel of this colony. A Magistrate and Collector of Customs with a couple of Clerks in Scarboro and a sub-Inspector of Police and twenty constables would I think be sufficient for Executive administration of the Island. I would further suggest that the Tobago people should be invited to transfer themselves and their effects, free of passages given to them by the Royal Mail Steamers at the cost of the Tobago Treasury, and that I should be authorized by the Secretary of State to offer them one acre of Crown Land for every man, woman and child who responded to that invitation in the neighbourhood of Moruga which to me is the richest district in the island. By means such as I propose the Tobago issue would easily be settled."[34]

ROBERT W. LLEWELYN, ADMINISTRATOR OF TOBAGO (1885-1887)

The dire state of the economy of Tobago and its associated administrative problems in the period leading up to the Union may be gleaned from a report by the administrator, Robert B. Llewelyn, for the year 1885:

"From what I have been able to learn the present Government House, pleasantly situated on a hill 415 feet above the sea, about 13/4 [one and three quarters] miles from the town of Scarborough, was planned and commenced in the year 1828 when Tobago was a flourishing independent Colony, having its own Governor, and the house as originally planned, was warranted by the then condition of the Island.

About three years after it was commenced and when the brick walls were erected three-fourths of the height

---

[34] Craig-James, Dr. Susan E., *The Changing Society of Tobago 1838-1938, Vol. I, 1838-1900,* Port-of-Spain, Trinidad: Paria Publishing, 2008, p. 292.

required for a two storied building Tobago ceased to be an independent Colony and was grouped with the Windward Islands a Lieut. Governor being appointed here instead of a Governor.

It was then I believe decided not to erect the upper story [sic], originally intended for the bedrooms, but to make the ground floor suffice, the result being that the best accommodation of the house was retained as planned for Dining, Dancing and Billiard Rooms, whilst the bedrooms have been partitioned from what was no doubt originally intended for ante-rooms, card rooms, &c, and the offices of the Governor and his staff.

Such a house can never be made suitable family residence for an administrator with a very small salary, who [sic] has now many other offices to hold requiring his daily presence in Scarborough, and who cannot afford to entertain in the large rooms provided for that purpose.

Living at such a distance from Town entails the necessary keeping three or four horses, and many servants, and in the interest of the Public Service, I think the administrator, with the numerous duties now attached to the appointment should live nearer his Office and the Public Institutions, over which, with the present reduced number of Officers, it will be necessary for him to keep a close and constant supervision.

Government House is in a dilapidated, I should say dangerous condition, that it will take at least £1,000 and probably £1,500 to put it in thorough order. And then if this were done, I think it is my duty though perhaps hardly necessary, to point out that the Administrator, with a salary of £600 per annum, would not be able to afford to live in a house that was planned for a governor or Lieutenant Governor with more than double the income.

*For these reasons I am afraid I cannot recommend that
any money should be spent in repairing the present
Government House, but that a more suitable and modest
residence for the Administrator be provided nearer
Scarborough, and I would suggest that some of the
old military buildings at the Fort be repaired with the
permission of the Imperial Government.*

*I am aware that there is a feeling of sentiment amongst
many against giving up the old house that has for 50
years been occupied by the Governors of this colony. Such
feeling I admire and respect. But the hard fact presents
itself that money is not as plentiful in Tobago as formerly,
and that the resources of the Colony do not permit of,
what I may perhaps call, the grandeur of former days
being now maintained.*"[35]

THE UNDERLYING CONSTITUTIONAL ISSUE

Most noteworthy of Tobago during the period was the uncertainty of
its constitutional status. This uncertainty was not unlike the instability
that dogged the island throughout the seventeenth and eighteenth
centuries. Recaptured from the French during the Napoleonic
wars and formally ceded to Britain at the Peace of Paris in 1814,
the colony enjoyed self-government until 1833. In that year Tobago
became a member of the new Windward Islands Group including
Barbados, St. Vincent, and Grenada with a governor-general based
in Barbados. In 1834 St. Lucia was admitted to the group. That
arrangement in which Tobago was associated with other islands
of the British West Indies was not a new one. The administrative
reforms during the nineteenth century resulted in the changes from
governor to lieutenant governor to administrator. In the institutions
we saw the change from a self-governing colony to that of Crown
colony; the change from a bicameral parliament to a single-chamber
Assembly; and finally the proposal to be annexed to Trinidad to

---

[35] *Minutes of the Proceedings of the Legislative Council of Tobago,* 7 April 1886.

form one colony. At the root of the constitutional problem in Tobago was a continuing conflict between the executive and the legislature.

In 1846 Governor-in-Chief Sir Charles Grey, in recognition of the incipient constitutional problem, had suggested that either the franchise be widened or that the Assembly be suspended and replaced by an Executive Council:

> *"In January 1853, the Privy Council, tired of its recommendations to the Assembly being ignored, drafted a letter to the solicitor general directing he simplify and clarify the Land Tax Act."*[36]

In 1855 there was a Memorial from the Assembly praying for the removal of Lieutenant Governor Shortland.

THE QUEST FOR STABILITY

Changes began with the revolutions in America, in France, and in Haiti. In 1792 Pitt the Younger, British prime minister, remarked in a speech in the House of Commons (in fulfilment of a promise made to Wilberforce) that in the West Indies in 1722, the Legislature passed a law whereby a slave who ran away was punishable by death in the first instance.[37] Britain abolished its slave trade in 1807 followed by a period of amelioration of the conditions of the slaves. Slavery was abolished in 1834 throughout the British Empire. With the abolition of slavery the Colonial Office moved to protect the emancipated population as it had ultimate responsibility for the colonies at the same time that it paid compensation to the slave owners adversely affected by the abolition of slavery. Notwithstanding this the Legislatures of the West Indies moved to preserve the white dominance by restricting the franchise and, moreover, by placing the burden of taxation on the peasants. In any event the Legislatures were voted in by small numbers of voters; in 1854 there were 134 persons eligible

---

[36]   Craig-James, Dr. Susan E., op. cit., 2008, p. 232.
[37]   MacArthur, Brian, *The Penguin Book of Historic Speeches,* London: Penguin Books, 1996, p. 142.

to vote. The arrangement clearly lacked political legitimacy, and the crunch came in 1865 with the Morant Bay riots in Jamaica when constitutional government collapsed. The imperial government then moved to impose Crown colony government throughout the region, and in the case of Tobago this was done in 1876. The status of the colony was modified to that of a Crown colony with the abolition of the elective assembly and the Legislature reduced to the status of a Legislative Council

The collapse of the economy meant that drastic measures were required: one such measure would require a radical reform of the Tobago Constitution. It was inevitable that an objective examination of the economic and administrative problems of the colony would lead to some form of political or constitutional reform. And curiously the vision of that unknown Dutchman made around 1667 was about to become a reality because of the forced circumstances in which Tobago found itself at the end of the nineteenth century.

THE NEW CHALLENGE

Despite the rapidly changing world in which Tobago found itself throughout the nineteenth century, certain things about the government required constant attention. If we accept Rostow's idea[38] of politics as an eternal triad of competing imperatives—security, welfare, and constitutional order—in respect of Tobago in 1886, we find the following:

The security problem had been settled in 1815 after almost two hundred years of continuous turmoil. The age of buccaneerism had ended with the Treaty of Ratisbon, and there were no longer raids from Amerindians or usurping European powers. The Amerindians, where they had not been decimated or integrated into the colonies, were confined to the island of Dominica by informal treaty. Moreover, after the Napoleonic wars the Congress of Vienna had

---

[38]   Rostow, W. W., *Politics and the Stages of Growth*, Cambridge: Cambridge University Press, 1971, p. 7.

27

produced a period of enduring calm among the countries of Europe during which the focus of the imperial power was on administration rather than acquisition.

The economic bankruptcy of Tobago throughout the nineteenth century, however, meant that the welfare of its people had assumed greater prominence for the administrators. The development of the island depended upon absentee landowners, and to crown it all the island was ruled by a colonial government. While the economic condition was certainly a handicap, the welfare of its people was also hampered by the political system in which the ruling plantocracy was in overt social and economic conflict with the majority of the people. Emancipation meant new rights for the mass of the people, leading eventually to a greater say in their self-determination. Naturally the proprietors, jealous of their ancient rights and privileges, saw this as an affront to their authority and reacted against it; they resisted amelioration; resisted emancipation; and to some extent neglected their duties as members of the Assembly. The resulting deterioration in the social class struggle culminated in the Belmanna riots of 1876.

The overarching problem, however, was the constitutional issue. The sad truth was that Tobago in 1887 was a failed British slave colony. Unlike Jamaica after the Morant Bay riots, the imposition of the Crown colony constitution had no impact. The economic woes pushed the leadership in Tobago more and more into a position where they could not compromise; they simply had nothing to offer. In Barbados, by contrast, where huge capital sums had been accumulated during the halcyon days of sugar, where a majority of the estate owners were resident in Barbados, and where the slaves, despite the harsh conditions, had accommodated to their masters after a long period of association, when the crunch came in 1885 a social compromise was reached, concessions were granted to the emerging middle classes, and Crown colony government was avoided.[39]

---

[39] James, C. L. R., *The West Indian Intellectual*, in Thomas, J. J., *Froudacity*, London: New Beacon Books, 1969, p. 38.

Insofar as it was a failed British colony, Tobago was not unique in the British West Indies. Indeed, the Turks and Caicos Islands had had a similar tortuous experience:

- Discovered by Ponce de Leon in 1512.
- In the sixteenth, seventeenth, and eighteenth centuries, passed between the Spaniards, French, and British without being settled.
- In 1647, the Bermudans developed a salt industry.
- In 1779, the Bahamians took control after trying to tax the salt industry.
- After hurricanes in 1813 and 1815, the islands were virtually abandoned.
- In 1848, while a British possession, petitioned successfully to be supervised by Jamaica.
- In 1873, annexed by Jamaica after the arrangement of 1848 proved to be a financial burden.[40]

As was inevitable in the circumstances in which Tobago found itself, the focus would shift to administration and constitution reform. Tobago needed a radical change in its constitutional arrangements, and this imperative propelled Tobago towards the union with Trinidad. Not surprisingly, the Colonial Office would propose the relationship between Jamaica and the Turks and Caicos Islands as a model for such a union.

---

[40] Author's Note: The Turks and Caicos Island underwent more turmoil in the twentieth century. The Constitution of 1959 gave Jamaica almost feudal authority over the islands. After the demise of the West Indian Federation in 1962 the islands were ruled from 1965 by the Bahamians, their natural neighbours. They finally became a British Overseas Territory in 1974 and have been governed directly by Britain since 2009.

Map of Tobago

King George III of Great Britain and Ireland

CHAPTER II

Tobago: Constitution and Society

The History of Tobago in the 19th century is the story of a steady economic decline and of the absurdity of self-governing institutions in an island of some 12,000 persons.

Dr E. E. Williams, *History of the People of Trinidad and Tobago*

TREATIES

THERE IS MUCH UNCERTAINTY over the constitutional status of Tobago before 1763. This matter is treated fully in Appendix II below.

TREATY OF AIX-LA-CHAPELLE 1748

The parties to this treaty, signed on 17 October 1748, were Britain, France, and the States General of the United Provinces. The treaty achieved little and returned almost everything to the status quo ante bellum. Thus there was no change in Tobago arising from the treaty, but its status as determined by earlier treaties was confirmed.

TREATY OF PARIS 1763

The Treaty of Paris 1763 ended the Seven Years War fought in continental Europe, America, the West Indies, Africa, and India. Signed on 10 February 1763 by French and British diplomats, Tobago was ceded to Britain.

In 1781 Tobago was captured by the French during hostilities associated with the American War of Independence

TREATY OF PARIS, 1783

The Treaty of Paris 1783, signed by Britain, France, and Spain, acknowledged the independence of the United States of America; Tobago was ceded by Britain to France.

During the Revolutionary War against France Britain captured Tobago in 1793.

TREATY OF AMIENS 1802

Tobago was formally ceded to France.

From 1802 to 1803, it was a French Possession.

From 1803 onwards, it was a British possession.

TREATY OF PARIS 1814

Tobago was formally ceded to Britain.

Tobago from 1814 to 1888 retained its status as a British colony.

COLONIAL ARRANGEMENTS, 1833-1888

- 1833: Tobago formed part of the Windward Islands government including St. Vincent and the Grenadines, Grenada, and Barbados, with the governor general based in Barbados.
- 1834: Slavery abolished throughout the British Empire.
- 1837: Windward Islands group joined by St. Lucia.

- 1855: Advisory Council to the Governor formed; elective Legislative Assembly and executive Council. New elective franchise.
- 1871: Franchise Extension Act.
- 1874: The Single Chamber Act changed the form of the Legislature of the island from two chambers to a single Assembly.
- 1876: Constitution Act 1876 abolished the elective principle; Tobago became a Crown colony.
- 1885: Barbados separated from the Windward Islands group.
- 1885: Windward Islands group was composed of St. Vincent, St. Lucia, Grenada, and Tobago, with governor based in Grenada.
- 1886: The imperial government proposed that Tobago be annexed and form a united colony with Trinidad.
- 1887: Resolution passed by Legislative Council in Tobago in favour of annexation.
- 1887: Resolution passed by Legislative Council in Trinidad in favour of annexation.
- 1887: Trinidad and Tobago Act 1887 passed by the British Parliament.
- 1888: Order in Council issued establishing the colony of Trinidad and Tobago from 1 January 1889.

THE CONSTITUTION 1763-1888

Tobago received its first formal constitution with the royal proclamation followed by the British settlement in 1763. For much of the seventeenth and eighteenth centuries the status of Tobago was in a state of flux between Holland, France, and Britain for the most part. In 1748 at the Treaty of Aix-la-Chapelle, France and Britain confirmed that Tobago would remain one of the neutral islands. The peace achieved by that treaty was short lived, and within eight years the two countries were at war again. At the end of the Seven Years War (1756-1763), fought on the continent of Europe and in the Americas, the British emerged as indisputable victors, and there was a major redrawing of the map of the world. In the Treaty of Paris, 1763, Tobago was ceded by France to Britain. Later that same year, George III, the reigning British monarch, issued Letters Patent to establish four separate governments in those territories acquired at the Treaty of Paris: Quebec, East Florida, West Florida, and Grenada. The latter was composed of the islands of Grenada, the Grenadines, St. Vincent, Dominica, and Tobago and was on occasions referred to as the South Charibee Islands. Considering the size of its population Tobago possessed a somewhat large administrative structure that eventually had a bearing on the viability of the island as a colony.

THE EXECUTIVE

From 1763 to 1781, the head of the executive in Tobago was the governor-in-chief or governor general of the South Charibee Islands and was based in Grenada. In addition to being governor of Tobago, he was also governor of St. Vincent and the Grenadines and Dominica. Of all the islands in the group Grenada had its own governor in Mr George Scott. The first governor of Tobago was General Robert Melville. By Letters Patent he was authorised to:

- Make, constitute, and ordain laws, statutes, and ordinances with the consent of the people for the peace, welfare, and government of the colony as might be found agreeable to the laws of England.
- To erect and constitute, with the advice of his council, courts of judicature and public justice, for the hearing and determining of all causes criminal as well as civil according to law and equity as might be agreeable to the laws of England.

The governor general would be advised by a Council.

General Robert Melville was appointed governor general; he held a commission as vice admiral and was based in Grenada.

The Governor (1781-1783) and (1802-1803)

General Philbert de Blanchelande was the first French governor.

Major General Cornelius Cuyler recaptured the island for the British in 1793.

1794-1802 and 1803-1833

On 4 January 1794, Tobago was formed into a separate government, severing its British ties to the Windward Islands, with a Legislative Council appointed by the Crown and a representative House called the Assembly. George Poyntz Ricketts was appointed the captain general and commander-in-chief.

From 1833 to 1885 the governor-in-chief was based in Barbados, and from 1885 to 1888 was based in Grenada.

The Lieutenant Governor (1763-1781, 1833 to 1880)

The governor, based in Grenada, was authorised to appoint as lieutenant governor a person normally resident in the island of Tobago. He was the deputy of the governor general, and in the absence of the latter he carried out the duties of the governor. In that regard he had all the powers of the governor except the authority to make certain appointments and the right to grant pardons. In particular he was vice-admiral of the colony. The president of the council acted as lieutenant governor in the absence of the latter. The first lieutenant governor of Tobago was Alexander Brown (1763-1766). Augustus F. Gore (1877-1880) was the last lieutenant governor of Tobago.

The Administrator (1880 to 1888)

When Augustus F. Gore left for St. Vincent in 1880, the post of lieutenant governor in Tobago was abolished. The person who replaced Gore as the most senior official on the island was Edward Laborde in the new post of administrator. The administrator had somewhat less responsibility than the lieutenant governor, and his responsibilities included those of the colonial secretary.

THE PRIVY COUNCIL (1855)

The Privy Council of Tobago, created in 1855, was an advisory council to the governor and comprised of a maximum of nine members, known as Privy Councillors.

THE EXECUTIVE COMMITTEE (1855)

The Executive Committee was comprised of one member of the Legislative Council and two members of the Elective Legislative Assembly. These members were elected by the lieutenant governor and held office at his pleasure. The function of this Committee was to advise and assist the lieutenant governor in the general administration of the affairs of the island and to propose and perfect all estimates of revenue and expenditure. Its members sat as Privy Councillors by virtue of their office and ceased to be members on retirement from the Committee.

In 1877, the Committee consisted of the attorney general, the colonial secretary, the treasurer, and other persons as might from time to time be appointed by Her Majesty.

THE LEGISLATURE

In September 1767, the Crown was petitioned for an Assembly and an Executive Council, and these were established in 1768.

- The Legislature was comprised of two chambers (1768 to 1874).
- An upper chamber called the Council was created by Governor-in-Chief Robert Melville in February 1768. The council was chaired by the lieutenant governor and comprised of eleven members and a secretary.

- A lower chamber known as the Assembly was established in July 1768. It was comprised of thirteen elected members: two each from the parishes of St. Patrick, St. David, St. Andrew, St. George, and St. Mary, and one each from the parishes of St. Paul, St. John, and the town of Plymouth (abolished 1876). It was presided over by a speaker. In 1769, the regulations, among other things, were modified by the Colonial Office to increase the membership of the Assembly to fifteen: two from each of the parishes and one from the town of Plymouth.
- In July 1769, the Representative Assembly considered the matters of claims for accustomed privileges of debate, freedom from arrest, and settled the rules of procedure for debate.
- Ordinances passed in the island were forwarded to the governor-in-chief for his assent. On his assent the ordinances became law unless they were vetoed by Her Majesty the Queen in Council.
- The Legislature was established by a commission issued by Governor Melville in February 1768 for a period of three months. Elections were held; laws were passed; an act was passed to settle the rate of interest and of damage on protested bills; an act was passed for declaring slaves to be property; an act was passed for the establishing of a register office; an act was passed for the good order and government of slaves; an act was passed for the regulation of tippling houses. The governor gave his assent; however, the Crown disallowed them and dealt with the maters by royal proclamation issued in February 1769.
- In 1855, the Legislative Council was reformed. Members were seven in number; subjects of Her Majesty; resident in the island; age twenty-one and over; and held their seats for life or may resign and forfeit their seats on bankruptcy, on insolvency, on defaulting on their public duties, or on being convicted of a felony or other indictable offence. The lieutenant governor could be authorised to summon persons to fill vacancies provided the number was not less than or exceed seven. The membership of the Assembly was

increased to sixteen by the addition of a seat for the town of Scarborough.

- In 1874, the Single Chamber Act reduced the form of the Legislature from two chambers to a single chamber called the Assembly. The new Assembly was presided over by the governor and included six members nominated by the governor and eight members elected from Scarborough and one each of the seven parishes on the basis of the old franchise.
- In 1876, the Constitution Act made Tobago a Crown colony. The representative body, the Legislative Assembly, was abolished. Replacing it was the Legislative Council which included the ex-officio members the administrator, the attorney general, the treasurer, and any other person who the queen might appoint. In 1884, there were three unofficial members.

MEMBERSHIP AND FRANCHISE

FRANCHISE RULES 1768

The first parliamentary elections were held in 1768 under the newly minted rules. To be eligible for election to the Assembly, a candidate had to be Protestant, British, twenty-one years of age, and in possession of fifty acres of land or of a town property with an annual rental value of £50.

To be eligible to vote, a person had to be male, Christian, British, twenty-one years of age, and in possession of at least six acres of land with an annual income value of £20. Elections were scheduled to take place every three years. That meant that about thirty-five persons on the island had the requirements of becoming a member of either house. Indeed, of the thirteen seats of the lower Chamber, only one was contested at the first election held in 1768. Members of the Legislature, like all other officials, were required to take oaths of allegiance, abjuration, and supremacy: this was stipulated in the Royal Proclamation that created the government of Grenada in 1763.

The census of 1770 estimated the population as follows: Whites: 447, Negroes: 3,090.

THE FRANCHISE IN 1855

The elective franchise was limited to male subjects, natural born or naturalised, or denizened[41], who had attained the age of twenty-one years and were seized or possessed of real property, within the town or parish in which that elector voted, of an annual value of £10, held on his own right, or of his wife, or for a term of one year or upwards.

The manager or overseer occupying a house on an estate, which estate was of annual rental value of £50, was to be deemed a tenant, and as such entitled to vote for the parish in which the estate was situated.

The qualification for being a member of the Assembly was limited to male subjects, natural born or naturalised, or denizened, who had attained the age of twenty-one and be seized or possessed of real property situated in the island, held in his own right, or that of his wife, in fee simple, or fee tail, or for the life of himself, or his wife, or for the term of one year upwards, of the annual rental value of £50, or his being in actual receipt of a clear yearly income of not less than £150.

The elections to the Assembly would take place every three years.

FRANCHISE ACT OF 1871

Franchise extended to all landowners with an annual rental value of £5. A registry of voters was established. The provost-marshal was the returning officer.

Henry Isles Woodcock, a former chief justice and historian, makes a fuss over the problems about the status of the law in Tobago as

---

[41] Refers to foreigners admitted to certain rights in Tobago as an adopted country.

the country changed allegiance between France and Britain. He resolves the problem by taking refuge in the notion that freeborn British subjects took the common law with them wherever they went. This concept gave rights to one set of persons while denying them to others and was the germ for the racial discrimination that was prevalent throughout the British Empire.

From 1874, the bicameral system was replaced by a single chamber called the Assembly. The membership comprised the governor, six members nominated by the governor, and eight members elected by the people. As was customary, the proclamation appointing the governor general authorised him with the help and consent of his Council to summon an Assembly as soon as it was expedient to do so.

THE JUDICIARY

The Chief Justice was head of the Judiciary.

In July 1769 the Legislature passed an act for the establishment of a **Court of Common Pleas (1794).**

The Court Act of 1794 established the Court of Common Pleas, comprised of the chief justice and three assistant justices any one or more of whom could exercise the power of the court.

The Court of King's Bench 1829, replacing the Court of Queen's Bench and Grand Sessions, was created by the Court Act of 1794. This court, responsible for the criminal jurisdiction, was comprised of the chief justice of the common pleas and two puisne judges, any one or more of whom could exercise the power of the court and provided for slaves the benefit of trial in cases more serious than misdemeanours. In 1843 the act was amended to extend the jurisdiction of the courts to issuing of the prerogative writs of *certiorari, mandamus,* and *prohibition* in all similar cases where the writs may have applied in England.

THE COURT OF APPEAL

In 1856 an act was passed that permitted the Courts of Queen's Bench and Common Pleas to hear appeals from the justices of the peace. Under Governor Drysdale the superior courts of Tobago, that is, the Court of Queen's Bench, the Court of Common Pleas and the Court of Appeal were placed on the Circuit Appeal Court. The latter was composed of all the chief justices of the Windward Islands and had a quorum of three. Although it was intended that the court would visit the islands twice a year, the Tobago Appeal Court Act of 1858 sanctioned that the itinerant court would only visit when an appeal had arisen.

THE COURT OF CHANCERY

The Court of Chancery was created to deal with matter of equity. By statute of 1853, the court was modified to have the same equitable jurisdiction as the Lord High Chancellor of Great Britain, the Lords Justices of Appeal, the Vice-Chancellors, and others of Her Majesty's justices exercising equitable jurisdiction in Great Britain and to handle the equitable jurisdiction.

COURT OF THE VICE-ADMIRALTY

The lieutenant governor was vice-admiral of the island. In the case of vacancy in the office, the chief justice was appointed judge until notification was received from the admiralty that a formal appointment had been made. The chief justice also had the authority to appoint with the approval of the lieutenant governor a registrar or marshal in the event of a vacancy until notification of the post had been filled by the admiralty.

THE ECCLESIASTICAL COURTS

THE COURT OF THE ORDINARY

The Church of England was the established church from October 1763 and fell under the jurisdiction of the Bishop of London. That was inferred from an opinion given in 1784 by the law officers to Lord Sydney, who was serving as home secretary in the Pitt Cabinet.[42] The Letters Patent appointing and authorising the governor had stipulated that the civil laws and equity administered must be agreeable to the laws of England. Nominally the governor-general was the Ordinary, that is, he presided over the consistory court for his diocese. That was the normal court for ecclesiastic causes including defamation and wills.

An act was passed in 1844 to establish three rectories.

An act was passed in December 1856 to enforce church discipline and to establish vestries in the rectories, to repeal all earlier acts on the subject, and to introduce the Ecclesiastic Law of England.

An act was passed in 1862 to improve the Court of the Ordinary and declared:

> *"The Governor of the Island is Ordinary of the same, and hath sole jurisdiction in the court of Ordinary of this island."*

The term "governor" used in the legislation was taken to apply to the officer administering the government, whatever his rank or title might be, with the goal of authorising the chief justice to act as assessor to the governor in all matters and causes that were contested in the court of the Ordinary. In England, where there were few cases, eminent barristers acted as Ordinary in several dioceses.[43]

The Concurrent Endowment Act of 1873 disestablished the Anglican Church in Tobago from 1874.

---

[42]   Douglas Archibald, Rupert, *Tobago: Melancholy Isle, Vol. III, 1807-1898*, Port-of-Spain, Trinidad: Westindiana, 2003, p. 17.

[43]   Kiralfy, A. K. R., *Potter's Historical Introduction to English Law*, London: Sweet and Maxwell, 1970, p. 223.

COURT FOR THE SALE OF ESTATES

The Court for the Sale of estates became necessary in Tobago with the steady abandonment of estates. Where 57,408 acres were granted to the first British settlers, in 1884 not more than 10,000 were under cultivation. The court dealt with matters of escheat, and of estates abandoned forfeited by the Crown in lieu of payment of taxes.

ADMINISTRATIVE DIVISIONS

In January 1765, the island was divided into seven divisions with the following corresponding parishes: St. Patrick, St. Andrew, St. David, St. George, St. Mary, St. John, and St. Paul.

In 1844, the island was divided into three rectories and those divisions were also used for secular purposes with a stipendiary magistrate assigned to each rectory.

THE ECONOMY

PRODUCTION

The decline of the sugar industry was hastened by several factors not all unrelated. Firstly, after the Peace of Paris 1814, Mauritius, which was ceded to Britain, became a major player in the sugar market. Secondly, in the West Indies after abolition, women and children withdrew from the labour force. This scenario was a double blow to the sugar producers in the British West Indies. On the one hand, the abolition of slavery created a shortage of labour, and on the other, the industry had to compete with producers in places like Cuba, where slavery had not been abolished. Thirdly, despite the abolition of slave trade in 1807 and the abolition of slavery throughout the British Empire slavery in 1834, slavery continued to flourish in Spanish Cuba. The outcome was that with new technology in Cuba, in combination with the slave labour, Cuban sugar then became one of the cheapest in the world. In 1862, the slave trade dwindled to a trickle after the United States, in the midst of the Civil War, signed a treaty with Britain conceding the right of searching vessels at sea, a move that was necessary for enforcement of the ban on the slave trade. Cuba abolished slavery between 1880 and 1886 and Brazil between 1883 and 1888.

THE MARKET

Whereas towards the end of the eighteenth century Tobago was producing indigo and cotton in addition to its staple of sugar, for most of the nineteenth century Tobago's was a one crop economy producing sugar and its derivatives, molasses and rum for export. Thus Tobago enjoyed its halcyon years during the period of the French occupation, 1781 to 1793. At the Treaty of Paris in 1783 the French West Indian colonies of Haiti, Martinique, and Guadeloupe were thought to be amongst the richest in the world, and their intrinsic value had a great influence on the course of the treaty negotiations and ultimately on the partition of the Western world. The French attitude to the development of Tobago[44] was somewhat different from the laissez-faire posture of the British. The French administration imposed fiscal discipline by insisting that the budgets be balanced, introduced a slew of measures to raise taxes, and reduced the duty on imported slaves.

Produce comprised sugar, rum, molasses, shrub, indigo, cotton, turmeric, and ginger. Indigo, the source of a dye used in colouring cotton and wool, declined. By 1886 when Baeyer in Germany produced a synthetic version, the indigo industry was already dead in Tobago.

The Tobago economy flourished during the French occupation.

---

[44] "The metropolitan country itself offered incentives to development. The governor was advised by the Minister of Colonies in 1786 that 'it is the desire of the government to do all that is possible to help he people and to assist agriculture and commerce in Tobago." Williams, Dr. E. E., *History of the People of Trinidad and Tobago,* New York, NY: A & B Publishing, 1993, p. 57.

DECLINE OF THE WEST INDIES

After the Napoleonic wars a period of deflation ensued, and in international trade, the price of sugar fell dramatically. In this period there was a marked reduction in British exports to the region. This reduction masks the decline in the availability of capital goods at a time when the industrial revolution was taking root throughout the world; the absence of capital goods had the effect of placing greater emphasis on labour in the production process. The impact on the Tobago economy was devastating. In 1823 the Tobago House of Assembly petitioned the imperial Parliament, pointing out the dire economic conditions that existed in the colony. As fate would have it, that was the state of affairs for most of the nineteenth century. After abolition the use of slave labour in the southern United States expanded with the result that the cotton industry of the West Indies was almost completely obliterated. Between 1784 and 1786 almost half of the £1,814,000 worth of cotton imported into Britain came from the West Indies; between 1834 and 1836 the value had increased to £14,494,000, and 80 percent of this came from the United States.[45]

After 1850, coconuts became the second most valuable agricultural cash crop exported in Tobago, but despite this in the 1880s over 82 percent of the estates in Tobago were still producing sugar.

The Civil War disrupted the production of cotton in the southern United States. As a consequence the cotton industry enjoyed a short lived revival during the 1860s.

Given the reported abundance of fruits, ginger, cotton, cacao, indigo, fish, and fowl, it is surprising that the economy emerged with a sugar producing monoculture.

The only possible explanation for this is that the marginal profits accruing to a unit of labour from the sugar industry was so much

---

[45] Cain, P., *Economics in the Metropolitan Context*, in Porter, Andrew (Ed.), *The Oxford History of the British Empire Vol. III: The Nineteenth Century*, Oxford: Oxford University Press, 1999, p. 33.

greater than that from alternative production. And this would be so only with a shortage of labour.

The sugar industry collapsed under the burden of a plethora of factors.

The introduction of beet sugar changed the game entirely. The countries of Europe that developed the technology for sugar production from beets also introduced a system of bounties that subsidised the production and drove down the price of sugar on the world market. Sugar production in Tobago in 1882 was just under 6 percent of the production in 1822. Molasses production, which was highly variable, at 77,260 gallons in 1882 had increased to 142 percent of the production in 1822 but only 40 percent of the peak production achieved in 1832. Sugar had become the staple of cultivation to the exclusion of cacao, coffee, coconuts, cotton, and spices.

TECHNOLOGY

During the French occupation, giraffes were imported and used as draught animals. Subsequently, changes were made to the outmoded technology. The first was the introduction of the metayer system and the second was attempts to improve the technology through the spread of technological information and upgrading of the production process. Thus by 1846 one third of the mills in Tobago were steam driven. But sugar production continued in some discrete mills. The lack of transportation infrastructure precluded centralisation, as had occurred in Trinidad.

OUTMODED PLANT MANAGEMENT

The Tobago Agricultural Society was founded by Governor Sir William Young in 1807 but no longer existed when he died in 1815. The factors of outmoded technology and of rundown plants would have made sugar production in Tobago uncompetitive. But there were other factors. For example the more fertile soils of Trinidad and British Guiana gave higher yields than in Tobago. The close proximity of these two new sources would have been a disincentive to investment.

LABOUR

It was felt that the simplest way to overcome the shortage of labour in Tobago was through the process of immigration. To that end a series of acts, three in number, were passed between 1852 and 1861 to bring about the desired transformation of the labour force: the first, in 1852, was for the better protection of persons under the care of and control of others, as apprentices, servants, or liberated African immigrants; the second, in 1857, was to remove doubts as to the rights of the liberated Africans in Tobago: Africans domiciled or resident were deemed natural born subjects of Her Majesty; and the third, in 1861, sought to amend and consolidate the laws regulating and making provision for the treatment of liberated African immigrants. To compensate for the losses incurred by the sugar industry in the West Indies, the British government in the aftermath of the abolition of slavery was supplying at no cost to the West Indies liberated Africans from Sierra Leone and St. Helena. In 1862, the secretary of state, the Duke of Newcastle, indicated that the imperial government had withdrawn the subsidy on immigrant labour and directed that the colonies find the means of financing the cost of immigration, arguing that the colonies ought to pay for the benefits that would accrue from the improved supply of labour. Nevertheless, by that time the sugar producers were facing fresh competition from Europe. Labour was undoubtedly one of the biggest bugbears that hampered the Tobago economy. With the lowest wage rates in the region there was great difficulty in attracting liberated slaves from the neighbouring islands. Unlike Trinidad it was in no position to finance the supply of indentured labourers from India.

The straw that broke the camel's back came in 1884 with the demise of Messrs Gillespie & Co. Ltd, a London-based firm that controlled the majority of the businesses in Tobago, although the island was on the verge of bankruptcy during most of the nineteenth century.[46]

---

[46] Douglas Archibald, Rupert, *Tobago: Melancholy Isle, Vol. III, 1807-1898*, Port-of-Spain, Trinidad: Westindiana, 2003, p. 1.

In addition, the entry of new producers in Mauritius and the cultivation of beets in Europe after Napoleon blockaded Europe changed the character of the market in sugar. Thus an economy that was short of labour for most of the nineteenth century at the time of the union became one of great unemployment, adding to the woes of the colony.

In addition on account of its small size and population, the economy had to face up to the chronic West Indian problem of scarcity of labour, more so, since 1834. The wage rates in Tobago were amongst the lowest in the West Indies and so could not attract labour from the neighbouring colonies. The new imperial policy sent British citizens to the Pacific but did nothing to attract people to the West Indies. There was even a difficulty in recruiting top rate diplomatic staff for the administration in the area.

REVENUE AND CAPITAL

The Caribbean sugar industry suffered a body blow in 1846 with the passage by Lord Russell of the Sugar Duties Act, designed to equalise the duties on all sugar by 1851 while reducing the preferential rates payable to West Indian sugar. The attempts to import labour failed. Wages in Tobago were lower than those West Indian countries that had a surplus of labour.

The Gillespie & Co., when it collapsed, was estimated to control 80 percent of the produce and exports of the colony while owning thirteen of the operating estates, and it carried on other business that included shipping. The economic woes of the island were everywhere manifest: as we saw above the shortage of funds hampered the maintenance of the official residence of the administrator, and there were little funds for education and for road maintenance. It was not unexpected, therefore, certainly not in Tobago, when the Colonial Office sent dispatches to the governors of Tobago and of Trinidad requesting the consideration of annexation of Tobago to Trinidad.

TRANSPORT AND COMMUNICATIONS

One of the striking shortcomings of Tobago, according to Gorrie, was its poor infrastructure. Sir John Gorrie was chief justice of Trinidad from 1886 before becoming the first chief justice of Trinidad and Tobago; he commented on the Report of the Tobago Metairie Commission of 1890, making a striking observation:[47]

> *"Turning to the condition of Tobago, Gorrie noted how impoverished the island was after 50 years of metayage, how wretched its infrastructure and social services; and asked whether the Service Commission would not have enquired how the system discouraged agricultural enterprise generally."*

From 1875 the Royal Mail Steamship Company paid a monthly visit to Tobago. Although petitioned to pay the subsidy so as to double the frequency of visits to Tobago, the imperial government refused or overlooked the request. With its poor finances Tobago could not afford to pay the subscription fees to the West Indian and Panama Telegraph Company in 1871. Tobago missed the bus again in 1875 when the system was upgraded and so lost a very important opportunity to link Tobago with the outside world. In modern economic terms this is considered a severe drawback and adds to our understanding of the failure of the Tobago economy during the nineteenth century.

There were a few marine hazards that hampered communications by sea. There was a narrow, rocky channel that separated Tobago from Trinidad. The two principal ports were at Courland Bay and Scarborough. According to the British Admiralty, the harbour at Scarborough had formidable dangers,[48] and it recommended that

---

[47] Brereton, Bridget, *Law, Justice, and Empire: The Colonial Career of Sir John Gorrie, 1829-1892*, Kingston, Jamaica: University of the West Indies Press, 1997, p. 285.

[48] "There is a suitable depth of water for merchant ships but the anchorage is in most parts foul:—the reefs an shoals scattered on the chord of the Bay, and in the offing are numerous and require pilotage in and out." From *Young's*

the mail be delivered at Courland Bay. The latter was not without difficulties, and in 1846, the HMS *Eagle* ran upon a sunken rock in Courland Bay. In 1872, a new landing stage was installed at Scarborough, and the mail was delivered there instead of at Courland Bay. In addition to the woes with communicating with the external world, Tobago, unlike the other islands of the Windward Islands, did not have internal postal communications, a problem that was associated with the absence of adequate roads.

ROADS

The overland transport was not much better than transport by sea, with a dearth of suitable carriages on the island: for example, for the nine-kilometre journey between Scarborough and Courland Bay, ladies and children were carried in open carts. There were few roads to the interior of the island, and that explains the small acreage of privately held land under cultivation.[49] Indeed, between the many villages located at the bays on the coast line, communication was done by small boats at sea. In the 1880s, the coffers of the government were so depleted that the pay of road workers was cut to save costs and subsequently ordered to be reinstated by the secretary of state. Road work had to be carried out by the private estates.

POSTAL SERVICE

The Tobago post office was established in 1793 after the island was recaptured from France. With the ongoing Revolutionary and Napoleonic wars, the two mail packets were very irregular in their delivery of mail. Mail was delivered at Courland Bay and taken overland nine kilometres to Scarborough. In 1861 Lieutenant Governor Drysdale used the Trinidad Post Office Memorandum to reorganise the Post Office and Tobago joined the Postal Union in

---

Journals, cited in Douglas Archibald, Rupert, *Tobago: Melancholy Isle, Vol. I, 1498-1771,* Port-of-Spain, Trinidad: Westindiana, 1987, p. 115.

[49] "One of the chief reasons why a great deal of the best land lay abandoned and unproductive was the difficulty of access, in the absence of roads, to the interior of the Island." Douglas Archibald, Rupert, *Tobago: Melancholy Isle, Vol. III, 1807-1898,* Port-of-Spain, Trinidad: Westindiana, 2003, p. 195.

1880. But it must be recalled that Tobago was then only an outpost for the administration in Barbados.

THE SOCIETY

Once the British colonisation began, the Amerindians seemed to have vanished from the pages of history in Tobago. If they did not abandon the island, there was little attempt to accommodate them or incorporate them into the new colony. But their disappearance from the island may have been due to a West Indian policy agreed to between early rulers from France and Britain to relocate the natives in Dominica, with that island being treated as a neutral island. In any event that neutrality ended with the Treaty of Paris of 1763, when Dominica formed part of the British colony of Grenada comprised of Grenada and the Grenadines, St. Vincent, Tobago, and Dominica.

SLAVERY

Tobago joined Barbados and the other British colonies in the West Indies as a sugar producing slave colony. Industry in these colonies was dominated by the production of sugar, with the bulk of the labour provided by the slaves. One of the earliest enactments of the Assembly in 1769 was to legitimise Negro slavery in the new colony. According to Douglas Archibald, these early laws, although assented to by the governor, were disallowed by the Crown as being objectionable for constitutional reasons, and the matters they dealt with were disposed of by Royal Proclamation in 1769. Slavery was introduced to the West Indies by the Spaniards after the native Amerindians refused to cooperate with the conquistadores.

While exploring the African coast from early in the fifteenth century, the Portuguese traders in the period were taking 800 slaves per annum. By the end of the fifteenth century, it was estimated that 10 percent of the population of Portugal were Africans. There was a dire shortage of labour in the south of Iberia in the aftermath of the *reconquista*, and Negroes filled many jobs on the docks and in farms in both Spain and Portugal. Faced with the labour problem that arose from the enterprise of exploiting the new and fertile lands and the rich mineral, the Spaniards first tried to enslave the Amerindians, and when that failed they tried to adopt them in a nominally quasi-feudal system. When that failed the Spanish intellectuals recommended Negro slavery which thereafter became a modus operandi in the West Indies. The British who joined the enterprise with little or no moral consideration for the slaves quickly dominated the slave trade. By 1770 the population of Tobago was comprised of 238 whites and 3,090 Negroes.

> *"Thus Tobago in 1790 was essentially an African population and fundamentally a slave society. Of every 100 people in the community, 94 were African slaves. A further two [percent] had a large admixture of African blood, though they were free."*[50]

Emancipation eventually resulted in new social and economic structures in Tobago as elsewhere. Where the slaves were previously part of the capital of the producers, they became a true labour force with its attendant problems of management and productivity. Until then, in the allocated labour system, most of the peasants lived on the estates with houses, provision grounds, and medical attention as part payment under a system of annual hiring. Within the slave community there was no such thing as kinship, family ties, or clans. In such an atomised society there was a lack of solidarity and a sense of interdependence. The riots in Tobago increased after emancipation and indicated a growing sense of community, a natural accretion from the abolition of slavery. Under the latter regime there was no communal life; slaves could be and were regularly moved from estate to estate where they were housed and thus had no permanent place of abode and could develop no lasting relationships. Thus slavery defined the human rights and was the basis of social relationships in Tobago. It was a matrilineal system[51] in which the children, whose

---

[50] Williams, Dr. E. E., *History of the People of Trinidad and Tobago*, New York, NY: A & B Publishing, 1993, p. 58.

[51] "The planter claims his native slaves, in right of his property in the mother, —the rule in the colonies being **partus sequitur ventrem**; whereas in the law of villeinage, the rule, as to the condition of the issue, was **partus sequitur patrem**. By the application of this law every mulatto would be enfranchised;

mothers were slaves, were all slaves under the law in perpetuity. While the same was not true of the children whose mothers were free and whose fathers were slaves, the latter relationship was thought to be abhorrent.

> *"In a community where the ties of family, of caste, of class and craft fraternities, no longer exist, people are too much disposed to think exclusively of their own interests . . . Far from trying to counteract such tendencies, despotism encourages them, depriving the governed of any such solidarity and interdependence. It immures them, so to speak, each in his private life."[52]*

By 1855, however, the majority of freed people had acquired their own homes, however crude, on land held under various types of rented tenure, devised by the land owners as a means of compensating the workers for their labour. This made some of the peasants independent of the planters and was the genesis of further antagonism between the groups.

Tobago in the period before emancipation was relatively calm when compared with the other West Indian slave societies. After emancipation, however, the new freedom of the peasants and the intransigence of the plantocracy experiencing increased hardship led to a definite polarisation of the society. This manifested itself in some riots between 1852 and 1876.

THE LAND TAX RIOT OF 1852[53]

The decline of the sugar industry led inevitably to an abandonment of the sugar states and to a decline of land use. Particularly in the

---

since the paternal ancestor except in a case which it would be shocking to suppose, must have been a white and consequently a free man." Stephen, Dr. James, *The Slavery of the British West India Colonies Delineated, Vol. I, 1824*, Cambridge: Cambridge University Press, 2010, p. 23.

[52] De Tocqueville, Alexis, cited in Lienhardt, Godfrey, *Social Anthropology*, Oxford: Oxford University Press, 1966, p. 62.

[53] Craig-James, Dr. Susan E., op. cit., pp. 103-104.

Windward district, where land was not suitable to the cultivation of sugar cane, lands were unclaimed and yielded no revenue. With the loss of revenue the Assembly imposed new taxes on personal income and on carts for hire. In 1849 the land tax was set at 5 shillings per acre. In 1852 the Land Tax Act proposed to appropriate half of land taxes to pay for the immigration of workers while abolishing export duties on plantation produce. The burden of these new measures drove the peasants to despair. In November a riotous crowd went to Market Square in Scarborough while between seventy and eighty persons stormed the office of the treasurer and defiantly threw down their tax schedules while declaring that they refused to pay. Others armed with bludgeons threw stones into the courthouse building that housed the Assembly and fought with the superintendent of police. The situation was resolved when Henry Yeates, the president of the Legislative Council, gave his interpretation of the act in such a way as to remove the burden of taxation from renters, located labourers, and metayers and placing the burden squarely on employers and owners.

In 1854, there were 966 freeholders of land but they were mostly small holdings and only 43 met the voters' requirements of ten acres or an annual rateable value greater than £30.

THE MASON HALL DOG TAX RIOT OF 1867

In a desperate effort to increase the revenue, the Legislature in May 1867 authorised a tax of 6 shillings per dog of any age payable annually. In addition costs for those convicted of having unlicensed dogs after a stipulated period was set at 20 shillings. The tax was resisted by the villagers. Using a primitive public address system in the form of conch shell signal, the villagers were alerted as the police attempted to issue warrants at Mason Hall. The police had to retreat from the village and were warned not to send soldiers and that the governor himself should not put in an appearance. In 1868, the tax was modified and reduced to 4 shillings. In 1878, it was reduced to 2s 6d after neglect by taxpayers and collectors showed that little revenue was being earned by the tax.

THE BELMANNA RIOTS OF 1876

The collapse of the sugar industry in 1884 was the spark that ignited the Belmanna riots. Property values declined rapidly, and the sale of the estates by absentee landowners brought a wave of speculators from Trinidad, Barbados, and Tobago. These new owners had no ties to the old peasants and in all likelihood had a poor understanding of the metayer system and further exploited the workers, who were still living in conditions that had hardly changed since the abolition of slavery, because of the shortage of funds in the country. The result was the Belmanna riots[54] that lasted three days and were quelled by the visit of a warship from Barbados that brought the Second Company of the 2nd West India Regiment. Apart from Constable Belmanna, who was called into the fracas, several persons suffered injuries and forty persons were indicted for murder; sixteen were condemned to death but their punishment was mitigated with varying periods of imprisonment.

THE FRENCH OCCUPATION 1781 TO 1793 AND 1802 TO 1803

In 1779, Grenada was captured by French forces during the American War of Independence. France, the oldest ally of the United States of America, had engaged the British in the Caribbean and captured Grenada. This immediately severed the link between the governor-in-chief based in Grenada and the lieutenant governor based in Tobago. Two years later Tobago fell to the French and remained so despite the fact that by the Treaty of Versailles in 1783, Grenada was returned to the British. In the wake of its dominance in 1763, the defeat of the British in the Caribbean was seen in Britain as very humiliating. It served to embolden their resolve a decade later during the Revolutionary and Napoleonic wars. Under the French

---

[54] "The Police were generally beaten very severely, but Corporal Belmanna most brutally—so much so that he died from the wounds inflicted on him." Williams, Dr. E. E., *History of the People of Trinidad and Tobago*, New York, NY: A & B Publishing, 1993, p. 134.

in Tobago, the constitution remained essentially the same with the one exception that appeals from the Court of Chancery went to the Court of the French king. This is seen in the following excerpt from the terms of capitulation to the French:[55]

> "It was among other things provided that the inhabitants should preserve their civil government, laws, customs, and ordinances, and the persons who then administered justice were continued in their functions until the peace, so long as they should conduct themselves properly. It was further provided that the Court of Chancery should be held by the members of the Council in the form established until the peace; but appeals from that court were to be made to the Council of His Most Christian Majesty. The inhabitants in general and clergy were protected in the enjoyment of their estates, and everything in their possession as well as all privileges, rights, honours and exemptions, and in the free exercise of their religion; and to the clergy it was insured the enjoyment of their benefices. It was declared that the free Negroes and mulattoes should be maintained in their liberty, but that thereafter no slave should be franchised without the permission of the governor General. The inhabitants who were absent, even those in the service of His Britannic Majesty, were maintained in the possession of their property which they were allowed to manage by their attorneys. And all were allowed to dispose of their estates real and personal as they should think fit; and they were at liberty to send their children to England, or elsewhere to be educated, and to receive them back again."

In April 1793 Tobago was recaptured by Major General Cornelius Cuyler for Britain. He appointed a military governor and a Council of nine members. At the Treaty of Amiens in 1802 Tobago was

---

[55] Woodcock, Henry Isles, *A History of Tobago*, Frank Cass Library of West Indian Studies, 1971, pp. 55-56.

returned to France and in September of that year General F. Sabuguet was appointed captain general and Governor by Bonaparte.

EDUCATION

In 1823, there were three primary schools in Scarborough and one in Plymouth. By 1827, the well-to-do had established a few fee paying private schools. The expense barred the growing numbers of blacks and free coloureds. There was a public meeting and appeal to the government for assistance. A free school started under the aegis of a Committee of Free Blacks and Coloureds, and housed in a Wesleyan church chapel was officially opened in 1828 with an annual grant of £100 from the Assembly.

After emancipation the Mico Charity based in Jamaica made an annual grant for the education of the former slaves in Tobago and throughout the British West Indies; however, that ended in 1848. The thrust to educate benefited from the denominational rivalry, and in 1850 there were fifteen schools. In 1875, a board of education was appointed by the lieutenant governor and included one minister and two laymen from each of the principal denominations. By then the number of schools had grown to twenty: eight Anglican, seven Wesleyan, and five Moravian. Over the years the government had played an increasing role in the education by increasing the grants to the schools. In 1876, the total education grant amounted to £1,000. The education system, like everything else in Tobago, was constrained by the dire state of the economy.

PUBLIC HEALTH

At the advance towards the end of the nineteenth century the government instituted a few measures for improving individual and public health and care for the indigent. A hospital was established in 1876. The Royal Commissioners in 1883 described the hospital as the worst they had visited in the West Indies. There was no facility for treating the mentally ill, who were either sent to Grenada for treatment or else confined in the local jails.

RELIGION

The proclamation that created the colony of Tobago required of the governor general:

> *"That he and all of his officials would be required to take not only the oath of allegiance, but also that of abjuration and supremacy, and make and subscribe to the test as required by 25 Car.2nd."*

In the instruction accompanying the Royal Commission the sovereign declared:

> *"That as the end that the Church of England might be established both in principle and practice."*

From the establishment of the government of Tobago in 1763, it may be inferred that the Church of England was the established church in Tobago.[56] Consistent with that was the division of the colony into parishes and rectories. The Society of Wesleyan Methodists established a mission in Tobago in early 1818. Concern by John Hamilton of the Riseland estate for the spiritual needs of the slaves led to the establishment of the Moravians (United Brethren) in 1790. The Presbyterians had a short lived experience, having made provisions for a preacher in 1834, but by 1841, the congregation was dissolved and the kirks leased to the Anglicans. In 1881, in a population of 19,051 there were 2,865 Anglicans, 4,612 Moravians, 4,016 Wesleyans, 13 Roman Catholics, 11 Presbyterians, 27 of other forms of worship, and 507 of whom the religious allegiance was unknown. In retrospect the fate of the Presbyterians was symbolic of the problems that confronted the island. The small island could not viably support and mirror all the institutions that were possible in a larger country. In 1874, the Church of England was disestablished after the passage of the Tobago Concurrent Endowment Act of

---

[56]   Douglas Archibald, Rupert, *Tobago: Melancholy Isle, Vol. III, 1807-1898,* Port-of-Spain, Trinidad: Westindiana, 2003, p. 18.

1873. The denominations played a crucial role in the development of education in Tobago.

Flag Badge of Tobago c. 1880

CHAPTER III

Making the Decisions I: Tobago and Trinidad

---◆◇◆---

If men could learn from history, what lessons it might teach us! But passion and party blind our eyes, and the light which experience gives is a lantern on the stern, which shines only on the waves behind us.

Samuel Taylor Coleridge,
Specimens of Table Talk, Vol. II

---◆◇◆---

THE CONVENTIONAL WISDOM SURROUNDING the decision to form the union between Trinidad and Tobago holds that the decision was forced on the two Crown colonies by the imperial government. The rationale for this, according to Dr Williams, was:

> *"The British government washed its hands of the matter and divested itself of any special responsibility for Tobago by making available to the Government of Trinidad the sum of £4,000 in part repayment of a loan of £5,000 which had been made from Trinidad to Tobago."*[57]

---

[57] Williams, Dr. E. E., *History of the People of Trinidad and Tobago,* New York, NY: A & B Publishing, 1993, p. 150.

*"It was power without responsibility. It was power for the
mere sake of power."*[58]

If we are to dismiss Dr Williams's remarks as cynical, we must
re-examine the relationship that existed between the two colonies prior
to the decision making process together with the participants and the
economic and political environment in which the decision was made.

NASCENT RELATIONSHIP WITH TRINIDAD

The official records of Spain show that in February 1569, Trinidad
and Tobago was considered as one colony with one Treasurer and one
captain general.[59] However, early in the nineteenth century Tobago's
relationship with the European powers and other British West Indian
islands had been settled, and there was little formal or informal
relationship with its closest neighbour to the southwest. Because of
its political affiliation from the time of its settlement in 1763 by the
British, Tobago shared communications with Grenada and Barbados
and Britain and some trade links with the North American colonies,
before independence in 1776, and with the United States thereafter.
As a French colony it had developed links to metropolitan France and
the French possessions in the West Indies. The island had belonged
to Spain from its discovery like Trinidad, where no gold was found
and consequently there was no sustained effort of colonisation. On a
number of occasions the Spanish rulers from neighbouring Trinidad
intervened to drive usurpers off the island, to maintain Spanish
sovereignty over the island, and to avoid their own security from
being jeopardised.

The vision of a political link between the two most southerly
islands of the West Indian archipelago goes back to the middle of
the seventeenth century. Although no more than thirty kilometres
separate the two islands, there was little contact with Spanish

---

[58] Ibid., p. 167.
[59] Garcia de la Torre, Francisco, (Ed. & Translator), *Spanish Trinidad by
Francisco Morales Padrón*, Ian Randle Publishers, Kingston, Jamaica,
2012, p. 259 (Note 66).

speaking Trinidad to the south. Because of Spain's neutrality during most of the period there was very little interaction with the largely neglected island to the south. During the French occupation of Tobago there was a relationship with Martinique and France. There was by contrast very little formal contact between Tobago and Trinidad.

The close proximity of the two islands suggests some familial ties originating with the Amerindians. Just as there were ties established between families in eastern Venezuela and southwest Trinidad long before the coming of Columbus, so there must have been ties between the Amerindian tribes of Tobago and those of north Trinidad. The abortive attempt of the Dutch in Tobago in 1628 and the resistance by the Spaniards and Amerindians in Trinidad showed that there were links between the two islands. It was only a matter of time, however, before the natural link between the two islands would be cemented, firstly in a commercial union and ultimately in a political union.

In 1628, Don Luis de Monsalves, governor of Trinidad, with a small expeditionary force that included a number of Amerindians, drove the Dutch out of Tobago. The Dutch were the first Europeans to try to settle Tobago after noting the indifference of the Spaniards or thinking that the island was abandoned.

- In 1636, the Dutch under Jan de Moor were again driven out of Tobago by Don Diego Lopez de Escobar, governor of Trinidad.
- The Treaty of Breda, 1667, prompted the Dutch to reoccupy Tobago. Pieter Constant was sent as governor, and in a memorial prepared on that occasion for the information of the governing bodies in the United Provinces, an unknown author wrote ominously of the relationship between Trinidad and Tobago:

> "The inhabitants of Tobago will in time have a good trade with the inhabitants of the Island of Trinidad which lies in the sight of them, as likewise with the River Orinocke for cows hides, tobacco, citron, etc.,

for as much as they sail to the said Island in a very short time.'[60]

- In 1772, a number of slaves in Tobago fled their masters and found their way to Trinidad and Margarita. In 1773, Carlos III, king of Spain, declared that African slaves in Trinidad who had escaped from Tobago were not to be treated as slaves, and that they should be employed in public works.[61]
- The governor of Trinidad was frequently appealing to the authorities in Caracas and Spain for men and arms to defend the island. In addition, Spain's neutrality during the American War of Independence made Trinidad a haven for pirates who, contrary to the Treaty of Ratisbon, were harassing British shipping in the Caribbean. In September 1777, Pascal Bonavita, a pirate who held an American congressional commission, entered Man of War Bay in Tobago, captured a schooner, and took thirty-seven Africans and two Caribs to Trinidad, where he traded them. An attempt by the British authorities to recover the property failed. Don Manuel Falquez, the governor of Trinidad, in washing his hands of the matter, advised the British officers to take their complaint to Martinique, where the Americans had diplomatic representatives.
- In 1786, during the French occupation, Roumé de St. Laurent was made Ordonnateur of Tobago. A year later he enticed the governor of Tobago, Count Dillon, to write to the governor of Trinidad, Don Chacon, to establish a system of mutual aid between the two islands. Considering the great influence that both St. Laurent and Chacon had in establishing the French community in Trinidad, that move must be seen as a great diplomatic initiative to unite the two islands. In considering a possible shipping route between the two islands Chacon pointed out that turtle fishers went from Band de L'Est in northeast Trinidad to Great Courland Bay in Tobago.

---

[60] Douglas Archibald, Rupert, *Tobago: Melancholy Isle, Vol. I, 1498-1771*, Port-of-Spain, Trinidad: Westindiana, 1987, p. 43.

[61] Douglas Archibald, Rupert, *Tobago: Melancholy Isle, Vol. II, 1782-1805*, Port-of-Spain, Trinidad: UWI School of Continuing Studies, 1995, p. 12 footnote.

- However, the relationship between the two islands would fluctuate as the relationship between France and Spain changed during the Revolutionary and Napoleonic wars. The French revolution of 1789 marked a change in the relationship. French republicans throughout the West Indies were seen as modern day terrorists, and in any event, when Spain joined the first coalition in the Revolutionary War with France in May 1793, the British had by then recaptured Tobago.

- In 1798, one year after the conquest of Trinidad, a committee of both houses of the Legislature in Tobago met and recommended conditions for the amelioration of the slaves along the lines of the *Code Noir* in Trinidad.

- In 1801, Tobago was authorised to carry out free trade with the Spanish colonies on the main. However, because of the location of Trinidad most of the trade passed through the latter, and Tobago did not achieve the full benefits of her endeavours.

- Not long after the Peace Treaty of Paris, in 1818, consultation between Governor Sir Frederick P. Robinson in Tobago and Governor Woodford in Trinidad led to a decision to grant land in the region of Valencia in northeast Trinidad to 180 soldiers of the soon to be demobilised 6th West India Regiment—then based in Tobago. The West India Regiment, comprising free Negroes and slaves conscripted from the plantations, was first raised in 1795, and by 1799 the number had risen to twelve. The regiments served mainly in North America and the Caribbean during the Napoleonic wars. This newest set of immigrants to Trinidad from Tobago served to strengthen the archaic ties of the Amerindians between the two islands. Such migration was not unusual for Trinidad where the curtailment of the slave trade had added the importation of labour from China and Madeira to augment growing polyglot society.

- In 1824, Trinidad and Tobago joined Barbados, Grenada, St. Vincent, Dominica, Antigua, Montserrat, St. Christopher, Nevis and the Virgin Islands, St. Lucia, and the Grenadines as the creation of a Bishop's See of the then established Anglican Church, known as the Bishopric of Barbados and the Leeward Islands. The bishop, known as the Bishop of Barbados and the Leeward Islands, was an ex-officio member of the Legislative Council of Trinidad established in 1831. In 1842 the diocese was split into three bishoprics, one of which was known as the diocese of Barbados, which included Barbados, Trinidad, Tobago, Grenada, St. Lucia, and the Grenadines.

- After the devastating hurricane of 1847 in which the barracks at Fort King George were severely damaged, the company of the 19th Regiment that was in garrison there was sent to Trinidad for their safety on the arrival of the first sloop. The commanding officer was fearful for their health with the exposure to the elements during the height of the rainy season.
- In 1861, the lieutenant governor of Tobago, James V. Drysdale, used the Trinidad Post Office Memorandum as a basis for establishing a postal service in Tobago. Prior to that the service was administered from Barbados.
- In 1878, there was correspondence between Lieutenant Governor Gore in Tobago and Governor Irving in Trinidad with a view to establishing a bimonthly mail service between Tobago and Port-of-Spain via the route Tobago, Toco, Arima, Port-of-Spain. The feasibility of the project was tested by the chief of police of Trinidad traveling over the proposed route. The proposal, nevertheless, was not implemented and it was not until 1885, when a contract was established with the Royal Mail Steam Packet Company, that a regular mail service was established between Trinidad and Tobago.
- In 1880 Lieutenant Governor Gore suggested that Tobago be administered in a joint arrangement with Trinidad. He thought that the idle land and lower wages available in Tobago would induce speculators from Trinidad to develop cocoa plantations in Tobago.
- In 1880, John McCall, the largest merchandising firm in Tobago, in recognition of the growing trade between Tobago and Trinidad ran a cutter as a passenger vessel between the two islands.
- In 1881, agents in Scarborough procured a steamer of 100 tons that opened up considerable intercourse with Grenada, the administrative centre, Barbados, and Trinidad.

- The size of the population of Tobago in 1881 was 18,051. When compared with the population of 1871 at 17,054 that figure points towards the high infant mortality rate in Tobago. But it also conceals the fact that relatively large numbers of men of the labouring class were migrating to Trinidad where jobs paid better. This migration between the two islands was the continuation of a custom that predated the discoveries of Columbus.
- After the abandonment of the sugar estates in 1884, speculators from Trinidad, attracted by falling land prices in Tobago, attempted to bring new life to the industry. Unfamiliar as they were with the metayer[62] system, it appeared that their intervention served only to aggravate the strained relations between the metayers and the planters with an accumulation of matters awaiting judgement in the courts.
- By 1886, a growing trade by sloop and schooner had been established between Trinidad and Tobago.[63]
- In 1886, the governor of Trinidad proposed to the Colonial Office that the people of Tobago be invited to transfer themselves to Moruga in Trinidad.

Concrete moves to strengthen the formal relationship between Trinidad and Tobago began to materialise in Trinidad in 1886 when the governor, Sir William Robinson, under the authority of the Customs Ordinance of 1880, issued an order for the admission and clearance at Toco of vessels and their cargoes from the island of Tobago:

ORDER FOR THE ADMISSION AND CLEARANCE AT TOCO

Government House,
25 February, 1886

Vessels from Tobago in ballast, or laden with free goods and passengers only, will be allowed to enter

---

[62] A derivative from the French *métayer* a sharecropper. In Tobago the word had variants in *metairie* and *metayage*.

[63] Craig-James, Dr. Susan E., op. cit., p. 292.

and discharge at Toco on the following conditions: (25th February, 1886)

- *That the vessel anchors at a distance of not more than six hundred yards from the nearest part of the Beach to the Toco Police Station.*
- *That permission be obtained from the Police Officer at Toco before communication takes place between the vessel and the shore.*
- *That the discharge takes place only between the hours of 8 am and 5 pm, and only at such place as the Police Officer may direct.*
- *That before discharge the vessel and cargo be entered with the Police Officer in such manner as he may direct.*

Vessels entering Toco from Tobago will be allowed to proceed from the former to the latter place with passengers and free goods only, on condition that they are previously cleared with the Police Officer in such manner as he may direct.

By Command,
J. Scott Bushe,
Colonial Secretary.

Thus, at the start of 1886 we witness the opening up of formal commercial relations between Trinidad and Tobago. The close geographical link would be a big factor in the event of a union between the two colonies. But there were other factors, cultural and historical: both colonies, some four hundred years after being discovered by Columbus, then shared the English language with English law. Both colonies, Tobago, because of its small size and the influence of the French occupation, and Trinidad, because it remained largely undeveloped by Spain, had to some extent escaped the turmoil that had characterised the relationship between the slaves and the whites in most of the other West Indian colonies: the slave revolt of Haiti of 1793; the slave revolt in British Guiana in 1823;

the permanent state of revolt in Barbados in the two decades before emancipation. The harmony between the races in Tobago was noted by Woodcock, a former chief justice, while the harmony in Trinidad was a key factor in attracting people as a means of overcoming its chronic labour shortage in a rapidly expanding economy. The establishment of the regular mail service led to trade and commerce and freer movement between the two islands. It was a development of which many of the residents of Trinidad were aware: the members of the Legislature and the press; the members of the police force; and traders based at Toco. The suggestion for annexation, when it came, surprised few people on the islands although the reactions were predictably different.

The principal participants in the creation of the union were the British Parliament; the Colonial Office; the Legislative Council of Tobago; and the Legislative Council of Trinidad. As best as can be reconstructed, the following is the sequence of events leading up to the union: In the first half of 1886, the governor-in-chief of the Windward Islands, with the concurrence of the administrator of Tobago, made a proposal to the Colonial Office. The proposal suggested that the colony of Tobago would be economically and efficiently administered if it were a dependency of Trinidad (June 1886). The matter was taken up with Her Majesty's government who expressed a desire to bring about the union; the Colonial Office put the proposal to the governors of both colonies (December 1886). The Legislatures took certain resolutions (January 1887 and March 1887); there were some negotiations between the secretary of state and the governors (March 1887); the British Parliament passed an enabling act (September 1887); and the Privy Council issued an Order in Council that made the union a legal entity (November 1888). In summary, the Tobago Legislature expressed to the imperial government the desire to be annexed to Trinidad, and the Trinidad Legislature consented.

THE TOBAGO LEGISLATURE

It is obvious that the compelling case for the union had to be made in Tobago. The colony was plagued with a political crisis for most of the nineteenth century. The crisis stemmed from the unending conflict between the executive and legislative arms of the government. This problem was discernible to several administrators long before the idea of annexation was made, and reading between the lines, we see that it was a major contributing factor to the several changes made to the Constitution of Tobago in the fifty years before the union took place. According to Administrator Henry Yeates in September 1853:

> *"The state of our Roads, the state of our Public buildings, the condition of our Jails, the bankrupt state of our Exchequer, all indicate a want of power in the Executive—principally attributable to the deficiency of its pecuniary means . . . [but also] to the injudicious concessions which have been from early times been made in these Colonies, in deference to the Representative Branch of the Legislature; by means of which it has come to pass that **the centralization of power which is the characteristic feature of Monarchical institutions has been in great measure lost, the Executive power weakened . . . , and the character of the Government superseded by the Oligarchy** . . . everything within this Colony betokens regression [my emphasis]."*[64]

During that same year similar sentiments were expressed by Chief Justice Edward D. Sanderson, who told the Privy Council:

> *"**I attribute the disastrous state of the colony, its bankrupt exchequer, and its legislation**, in which it is behind all other Colonies as respects the administration of justice, police, education and everything else necessary for the wellbeing of the people, **to the course which has been invariably adopted by the Executive Government . . . of***

---

[64] Craig-James, Dr. Susan E., *The Changing Society of Tobago 1838-1938, Vol. I, 1838-1900,* Port-of-Spain, Trinidad: Paria Publishing, 2008, p. 232.

*remaining perfectly inactive, awaiting measures to be
originated by the Council and Assembly. [my emphasis]"*[65]

The problem was equally evident during the administration of James
V. Drysdale, who was lieutenant governor between 1857 and 1864.
He opined that nothing concrete was achieved during his tenure,
dominated as it was by interchanges of addresses:

> "To sum up, the Executive Committee was, as Hume
> Wrong put it, 'a strange contrivance.' **It was difficult to
> find people who would not oppose the Executive, [and]
> who would also be acceptable to the Assembly and the
> Legislative Council.** The committee became a game of
> musical chairs, as it were, with frequent resignations,
> removals, dissolutions and reconstitutions; eleven
> changes were made in eight years, and on one occasion
> four months elapsed before three persons could be found
> to serve. **[my emphasis].**"[66]

A union with Trinidad would have the effect of transforming the
Constitution of Tobago, and the proposal, when it was made by Mr
Sendall the governor, was readily welcomed by the administrators.
The idea of having a political association with other islands in
the West Indies was not a new one to the people of Tobago, and
certainly not new to the people of the British West Indies. The
Leeward Islands group existed in varying forms in 1671, 1833, and
1871. From the British settlement in 1763 Tobago was associated
with Grenada, Dominica, and St. Vincent and the Grenadines in
a Windward Islands grouping then known as the South Charibee
Islands. From 1833 it was associated in a number of groupings with
Barbados, St. Vincent and the Grenadines, Grenada, and St. Lucia
as the Windward Islands. Outside of the period 1779 to 1814, while
France was at war with Britain, when it enjoyed the luxury of having
its own governor, the security of the island was inexorably embedded

---

[65]   Ibid., p. 232.
[66]   Craig-James, Dr. Susan E., *The Changing Society of Tobago 1838-1938, Vol.
       I, 1838-1900*, Port-of-Spain, Trinidad: Paria Publishing, 2008, p. 235.

in a larger grouping. The authority of the most senior official on the island varied with the form of the union. It will be recalled that the lieutenant governor did not have the powers of a commander-in-chief and the authority of the administrator, the most senior official when the union with Trinidad was considered was even less.

UPPER CLASS POLITICS

We may speculate with some confidence that at the time of the union there was little in public opinion to guide the legislators on the matter. Clearly there was no such thing as an organised political party, and such newspapers that existed had limited circulation in view of the low level of literacy, abetted by the physical difficulty of poor distribution facilities. There were, however, some signs of political awareness amongst the population of all classes. In particular the planters and merchants appeared to be a long-standing, close-knit cohesive force. For example, in 1823 there was unanimous disapproval by the planters of the measures by the British government to ameliorate the condition of the slaves in Tobago. Shortly thereafter there was a petition to the Crown from the same group seeking to remove the governor, Sir Frederick P. Robinson. In addition there was a reaction after the bicameral system was changed to a single chamber. After the new Council first convened in 1875, a public meeting was held at Scarborough at which the new arrangement was denounced as a violation of the long-standing rights of the people of Tobago. The planters were the instigators of this protest. The planters and merchants established the Tobago Chamber of Commerce in 1884, and its members enjoyed membership of the Tobago Legislative Council. This body represented the interests of the plantocracy and tried desperately to influence the legislation for the annexation. But the interests of the planters were narrow and self-seeking and obviously had very little concern for the plight of the mass of people in Tobago. Indeed, in 1876, the planters were in favour of becoming a Crown colony if only to frustrate the democratic aspirations of the Negro and coloured masses.

LOWER CLASS POLITICS

There were signs as well of growing cohesion amongst the lower classes. A public meeting was held in Scarborough in 1827 for the purpose of establishing a free public school for the education of all classes. Furthermore, the Land Tax riot of 1852, the Mason Hall Dog Tax riot of 1867, and the Belmanna riots of 1876 had shown that the peasants were prepared to take political action over harsh administrative measures whether coming from the government or the plantocracy.

> *"The riots displayed both the strength of the class antagonisms and the vulnerability of the dominant class, who discovered, in the words of the Privy Council, that they had been living on 'a half extinct volcano which only slumbered to awake to mediated destruction.'"*[67]

The instigation of the Belmanna riots has been attributed to the large number of Bajans employed on the estate, and the political awareness of the Bajans was something of which most members of the merchant and planter class were aware.

Where before emancipation the Negroes were indeed an atomised society, thereafter there was growing social and emerging political relations. Following the memorial of the assembly to remove Lieutenant Governor Shortland, ninety-three persons, comprising mechanics and labourers for the most part, sent a counter memorial in support while requesting drastic changes in the franchise rules. In their complaints of the assembly they said:

> *"Too long in its Mal-effusion of the law to no benefit to the Colony."*[68]

---

[67] Williams, Dr. E. E., *History of the People of Trinidad and Tobago*, New York, NY: A & B Publishing, 1993, p. 134.

[68] Craig-James, Dr. Susan E., *The Changing Society of Tobago 1838-1938, Vol. I, 1838-1900*, Port-of-Spain, Trinidad: Paria Publishing, 2008, p. 233.

The church played more than a passive role in the political life of Tobago if only providing suitable venues for holding political meetings.

If we were to conjecture as to attitude of the population as a whole towards the annexation, we would easily conclude that they would have voted in favour if only to alleviate the situation with leaders seen to be oppressive to their wishes. In any event the Legislative Council had elected members whose votes would be representative of their parishes. The authorities in Tobago were looking forward to a reduction in the administrative costs together with the ready access to the relatively larger market in Trinidad when they considered and passed the resolution for annexation, and much of the initiative for annexation had originated from former lieutenant governors and administrators of Tobago. Finally, the idea of strengthening relations between Tobago and Trinidad was not a bolt from the blue. As we have seen already, arrangements had been implemented for vessels from Tobago to discharge their cargo at Toco in northeast Trinidad, and talks were ongoing about improving the communications between the two islands.

The Legislature in Tobago took its first step when it was directed by the governor-in-chief to formally consider the proposal of the secretary of state for annexation.

EXTRACT FROM THE *TOBAGO GAZETTE*, DECEMBER 17, 1886

The following Notice received from His Excellency the Governor-in-Chief is published for general information.

R.B. Llewelyn,
Administrator.

Government Office,
2nd December, 1886.

Her Majesty's Government having had under its consideration the condition and prospects of the colony of Tobago and having regard to its geographical proximity to, and means of communication with, the colony of Trinidad, are of the opinion that it would be to the advantage of both Colonies that the Colony of Tobago be annexed and form part of the said colony of Trinidad Such annexation may be effected in either of the following modes namely:

- *The Colony of Tobago may be wholly or completely incorporated with the Colony of Trinidad; or*
- *The Colony of Tobago may be annexed to the Colony of Trinidad as a dependency, having a separate Treasury and sub-ordinate Legislature, holding to Trinidad the same relation that the Turk Islands hold to Jamaica.*

The former of the two schemes appears to be preferable. Her Majesty's Government are however desirous of ascertaining the opinions and wishes of the inhabitants of both Colonies upon the subject; and after a sufficient time has elapsed for a consideration of the question, resolutions in favour of incorporation of Tobago with Trinidad, or as a dependency, will be introduced into the Legislative councils of both Colonies.

Given the stipulation that a sufficient time ought to have been allowed for consideration of the matter, the Legislature seems to have moved somewhat hastily in deciding the matter on 19 January 1887.

RESOLUTION PASSED BY THE LEGISLATIVE COUNCIL OF TOBAGO IN FAVOUR OF ANNEXATION

At a meeting of the Legislative Council of Tobago held on the 19th day of January, 1887 under the presidency of His Excellency the Governor, the following Resolutions were put and carried unanimously:—

That this Council, having had under its consideration the notice published in the Government Gazette under the date 2nd December 1886, is satisfied that subject to certain conditions hereinafter mentioned, it would be of the advantage of both Colonies that the Colony of Tobago should be united with that of Trinidad so as to form one colony, to be called the Colony of Trinidad and Tobago, and that the Colony so considered should be governed by one Governor and be subject to one and the same code of laws.

That as an incident of such union this Council is of the opinion that the duties leviable in Tobago upon articles imported from abroad should be subject to the same as those in Trinidad, and that the traffic and intercourse between the two Islands should be absolutely free; but that the interests of Tobago imperatively require that all the internal taxes other than the duties aforesaid should be imposed and adjusted with such reference to local circumstances, and should not follow the laws of taxation in force in Trinidad, except in so far as local circumstances may admit of it.

That this Council is further of opinion that all revenues collected in and on account of Tobago should be wholly expended in the administration of the Island, and should not be absorbed in the general revenue of the United Colony; that no part of the public expenditure of Trinidad should be chargeable upon the revenues of Tobago, and no part of the public expenditure of Tobago upon the revenues of Trinidad except in so far as the two islands may by mutual consent, and upon terms to be mutually agreed, enter jointly upon any public enterprise for the benefit of both.

That the Chief Executive Officer representing the Government of the United Colony in Tobago should have associated with him a local Board, to be termed the Financial Board, whose duty it should be to advise the Governor in all matters relating to the internal taxation and expenditure of the Island, and that no tax leviable in Tobago (other than Customs Duties) should be imposed or altered without the consent of such Board.

> *That the Financial Board in addition to the Executive
> Office consist of three resident householders one of who
> be nominated by the Governor, and two to be elected by
> the general body of the householders of the island.*
>
> *That for the carrying out of these proposals this
> Council do move an humble address to the Crown praying
> that Her Most Gracious Majesty will be pleased to take
> such steps as necessary to effect the union of the two
> Colonies and to secure the faithful and lasting obedience
> of the conditions hereinbefore set forth.*

Certified a true copy,
Herbert H. Sealy
Clerk of the Council.

After the debate and unanimous resolution in favour of annexation, the Legislative Council on the same day debated and passed a second motion that, to this day, defies explanation. Mr Ebenezer Henderson, an unofficial member and a planter, tabled a petition by "certain Mercantile Firms and others" that modified the proposal of annexation by adding a conditional clause. It is puzzling to explain why the dissentient view should be presented only after the unanimous vote taken. In presenting the petition, Henderson affirmed his belief that the majority of the people supported the annexation although he felt that they did not fully understand the issues at stake. The second resolution asked that Tobago retain the option of reverting to its existing status in the event that the proposed union failed. Henderson thought that the people of Tobago favoured the union although he thought that they had not understood fully the issues at stake.

Supported by another unofficial member, Mr Edward Keens, a former president of the Assembly who had acted as governor, Henderson moved a resolution, the revised version of which was adopted. This second resolution which, in effect, added conditions to the earlier resolution remains curious, coming as it did only a few hours after the unanimous resolution for annexation supported by Mr Henderson and Mr Keens and is symbolic of the state of the Legislature at that time. The division of the vote is not recorded, and it appears that the Colonial Office objected to the resolution. However, on 11 May 1887, the Council, despite the protests of Henderson and Keens, withdrew the resolution. None of the subsequent correspondence from the governor of Trinidad, the governor-in-chief of Tobago, or the secretary of state bears any relationship to this resolution. In any event the matter which it raised was disposed of effectively by the secretary of state when frustration experienced by the authorities in Tobago in 1894 forced them to take up the same matter directly with the secretary of state.

RESOLUTION MOVED BY MR EBENEZER HENDERSON AT THE MEETING OF THE LEGISLATIVE COUNCIL OF TOBAGO ON 19 JANUARY 1887

"That inasmuch as the wish of the people of Tobago for union with Trinidad has principally been based on the representation of the Government and the assurances given to the people that material benefits will result to Tobago from such union, the Secretary of State for the Colonies to be respectfully asked in the event of such union taking place to afford the people a pledge that should it prove disadvantageous to the Colony, or otherwise undesirable to the majority of the inhabitants, this Colony shall on petition have granted back to it the form of self-government which now exists here."[69]

It is difficult to understand the decision of the authorities in Tobago to opt for financial independence given the dire state of the economy at the time. But perhaps they were aware of the higher rate of taxation in Trinidad at the time at £3 per annum, whereas in Tobago it was 15 shillings per annum. The economy in Trinidad could support the higher rate of taxation, but one purpose was for the development of infrastructure, in particular the Trinidad Railway, a development that

---

[69]   Craig-James, Dr. Susan E., *The Changing Society of Tobago 1838-1938, Vol. I, 1838-1900*, Port-of-Spain, Trinidad: Paria Publishing, 2008, p. 293.

had begun under the stewardship of Governor Sir Arthur Hamilton Gordon in 1866.

THE TRINIDAD LEGISLATURE

The motion to annex Tobago, before the Legislative Council of Trinidad in 1887, was the weightiest considered since the establishment of that body in 1831. Historically Trinidad's relations were with Spain, Venezuela, and (after the Cedula) Grenada and the other French-speaking West Indian islands. The British conquest established new relations between Trinidad and the other British West Indian islands through the supply of governors and senior civil servants and imported labour comprised of ex-slaves seeking a better standard of living in Trinidad. The Legislature, being a wholly nominated body, lacked some of the democratic traditions of the other British West Indian islands, although Trinidad was governed as a British Crown colony after Chacon capitulated to Abercrombie in 1797. The Legislative Council, however, was only established in 1831 and comprised official members and unofficial members nominated by the governor.

The challenge that faced the Crown colony then was to make a decision in the best interest of the people of Trinidad in the absence of a popular franchise. The absence of a fully representative basis in the Legislature would have skewed the decision, but on the record of the performance, the Trinidad Legislature had achieved its mandate creditably. Even a confirmed democrat like Dr Williams could only resolve the matter in a rhetorical question. Even so, the Trinidad Legislature gave the problem its best shot. The lack of a democratically elected assembly did not mean an absence of politics. In fact, the two main political interests dated back to the conquest and were represented in the Council. They were, on the one hand, the older Francophile and Catholic immigrants, land owners whose interests were then largely in cocoa production, and on the other, the British merchants and Protestants, whose interest lay in sugar production. Indeed, it is certain that although there was little general interest in political matters, there was a minority of persons, in a growing middle class, who took politics very seriously. For example, during that eventful year, James Anthony Froude, Regius Professor of History at Oxford, had published *The English in the West Indies, or the Bow of Ulysses*. In response to this, in 1889, John Jacob Thomas, a native intellectual of Trinidad published his historic polemic, **Froudacity.**

There is a modern tendency to suggest that the decision came out of the blue and was forced on the people. But the idea did not originate in a vacuum. It was only natural that relations between the two neighbouring British islands would increase. Only a year earlier in 1886, the governor of Trinidad, under the authority of the Customs Ordinance, had issued instructions for vessels from Tobago to be cleared at Toco. In addition the idea of developing a postage system had been broached and preliminary studies done on the feasibility of a tentative route. The governor of Trinidad at the time of the decision was Sir William Robinson who, for a while before taking up the post in Trinidad, had been governor in Chief of the Windward Islands group based in Barbados. That group included Tobago. In that capacity he had suggested to the Colonial Office the idea of a union between Trinidad and Tobago and it was his fate to be placed in a position to preside over the decision in the Trinidad Legislature. While the idea of union did not originate in Trinidad, the issue was well ventilated in the set of newspapers that existed at the time, particularly so in the *Port-of-Spain Gazette*, then the mouthpiece of the unofficials in Trinidad. The level of education was certainly better than in Tobago and there was a relatively large middle class. However, one legacy of the Picton administration was the unofficial colour bar[70] that silently blocked the social advance of all coloured people. The peculiar demographics of Trinidad at the time of the conquest was one of the reasons the island became a Crown Colony. But Picton on discovering the relatively large numbers of free coloureds many

---

[70] "The only mode of rendering these people useful, without their becoming formidable to the Colony is to have them where they are; to establish no artificial distinctions; to humiliate them by no marks of Degradation or Incapacity. You need not promote them to any office of importance or honour, but it is not necessary to show them, that you have raised an insuperable bar to their advancement or ambition." Picton's despatch to the Secretary of State in *Colonial Office Papers*.

of them with property and better off that the white merchant class, imposed an invisible colour barrier in the society which lasted for over one hundred and seventy years. Such a society could not have been created without the connivance of the leaders of the society. The society was transformed into one in which the Governor and the whites were at the apex of the social strata, with those at the bottom with a series of gradation in between. Within thirty years of the conquest Picton's unofficial colour bar had created a society that in the opinion of the secretary of state was strongly divided by castes. This was the condition of Trinidad in 1888 when the decision was being made on annexation.

With annexation on the agenda, there was another issue occupying the minds of the legislators in Trinidad at more or less the same time, for the Royal Franchise Commission, sitting in Port-of-Spain, was considering a change in the constitution to introduce a limited elective franchise. On top of the colour problem was imposed the problem of diversity of languages and races arising from immigration throughout the nineteenth century. There were thus two problems militating against granting the franchise: the first was the language problem and the second was the lack of knowledge about the political process. The first was best expressed in the minority report of the committee submitted by its chairman, Stephen Gatty, who was also the attorney general.

> "The educational test suggested in the Report of the majority would exclude a number of persons who cannot read, speak and understand the English language but who, nevertheless, on any property qualification alone would seem to be entitled to vote. This point received my very earnest consideration and in the end I felt bound to express my opinion that such a test would be necessary despite the apparent injustice. There are large numbers of persons who do not understand English and for a long time to come this condition of thing would be inevitable. No doubt the knowledge of English is spreading but in the Courts of Justice, the employment of Interpreters of Chinese, Hindoo, Tamil, Portuguese, Spanish, French

and Creole French is still absolutely necessary for the conduct of business. In some parts of the Country there are old Spanish Creole settlements far away from the centres of civilization, for the good roads have not yet reached them and these people cannot be said to read or speak or write the English language yet they form an important class and have very substantial interests in the colony. They are a class of peasant proprietors, quiet if left alone by agitators, aspiring to nothing but growing their cacao and fruit and living on their own land—many of these small holdings are heavily pledged to the town merchants who advance against their crops and buy the produce of their land. They are loyal and so far as I can learn have only local grievances as to roads etc. Politics are entirely unknown to them."[71]

Mr Gatty also highlighted a second problem in the lack of political education:

"I cannot image anything more fatal to the interests of this prosperous colony, than to attempt to rouse its peculiar heterogeneous population to desire to exercise political privileges and to take a share in the government before this spontaneous wish to do so, the result of a more advanced state of education and civilization, has arisen. Moreover, I see in the people no traces of the sense of grave responsibility which would underlie any system of election. So far as they have been given such powers in the election of the Borough Councillors and Road auditors they have shown the most meager appreciation of the value. The circumstances surrounding the signing of the Petition I regard as a warning example of the political immorality which in my opinion would certainly be repeated until the masses have more education (so far as the figures could be ascertained only 3,043 out of a

---

[71]   Gatty, Stephen, *Minority Report of the Royal Franchise Commission Trinidad*, 1888.

*total of 12,053 direct taxpayers in the country districts
can sign their names) and until they have learnt more
completely the duties and responsibilities attaching to
private life, I consider they are unfit to take a part in
politics."*[72]

Thus while in Trinidad the Legislature, in all probability, had the
best the country had to offer, it operated in an environment where
there was much indifference to and little understanding of changes
that would fundamentally alter the constitution of their country. The
12-to-1 vote in favour of the resolution in the Legislative Council
of Trinidad makes it clear that there must have been a great deal of
magnanimity in the part of the unofficial members of the Legislative
Council in Trinidad since very little argument was invoked to show
that Trinidad would benefit from the proposed union. But there is
no doubt that the reception for the decision was lukewarm. Perhaps
what contributed to the feeling of indifference was the notion that
Tobago would have its own treasury and that this would not be a
burden to taxpayers in Trinidad.

EXTRACT FROM THE MINUTES OF THE PROCEEDINGS OF THE LEGISLATIVE COUNCIL OF TRINIDAD 8 MARCH 1887

*Whereas Her Majesty's Government have expressed the
opinion after consideration of the condition and prospects
of the Colony of Tobago, and having regard to its
geographical proximity to, and means of communication
with this Colony, that it is expedient that the Colony of
Tobago should be annexed to and form part of the Colony
of Trinidad:*

*Resolved that this Council has no objection to
the administrative annexation of Tobago with this
Government, Tobago retaining, however, a separate
Treasury and a separate internal Financial Board, on
the understanding that such annexation is approved
and desired by Her Majesty's Government, and on the*

---

[72]   Ibid.

further understanding that no pecuniary charge is now or hereafter to be imposed on the Revenues of Trinidad for any service connected with the Island of Tobago, or the aforesaid annexation for the administrative purposes:

Resolved further that as an incident of such annexation there is no objection of the Islands being governed by one Governor and being subject to one and the same code of Laws and that duties leviable in Tobago upon articles imported from abroad should be the same as those in Trinidad, and that the traffic and intercourse between the two Islands should be absolutely free.

Seconded by the Hon. the Acting Colonial Secretary.

After discussion the Board divided.

Votes:

For - 12	*Against - 1*
Mr Fitt	*Mr Fenwick*
Mr Garcia	
Protector of Immigrants	
Mr Finlayson	
Director of Public Works	
Mr Guiseppi	
Acting Auditor-General	
Solicitor General	
Dr de Verteuil	
Attorney-General	
Mr Warner	
Acting Colonial Secretary	

Dr de Boissiere [an unofficial member] declined to vote, and Mr Fenwick gave notice of protest.

The Hon. the Solicitor General then moved that His Excellency the Governor be requested to communicate the above resolution to the Secretary of State for the

Colonies, with a respectful request that Her Majesty's Government will take the necessary steps for giving effect to the wishes of the two Colonies concerned.

Seconded by the Hon. the [Acting] Colonial Secretary and carried. Mr Fenwick dissentient.

Mr Fenwick, an unofficial member of the Legislative Council, was the lone dissenting voice. His opinion, that the arrangement as proposed was unviable, turned out to be accurate. Mr Fenwick pointed out a number of drawbacks in Tobago that would hamper the success of the union as proposed: the monoculture of the economy in an industry that was depressed; the shortage of revenues; the shortage of capital; the cost of inter-island shipping would have to be borne by Trinidadians; the administrative costs. He also predicted that the decision taken then would lead to the complete incorporation as the passage of time would reveal to be necessary. But a little thought would have produced the notions that the addition of capital, the diversification of the economy, and in particular the exploitation of the lower labour costs in Tobago would bring tremendous benefits to the union. As he had promised, Mr Fenwick presented his objections in writing and they were read into the records of the Legislative Council of Trinidad on 5 April 1887.

EXTRACT FROM THE MINUTES OF THE PROCEEDINGS OF THE LEGISLATIVE COUNCIL TRINIDAD 5 APRIL 1887.

The protest of the Hon. Mr Fenwick against the proposed annexation of Tobago to Trinidad was read (Council Paper No. 32).

No. 32   **Council Paper**   1887

PROTEST OF THE HON. MR. FENWICK AGAINST RESOLUTIONS IN FAVOUR OF PROPOSAL OF ANNEXATION OF TOBAGO.

I protest against the Resolutions with regard to the annexation of Tobago to the colony of Trinidad for the following reasons:

1. *Because the Colony of Tobago is, owing to the low prices obtainable for its principal, and almost only, staple, in a state of bankruptcy—with no prospect of better times in the near future—and the commercial credit abroad of the Colony of Trinidad will be injuriously affected by extending its protection to another colony in such circumstances.*

2. *Because administrative annexation, retaining for Tobago a separate Treasury, a separate internal Financial Board and all the machinery of a separate Government, while it will admit of some economy in official salaries, will not effect such reductions as to enable Tobago to keep its expenditure within the limits of its yearly diminishing revenue. If the Ordinance to repeal certain Duties of Customs, now under consideration of this Council, be passed, the small revenue, of about £8,000, now collected in Tobago will be reduced to less than one half of this sum.*

3. *Because if Tobago do benefit by a closer connection with Trinidad it can only be by the introduction into Tobago of Trinidad capital and of the enterprise of Trinidadians—all, and more than all, of which are urgently needed in Trinidad for the development of its own resources.*

4. *Because any attempts to bring about a closer connection between the two colonies will necessitate the establishment of a Steam Service, the expense of which Tobago is unable to bear even in part, and which would be altogether unremunerative to Trinidad if this Colony be called upon to bear any share of it. Though geographically nearer to Tobago than any of the neighbouring colonies, Trinidad is not so [as] convenient to the purposes of Trade as*

85

      Grenada or Barbados. The prevailing winds of these latitudes are favourable only for the voyage from Tobago to Trinidad—the return voyage being usually a long and tedious beat up against the wind, often occupying several days.

5. *Because the whole trade of Tobago with the British West Indies is too insignificant, even if Trinidad obtained it all, to benefit Trinidad to the slightest appreciable extent. The bulk of the existing trade with Trinidad—viz., ground provisions—will find no market here in another year or two if the cultivation of garden lots in Trinidad continue to increase at the same rate as during the past eight or ten years. Trinidad will require very soon to export instead of import ground provisions. The exportation from Tobago, during the year 1886, of an increased number of ponies, goats, pigs, and other livestock, so far from being the natural growth of a prosperous trade, is merely an indication of the distress to which proprietors, great and small, of that colony are now reduced.*

6. *Because Trinidad is put to expense indirectly by Tobago commanding the services of certain public officers paid by the Colony of Trinidad to devote their whole time and attentions to its interests. If these officials have the time to spare for the work of another colony it would appear that there has been, and is, much more room for economy in their various departments.*

7. *Because by agreeing to the act of administrative annexation this Council commits itself to a policy which must inevitably terminate in the complete incorporation, or absorption, of Tobago by Trinidad, so soon as the futility of the present arrangement is sufficiently demonstrated.*

8. *And because the second Resolution is not in accordance with fact—it being notorious that an*

*overwhelming majority of all classes in Trinidad
strongly disapprove of the annexation of Tobago.*

G. TOWNSEND FENWICK

LES EFFORTS HOUSE, TRINIDAD
MARCH 13th, 1887.

Mr. Michel Maxwell Philip

Although the Legislative Council in Trinidad agreed to the annexation, the opinion was not as uniform as that in Tobago if even we ignore Mr Fenwick's hyperbolic statement: "And because the second Resolution is not in accordance with fact—it being notorious that an overwhelming majority of all classes in Trinidad strongly disapprove of the annexation of Tobago." A huge question remained unanswered at the time: what benefit would accrue to Trinidad from the union? Nevertheless, on its third draft, moved by the illustrious Michel Maxwell Philip, the Legislative Council of Trinidad agreed to the annexation.

The Colonial Office having received formal notification and given acknowledgement of the resolutions of the Legislative Councils of the two colonies, the matter was then left in the hands of the British Parliament. It must be noted that the notification was not final. Exchanges between Sir Henry Holland, later the first Lord Knutsford, secretary of state, and the governor of Trinidad suggest that some negotiations were conducted in telegraphic exchanges as shown in Council Paper No. 45 of 1887 of the Legislative Council of Trinidad, as the following despatch indicates:

No. 45   **Council Paper**   **1887**

Despatch from the Secretary of State in Reference to the Annexation of Tobago

The Secretary of State to Governor Sir William Robinson, K.C.M.G.

Downing Street,
28ʰᵗ MARCH, 1887

Sir,
        I have the honour to acknowledge the receipt of your telegraphic Despatches, as noted in the margin, relative to the proposed annexation of Tobago, and to inform you that the Resolution to effect that object passed by the Legislative Council of Tobago, which I understand from your telegram of the 12ᵗʰ instant to have been substantially concurred in the Legislative Council of Trinidad, is approved by Her Majesty's Government, with the exception of one point, viz.: the constitution of the proposed Financial Board of Tobago, which they consider should consist of equal numbers of official and unofficial members, with a casting vote for the Chief Executive Officer, as they cannot consent to give the control of the taxation and Expenditure on the Island to a majority of the unofficial members.

With this modification Her Majesty's Government are prepared to take the necessary steps for giving effect to the scheme embodied in the Resolution.

I have, &tc.,
H.T. Holland

This note from the secretary of state confirmed the rejection of the proposal by the Tobago Legislature on the composition of the Financial Board. It is noteworthy that this and subsequent correspondence make no reference to the second resolution moved by Messrs. Henderson and Keens. The Legislative Council of Tobago, however, withdrew that resolution two months later on 11 May 1887.

CHAPTER IV

Making the Decisions II: Parliament and the Colonial Office

En politique, gouverner, c'est choisir,
Old French proverb.

THE BRITISH PARLIAMENT

IN 1888, THE ULTIMATE decision making authority for Trinidad and Tobago resided in the British Parliament. In the century and a quarter that elapsed after Tobago became a British colony in 1763, Parliament and its colonial policies had undergone several changes. Firstly, the geo-political situation had changed radically with the American Declaration of Independence, the Napoleonic wars, the Congress of Vienna, the abolition of slavery, the expansion of the British Empire, and the emergence of new powers in Russia, Germany, and the United States of America. Consequently, the evolving British Empire and its colonial policies had changed to the point where whatever significance Tobago enjoyed at the end of the Seven Years War had completely evaporated. Secondly, the international trade and its associated economics had seen mercantilism replaced with laissez-faire. Thirdly, the drive to evangelise the world that began with Columbus came to an abrupt end. Fourthly, the relationship between the Parliament and the Crown continued to undergo changes that left Parliament in the ascendency with greater responsibility in the management of the overseas territories.

THE CHANGING GEOPOLITICAL SCENE

THE CONGRESS OF VIENNA

The Congress of Vienna of 1815, whatever its demerits, came close to preventing a general European conflagration for a whole century of time. The wars fought in continental Europe and in the Americas during the previous two hundred years had ended: The War of the Spanish Succession; the War of the Austrian Succession; the War of Jenkins' Ear; the Seven Years War; the War of American Independence; the French Revolutionary War; and the Napoleonic wars. During those wars the possession of Tobago, Grenada, and other islands of the West Indies changed frequently. There were several harbingers of this coming transformation in world affairs: the American Declaration of Independence, the Haitian Revolution of 1804, and the initial declaration of independence of Venezuela from Spain in 1811 all presaged the movement towards self-government away from the colonising European powers.[73] The American Revolution, the French Revolution, the Rights of Man, the Haitian Revolution, and the abolition of the slave trade in British ships during the Napoleonic wars all pointed towards a new regime of human rights. They were tacit indicators of the transformation taking place in international affairs. Britain at the end of the Seven Years War was the unchallenged ruler of the seas.

---

[73] "On July 24, 1581, at the Hague, the States General proclaimed an end to the rule of Philip II as sovereign of the Netherlands. Acting in accordance with the right of self-determination, a new nation was born in Europe." *Encyclopaedia Britannica*, Macropaedia Vol. 6, 1975, p. 1088.

The Royal Navy had vanquished its Dutch and French rivals, and Spain had long ceased to be a challenge to her supremacy. The Navigation Act of 1651 had allowed the British to displace the trade then dominated by the Dutch. Despite the loss of the North American colonies Britain in 1820 remained the dominant power in the world. The exploration started by Columbus in 1492 continued throughout the nineteenth with the colonial drive by the European powers then shifted to Africa and the Pacific.

As the West Indies were enjoying a period of security unknown for over two hundred years the internal problems of governing the slave colonies took on greater significance and gave rise to the issues of self-government, of the abolition of slavery and of human and economic development.

THE ABOLITION OF SLAVERY

The state of human rights in the Caribbean during the eighteenth century was one of horrors throughout. The Barbados Slave Code embodied the despicable conditions under which the majority of the slaves lived, especially in the British colonies.[74] The atrocities of slavery in the West Indies and elsewhere must have been aired in private in Britain long before 1772.[75] The Barbados Slave Act of 1661, modified in 1676, 1682, and 1688, had served as a model for similar legislation in British colonies in Jamaica, Antigua, and South Carolina. After 1772, however, the matter was squarely in the public domain given Lord Mansfield's celebrated decision in that year.[76] It remains somewhat inexplicable why the British Parliament

---

[74] Dunn, Richard S., *Slaves and Sugar: The Rise of the Planter Class in the English West Indies 1624-1713*, W. W. Norton, 1973, pp. 238-241.

[75] Lady Jane Mico (d. 1670) in her bequest left a sum for the redemption of Christian slaves in Barbary. The funds were diverted to the building of schools for the education of emancipated slaves in the British West Indies in the 1830s. She was the widow of Sir Samuel Mico, a mercer who was familiar with the condition of the slaves in Barbary.

[76] Lord Mansfield was chief justice of England who handed down the landmark decision in *R vs. Knowles ex parte Somerset* that denied the legality of slavery according to the laws of England.

took more than thirty years to outlaw the slave trade and a further thirty to abolish slavery. There is also the opinion that what the case decided was that slaves could not be forcibly removed from Britain. Whatever is thought about the case then or today, in the wake of the decision there was a protracted debate about the issue, and apart from having the effect of freeing the slaves that then existed in England and Wales, the main impact was in the banning the trade and the amelioration of the condition of the slaves. There were winds of change all around: following Jefferson's eloquent statement in the Declaration of Independence in 1776, by 1783 all the former colonies north of Maryland in the United States had abolished slavery with a commitment to abolish in all states by 1803. Since Tobago was established as a slave colony in 1763, the abolition of slavery would have a profound effect on the society and colony as a whole.

Lord Mansfield, Chief Justice of England, c. 1772

THE GREAT DEBATE AND COMMITMENT

In 1783, Lord North, the British prime minister, while complimenting the Quaker movement on its humanitarianism, pointed out that the slave trade had become an economic necessity to Britain and every country of Europe. If the North government could be exonerated for a lack of knowledge of the state of government in the slave colonies and of the dire conditions under which the slaves laboured, that situation was changed after 1788. In that year Parliament and the executive government began extensive enquiries into the state of the laws in the slave colonies. Four years later, in making good his promise to Wilberforce to bring the slave trade to an end, an ill and exhausted Pitt the Younger, then prime minister, in an impassioned speech during a debate in the House of Commons told of the barbarous traffic in slaves before exacting from the British Legislature a commitment to end the slave trade. The debate loomed large during the Napoleonic wars when, in 1797, Trinidad was captured from Spain. Trinidad was then vastly undeveloped in comparison with the other British West Indian colonies, and its fertile lands posed the question of labour supply and the contingent issue of slavery. The demographic situation in Trinidad in addition presented problems that merited broader consideration. The difficulty of getting rid of this problem was inextricably linked to the British fetish over the property rights that resided with the slave owners and to some diffidence concerning the power of the imperial Parliament over the colonial assemblies.

THE SLAVES AS PROPERTY

The Parliament was somewhat prolix in taking positive action because of the controversy over property rights in the slaves. A clue to be taken from Lord Mansfield's decision was his deep concern for the property rights of slave owners. Mansfield estimated that there were about 14,000 slaves in Britain, and at £50 a head that would require compensation of £700,000. The unavoidable conclusion was that any change in the institution of slavery or of the slave trade would have entailed considerable costs.

The prevailing economic doctrine at that time was mercantilism with its emphasis on the protection of property, trade, and contract and ironically on liberty. This was alluded to by Fox in his debate on the India Reform Bill:

> *"Freedom, according to my conception of it, consists in **the safe and sacred possession of a man's property**, governed by laws defined and certain; with many personal privileges, natural, civil, and religious, which he cannot surrender without ruin to himself; and of which to be deprived by any power is despotism. This bill, instead of subverting, is destined to give stability to these principles, instead of narrowing the basis of freedom, it tends to enlarge it; instead of suppressing, its object is to infuse and circulate the spirit of liberty."[77]*

The parliamentarians were preoccupied with the costs involved in stopping the enterprise: loss of income to the treasury from a reduction in trade; loss of property by the slave owners, and the concomitant issue of the cost of compensation. There was in fact a great prolonged dilemma over compensation for the slaves as against compensation for the planters. Indeed, as James Stephen pointed out:

> *"Mr Pitt, in the debate of April 1791, took the same important distinction, and in the same identical case: for the indemnity of the planters, as a condition of the abolition of the slave trade."[78]*

In the first half of 1795, the king authorised his commander-in-chief in the South Caribbean, Sir John Vaughan, to raise two corps of one thousand Negroes each.[79] By 1799, the number of such regiments had grown from two to twelve, and for the most part they all served

---

[77] MacArthur, Brian (Ed.), *The Penguin Book of Historic Speeches,* London: Penguin Books, 1996, pp. 119, 120.

[78] Stephen, Dr. James, *The Slavery of the British West India Colonies Delineated, Vol. I, 1824,* Cambridge: Cambridge University Press, 2010, p. 392, 393.

[79] Douglas Archibald, Rupert, *Tobago: Melancholy Isle, Vol. II, 1782-1805,* Port-of-Spain, Trinidad: UWI School of Continuing Studies, p. 112.

gallantly during the Revolutionary and Napoleonic wars (although there were several mutinies). And they were still slaves. Law Officers in 1801 advised the Crown on the legal position of purchased Negroes in the regiments as follows:

> *"They are not in consequence of their being employed by His Majesty in military service become soldiers within the Mutiny Act; and* **we think they remain for all intents and purposes slaves . . . subject to the same laws as they would have been subject to had they been the property of His Majesty** *and employed in agriculture and public works."*[80]

The concern over the validity of slavery was not unique to Britain. In the United States of America, where slavery was strongly denounced in the Declaration of Independence, the issue threatened to abort the adoption of a new constitution and led eventually to the Civil War. This is borne out in the debate of June 1788 on the Slave Trade clause of the US Constitution.[81] Firstly, George Mason:

> *"This is a fatal section which has created more dangers than any other. The first clause, allows the importation of slaves for twenty years. Under the royal Government, this evil was looked upon as a great oppression, and many attempts were made to prevent it; but the interest of the African merchants prevented its prohibition. No sooner did the revolution take place, than it was thought of. It was one of the great causes of our separation from Great Britain."*

In part of his reply the eminent James Madison said:

> *"I should hold this clause to be impolitic, if it were one of those things which could be excluded without encouraging*

---

[80]   Ibid., p. 115.
[81]   Bailyn, Bernard (Ed.), *The Debates on the Constitution: Part II,* the Library of America, 1993, p. 706.

greater evils. The southern States would not have entered
the Union of America, without the temporary permission
of that trade. And if they were excluded from the Union,
the consequences might be dreadful to them as to us."

That debate makes it clear that the issue was the choice between preserving the union and the human rights of the slaves. But it must be noted that the pertinent question posed by the southern states was dependent upon the property rights and economic benefits they stood to lose. The sacrosanct nature of property rights militated against the abolition of slavery on both sides of the Atlantic. But the property issue alone cannot account for the delay by the British Parliament in taking executive action.

The Legality of Emancipation

There was the practical problem of enforcing a decision taken by the imperial government in colonies that were already, to an extent, self-governing.

Many of the colonies were ruled by self-governing assemblies and by that time had engendered reluctance on the part of the government in imposing imperial measures on the colonies. For example, after amelioration of the living and working conditions of the slaves was instituted in Trinidad, a Crown colony by Order in Council, Prime Minister Canning refused to impose the measures in Jamaica. His reason, stated with great eloquence, was:

> *"No feeling of wounded pride, no motive of questionable*
> *expediency, nothing short of real and demonstrable*
> *necessity, shall induce me to moot the awful question*
> *of the transcendental power of parliament over every*
> *dependency of the British Crown."[82]*

---

[82]   Porter, Andrew, *Trusteeship and Humanitarianism,* in Porter, Andrew (Ed.), *The Oxford History of the British Empire Vol. III: The Nineteenth Century,* Oxford: Oxford University Press, 1999, p. 205.

THE END OF THE BRITISH SLAVE TRADE

Two years after Trinidad was ceded to Britain at the Treaty of Amiens and more or less in the same year that the Constitutional Committee had set for the abolition of slavery in the United Stated of America, the participation by Britons in the slave trade was outlawed from 1 May 1807 [3 and 4 Will. IV, c. 73]. Nevertheless, the trade continued surreptitiously by other countries without similar commitment and flourished in Cuba, Brazil, and the southern United States of America until an Anglo American treaty was assented to in the 1860s that sanctioned intervention on the high seas and altered the course of history throughout the Caribbean. The end of the slave trade anticipated by the law of 1807 had the effect of creating an alternative market that thrived for another 55 years.

THE EMANCIPATION OF THE SLAVES

From 1823, Parliament was assailed by evangelists and humanitarians with petitions for emancipation. A bill was proposed in 1832, an act (3 & 4 Will. IV c. 73) passed in the summer of 1833, and on 1 August 1834 the slaves in all British colonies were emancipated. The act proved to be somewhat unsatisfactory as it stipulated varying periods of "apprenticeship" that would last until 1840 at the same time compensation was given to the former slave owners. With political agitation, the transitional period was cut short and the apprenticeship terminated in 1838. As Tobago was essentially a slave society, the emancipation had a most profound effect on the society and its economy. Although slavery was abolished throughout the empire, it continued to flourish elsewhere, as did the slave trade in the southern United States, Cuba, and Brazil, whereby the economics of the sugar industry had a devastating effect on the competitiveness of British West Indian industry. It was only after the end of the American Civil War, when the United States signed a treaty with Britain to allow intervention on ships on the high seas, that the slave trade dwindled to a trickle and eventually came to an abrupt end. But Britain itself was already benefiting from the cheaper sugar imported from Cuba, while the sugar industry was collapsing in the British West Indies.

THE EXPANSION OF THE BRITISH EMPIRE

Britain had outgrown the markets in the empire. The Industrial Revolution had moulded Britain into a workshop for the world.

After the emancipation of the slaves, the imperial government turned its attention to the Bantu peoples of South Africa, the Aborigines of Australia, the Maoris of New Zealand, and the islanders of the Pacific. There was general concern that lawlessness prevailed in these colonies despite attempts to introduce civil government; for the most part the indigenous peoples were badly treated. The House of Commons set up a committee to examine and report on the matter in 1836 and 1837. Nothing really came of it despite a report that identified a few policy measures. Everywhere indigenous customary rights to land were being extinguished:

What constituted "justice" or "the best interests" of indigenous peoples, emancipated slaves, or indentured labourers was also being debated and redefined.

Although the results of the committee were not put into practice, there emerged a new school of thought about the government of the colonies. Perhaps among these could be counted: Gladstone, later British prime minister, James Stephen, the Secretaries of State Lord Ripon and Lord Knutsford, and based on a speech that he gave at Couva early in the life of his governorship in Trinidad, Sir Arthur Hamilton.

THE EMERGENCE OF NEW POWERS

With the long period of peace, the technology from the Industrial Revolution that started in Britain in the middle of the eighteenth century was adopted by many countries: the steam engine and the replacement of horsepower by mechanical power, the railways, steam powered ships, the replacement of wooden ships with steel ships. The result was a whittling away of the competitive edge enjoyed by Britain on account of its early start.

THE NEW ECONOMIC ORDER

Accompanying these changes was the emergence of a new two-pronged foreign policy that would influence the course of development of the empire, the one humanitarian and the other economic and conveniently called Palmerstonianism. Lord Palmerston was foreign secretary during most of the period 1830 to 1851 and prime minister during most of the period 1855 to 1865 and was therefore very instrumental in formulating the new imperial policy during those thirty-five years. The impact of the American Revolution on British imperial governance was so extensive that whereas during the eighteenth century the main thrust of the empire was in the Atlantic, during the nineteenth century the thrust was predominantly in the Pacific. We may define Palmerstonianism as a policy of forceful intervention to spread market capitalism.

> "Commercial regulations [through the Navigation Acts] were replaced by free trade, while two sharply contrasting patterns of government evolved: white communities were moving from representative government to full control over their domestic affairs summed up by the term 'responsible government'; non-white populations were subject to government largely without their consent, supervised from London. To an ideology of liberty, reinterpreted by the American and French Revolutions, was added pride in the exercise of what was assumed to be a benevolent autocracy over non-European peoples."[83]

These changes were taking place at the time when rapid technological change was accompanied by new commercial and business laws.

The economic importance of the British West Indies declined rapidly throughout the nineteenth century. In 1815, the West Indies were contributing 17.6 percent of British trade, and a century later

---

[83] Marshall, P. J., *Britain Without America: A Second Empire?*, in Marshall, P. J. (Ed.), *The Oxford History of the British Empire Vol. II: The Eighteenth Century*, Oxford: Oxford University Press, 1998, p. 576.

that figure had dwindled to 0.47 percent. By the end of the century Britain was importing cheaper sugar from Cuba. In addition, with the expansion of the empire the commercial interests were diversified away from the North American colonies and the West Indies that dominated the trade in the eighteenth century.

RELIGION

The third area in which British colonial policy had changed since 1763 was in matters of religion. Religion in England had become a state issue immediately after the discoveries of Columbus and the Papal Donation; through the Act of Supremacy and the establishment of the Anglican Church, religion had become a pillar of the English Constitution and, after the Glorious Revolution and Act of Union, a pillar of the British Constitution and of the British Crown in particular. Britain, like Spain, but without any obligation to the pope, incorporated the spread of the Christian religion in its colonial policy. In an Ordinance of 1643 of both Houses of Parliament the chief governor of plantations and the commissioners were given the power to:

> "provide for, order, and dispose, all things which they shall from time to time find most fit and advantageous to the well-governing, securing, strengthening and preserving of the said plantations, and chiefly **to the preservation and advancement of the true Protestant religion amongst the said planters and inhabitants, and the further enlargement and spreading of the Gospel of Christ amongst those that yet remaineth there in great and miserable blindness and ignorance."** [84]

This was reminiscent of the last will and testament of Isabella at the start of the Spanish quest.

---

[84] Williams, Dr. E. E., *Documents of West Indian History, Vol. I*, New York, NY: A & B Publishing, 1994, p. 281.

Ecclesiastical law was enforced by the courts as part of the civil law. As the ideas of liberty in conjunction with the notion of human rights began to take root throughout the world, the principle of an established church was brought more and more into question.

The American Revolution rejected the concept of an established church as an encroachment on liberty:

> *"The establishment of religion had been a problem for Americans almost from the first years of settlement."*[85]

The attitude of the Americans was given concrete expression in the First Amendment to the Constitution in 1789. When the established church failed to take root during the nineteenth century, the Anglican Church was formally disestablished in Ireland in 1869. In Tobago, which in theory had an established church from 1763, the church was disestablished from 1874. In Trinidad, where the Ecclesiastic Ordinance of 1845 established the Anglican Church, the move turned out as Lord Harris had predicted, to be an embarrassment to the government until it was repealed in 1870. Despite the change in the colonies, in England the Anglican Church retained its status as an established church. In considering the union of the two colonies, the authorities would have noticed the dichotomy in religious allegiance. In Tobago there was some strong opinion against forming a union with a set of papists.

PARLIAMENT, THE CROWN, AND THE COLONIES

From ancient times the overseas territories were the king's dominions. This was also the doctrine of the Catholic Kings when Columbus's discoveries led to the foundation of the Spanish Empire in America and probably originated in ancient Greece.[86] However, early during

---

[85] Bailyn, Bernard, *The Ideological Origins of the American Revolution*, Harvard University Press, 1992, p. 247.

[86] "Since the death of Isabel the Catholic, the Grecian theory for the foundation of colonies had prevailed in the Council of Spain which was, that the

the seventeenth century, Coke, the chief justice, had asserted with remarkable eloquence the legislative supremacy of Parliament; this cast some doubts on the legality of the monarchical Prohibitions and Proclamations. During this continuum of change the absolute rule of the monarch evolved into the doctrine of parliamentary sovereignty.

The benign neglect of the dominions during the reign of the early Hanoverians ended at the accession of George III. Here we saw the split executive with the King-in-Parliament and the Privy Council on the one hand and on the other the emerging Cabinet that was using the Legislature in pursuit of its own political aims. Perhaps the most significant change to take place during the period was the continual erosion of the royal prerogative, with political power moving from the monarch to the Cabinet. When in 1763, George III issued his proclamation that created the government of Grenada of which Tobago was a part, he was functioning as a King-in-Parliament.[87] But between 1763 and 1889, when the union was consummated, the Cabinet had emerged as the centre of political power and had a much more powerful influence on colonial policy than when the American colonies were lost.

CONSTITUTION, LAW, AND GOVERNMENT IN THE COLONIES

From the Norman conquest England had had considerable experience with overseas colonies. Apart from the colonies in Normandy, there were the Channel Islands, Ireland, Wales, the North American colonies, and the West Indies. After the union with Scotland the evolving British Parliament naturally extended its arms over those

---

colonies were founded for the exclusive advantage of the metropolis, and foreigners had been severely excluded from these transatlantic provinces." Borde, Pierre-Gustave-Louis, *The History of the Island of Trinidad under the Spanish Government: Second Part: 1622-1797 (1883)*, Port-of-Spain, Trinidad: Paria Publishing, 1982, pp. 8-9.

[87] "Changes in British executive and legislative power had preserved the twinned royal and elective legitimacies then welded them together as King-in-Parliament." Steele, Ian K., *Governance of the British Empire,* in Marshall, P. J. (Ed.), *The Oxford History of the British Empire Vol. II: The Eighteenth Century,* Oxford: Oxford University Press, 1998.

foreign territories in the British Empire. Unlike both the Roman and the Spanish empires there was no legal framework encompassing the governance of the British colonies. In the Declaratory Act of 1766 the Parliament declared, in the face of growing North American intransigence:

> *"That the said colonies and plantations in America have been, are, and of right ought to be subordinate unto, and dependent upon the imperial crown and parliament of Great Britain; and that the king and parliament of Great Britain have and of right ought to have full power and authority to make laws and statutes to bind the colonies and people of America in all cases whatsoever."*[88]

One decade later changes were made in the application of this law. In *Campbell vs Hall* in 1774, while denying the right of the Crown to make laws for Grenada, which had an elected Assembly, it was established that in granting legislative powers to the colonial assemblies the Crown may reserve the legislative rights to the king or the governor. In 1790, the Law Lords gave an opinion that:

> *"By granting representative government to a conquered colony the Crown had divested itself of further legislative power over that colony with the result that if the Crown wished to enforce certain laws it had to do so with the cooperation of the colonial legislature or by recourse to the Imperial parliament."*[89]

Following on this, the Canada Constitutional Act of 1791 enshrined supremacy of the imperial Parliament in colonial affairs. The West Indian assemblies generated new ideas of self-government.

---

[88] (6 Geo. III, c 12) cited in Maitland, F. W., *The Constitutional History of England*, Cambridge University Press, 1974, p. 338 (1908).

[89] Millette, Dr. James, *Society and Politics in Colonial Trinidad*, Port-of-Spain, Trinidad: Omega Bookshops Ltd., 1985, p. 77.

CONCERN OVER GOVERNANCE IN THE WEST INDIES

The loss of the American colonies prompted a fresh approach to imperial control of the colonies. Until that momentous event, local assemblies were authorised, by charter or proclamation, to make laws consistent with the laws of England (later Britain), and there was a presumption that the English common law existed as was necessary.

In 1788, Parliament and the executive government in Britain began to enquire into the assemblies of the slave colonies of the West Indies. The Reports of the Privy Council and of the House of Commons revealed that the colonial legislators were unwilling or unable to give an intelligent and consistent account of their own servile codes. In consequence of this the government of the colonies came under greater scrutiny of the Cabinet and Parliament.

The opinion of the Law Lords of 1790 concerning the making of laws for the colonies alerted the Parliament to the risks attendant on the removal of the royal prerogative.

The governance of the colonies presented difficulties of their own because of the remoteness from the metropolis and the associated long delays in communication. The Spanish Empire had earlier experienced similar problems that gave rise to the rogue conquistadores. The rules applicable were that in colonies acquired by conquest or by cession, the laws of the colonies did not change; in new countries colonised by Englishmen, the latter were conceived as carrying with them the applicable parts of the common law and such legal systems that the king might authorise. This latter loose arrangement placed great authority and wide discretion in the hands of the viceroy or governor.

As a consequence of these events there were colonial policy changes in three main areas: human rights, economics, and religion.

CROWN COLONY GOVERNMENT

At the end of the Napoleonic wars a concerted attempt was made in earnest to deal with the scourge of slavery and to make good on the parliamentary resolution of 1792 to end the slave trade. Trinidad, ceded to Britain at the Treaty of Amiens in 1802, had only a rudimentary political institution in the Cabildo, was governed by Spanish law, and presented an opportunity to the imperial Parliament to consider a new form of government. To obviate the cruelty and the harsh treatment meted out to the slaves where the colonies had local assemblies and to manage the polyglot population, the Parliament decided on Crown colony government in Trinidad with a viceroy as governor exercising full executive powers and advised by a quartet as Executive Council.

With emancipation the deflation that took place when peace broke out throughout Europe increased the tension between the white rulers and the black former slaves throughout the West Indies. In Jamaica constitutional government actually collapsed in 1868, and the situation in Tobago was not much better. In 1876, the Tobago Constitution was modified, making it a Crown colony and removing the elective principle. By 1880, all the colonies of the British West Indies, with the exception of Bermuda, Barbados, and the Bahamas, were governed as Crown colonies.

PARLIAMENT AND TRINIDAD AND TOBAGO

Apart from its economic and humanitarian concerns Britain retained a strategic interest in the West Indies throughout the nineteenth century, and this despite the success of the Congress of Vienna. For some considerable time during the eighteenth century the British authorities had had their eyes on Trinidad, then a Spanish possession, as a strategic outpost for South America, both for commercial and military purposes. The British got the opportunity during the second revolutionary war in August 1796 when Spain, (because of the violation of her neutrality in Trinidad by Sir John Vaughan, commander-in-chief of the British forces in the South Caribbean), decided to become an ally of France in the second

Treaty of San Ildefonso, and declared war on Britain in October of that year. Indeed Spain had a long list of grievances for violation of her rights in the Americas by the British, which had signalled its intentions by sending a considerable squadron to the Caribbean.[90] As the British invading force sailed towards Trinidad, the governor, Don José Maria Chacon, who by then was fed up with the insurgency of the French immigrants and the indifference of the authorities in Spain, infamously burnt his superior armada at Chaguaramas and capitulated in February 1797. The British concern with South America did not end with the conquest and the new leader, Governor Picton, continued to agitate for a military intervention.

Until the capitulation of Trinidad, Tobago was the most southerly of the British West Indian islands. Thus, the strategic importance of Tobago declined once Trinidad became a British colony, with the latter having, in addition to its closer proximity to the South America, one of the safest harbours in the Caribbean and the advantage of being spared the ravages of the annual hurricanes. The problem of insecurity that had dogged the Caribbean for the past two centuries had vanished, and the principal concern was the economic viability of the islands.

It was clear, however, from the conquest of 1797 that there would be a change of colonial policy in Trinidad. The administrative and political difficulties experienced before, both in Canada and in Grenada, with governing peoples with mixed languages and laws had alerted the government to the lurking social problems in Trinidad. Moreover, the new spirit of humanitarianism required that Trinidad would not be granted the traditional Assembly like the other slave colonies of the West Indies. The imperial government thus opted for Crown colony government in which the relationship between the rulers and those ruled would be changed. Thus when in May 1809, George Smith was appointed as the first trained lawyer to the post of chief justice of Trinidad to re-establish the

---

[90] *Spain's Manifesto Against Britain*, cited in Borde, Pierre-Gustave-Louis, *The History of the Island of Trinidad under the Spanish Government: Second Part (1883)*, Port-of-Spain, Trinidad: Paria Publishing, 1982, pp. 456-459.

practice of Spanish law, he had other instructions for improving the government of the colony:

> "Steps were to be taken to achieve the eventual establishment of the Church of England, and to facilitate the religious instruction of mulattoes and slaves. A regular and abundant supply of slave provisions was to be provided for. All rights and privileges to which the Negro slave was entitled by Spanish law and the terms of the capitulation should be secured by him; to this end a liberal code of slave law should be enacted. The conditions of the free people of colour should be improved; their privileges should be improved and their education facilitated, since 'it is considered that upon the fidelity and attachment of this Class of Inhabitants the Security & Prosperity of the West India Islands may hereafter greatly depend.'"[91]

This initiative came two years after the abolition of the slave trade, and while for the most part it was an attempt to restore rights in Trinidad guaranteed by the Articles of Capitulation between the Spanish and British governments, it served a forerunner to the programme of amelioration of the condition of the slaves that was to take place throughout the West Indies some two decades later. Ironically conditions deteriorated after emancipation with a notable collapse with the Morant Bay riots in Jamaica in 1868. A quaint but expedient political compromise in Barbados retained the status of an independent Assembly in a fierce spirit of independence at that time.

Most of the British West Indies were transformed into Crown colonies. It was clear that with those policies Britain was intent on keeping Trinidad as a Crown colony, and eventually this new arrangement was imposed throughout the West Indies, Tobago included, as conditions got worse after the emancipation of the slaves. The progressive government in Trinidad, in addition to the natural advantage of proximity and the increasingly closer relationship,

---

[91] Millette, Dr. James, *Society and Politics in Colonial Trinidad*, Port-of-Spain, Trinidad: Omega Bookshops Ltd, p. 236.

provided the imperial government with the best option to save the failed colony in Tobago. When the proposal was made to form the union, both colonies were administered through the Colonial Office. Trinidad and Tobago were both Crown colonies, and the union was consistent with the policy of reducing the cost of administration. The Trinidad and Tobago Act of 1887 was the culmination of all the new policies towards the development of the colonies of Trinidad and Tobago.

Britain's leadership in the Industrial Revolution had transformed the country into a workshop for the world. This allowed the by then rich sugar planters to abandon the inefficient production in the colonies at the same time it sought to increase its markets through its imperialist expansion. In retrospect the policy was mere rhetoric and was really aimed at bolstering domestic production and consumption.

OPTIONS FOR THE IMPERIAL PARLIAMENT

Given the proposal coming from the Colonial Office and from both colonies, the Parliament had no option but to approve the annexation. Firstly there would have been no thoughts of independence. The lessons from the loss of the North American colonies and of the Haitian Revolution excluded any such consideration. Moreover, it was only in 1877 that the island was made a Crown colony to rescue its government from the tyrannical assemblies that dominated the British West Indies. In fact, an attempt to bring the Barbados government under the scrutiny of Crown colony government had failed in 1883.

Secondly, there was the matter of security. The nineteenth century had been relatively peaceful, but an independent Tobago would be as vulnerable as it was during the sixteenth and seventeenth centuries. In fact the tendency was, where politically feasible, to bring the colonies under direct control in the Crown colony system.

The third factor that militated against any thoughts of independence for Tobago was the collapse of its economy in 1884. Independence was not a feasible option. Finally, after seceding from the Windward

Islands group in 1885, Barbados had proposed to the British government to form a political union with Tobago. Tobago had been linked politically to Barbados since 1833 and economically since the seventeenth century when Barbados became dependent on wood imported from Tobago. The proposal itself, whatever its merits, was rejected.

And so in the autumn of 1887, the British Parliament passed the Trinidad and Tobago Act of 1887, authorising the formal union of the colonies into one colony.

TRINIDAD AND TOBAGO ACT 1887[92]

AN ACT TO ENABLE HER MAJESTY BY ORDER IN COUNCIL TO UNITE THE COLONIES OF TRINIDAD AND TOBAGO INTO ONE COLONY (16TH SEPTEMBER, 1887)

Whereas it is desirable that the islands of Trinidad and Tobago which are now separate colonies, should be united to form one colony:

And whereas the legislative body of the colony of Tobago has expressed its desire for the said union and the legislative body of the colony of Trinidad has expressed its consent thereto:

Be it therefore enacted by the Queen's most Excellent Majesty, by and with the advice and consent of the Lords Spiritual and Temporal, and Commons, in this present Parliament assembled, and by the authority of the same, as follows:

1. *It shall be lawful for Her Majesty by Order in Council to declare that the colony of Trinidad and the colony of Tobago shall from the date to be mentioned in such Order, be united with and form one colony, on such terms and conditions as Her Majesty shall in such*

---

[92]   Imperial Act, 50 and 51 Vict., cap 44.

> *Order in Council, or in any subsequent Order or*
> *Orders, think fit to appoint: Provided always that any*
> *such Order in Council made in pursuance of this Act*
> *shall be laid before both Houses of Parliament as soon*
> *as conveniently may be after the making thereof.*
>
> 2. *From and after the date to be mentioned in such*
>   *Order in Council the said colonies shall, subject to*
>   *such terms and conditions as Her Majesty shall think*
>   *fit to appoint, be taken to form one colony.*
> 3. *From and after the date aforesaid the St. Vincent,*
>   *Tobago and Granada [Grenada] Constitution Act*
>   *1876, shall be repealed so far as it relates to the island*
>   *of Tobago.*
> 4. *This Act may be cited as the Trinidad and Tobago Act*
>   *1887.*

One clear omission from the act was the name of the united colony. But thereafter the name of the colony, probably taking its cue from the short title of the enabling legislation, came to be known as Trinidad and Tobago.

THE COLONIAL OFFICE

The Colonial Office, more so than the British Parliament, with direct administrative control, strongly influenced the general progress and development in the colonies. Created by William III in 1696, in order to forestall parliamentary intrusion into royal authority, most of the imperial business in Britain was conducted through the Lords of the Committee of Trade and Plantations. Known commonly as the Board of Trade, it was an advisory body to the Privy Council and to the Parliament and was responsible for advising the administration (royal proclamations, review of laws passed by colonial assemblies, petitions, and legal appeals). In 1782, after the loss of the American colonies, the Committee was abolished and the onus of colonial work fell to the Secretary of State for War and Colonies until the offices were separated in 1854.

Almost simultaneous with the genesis of constitutional problems in Trinidad, a separate department for colonial affairs was established in 1801. The Secretary of State for the Colonies, a member of the British Cabinet, was the formal link between the British government and the colonial governors. Within the ambit of British policy, the Colonial Office was somewhat an orphan child. Competent ministers with strong ideas about the empire were rarely attracted to the department, and it was generally held in low esteem by the political big-wigs. This was consistent with the continuous erosion of the royal prerogative that retained a measure of control over the colonies, a trend that was hardly staunched during Queen Victoria's long reign. Despite its orphan status, the Colonial Office of all institutions had the best information and was therefore well placed to make the best judgements about the plight of the individual colonies and about the colonies collectively.

In Tobago the Colonial Office was confronted with three main challenges: firstly, the birth of a new society after the emancipation of the slaves with growing tension between the plantocracy and the peasants; secondly, the changed economic situation particularly after the collapse of the sugar industry in Tobago in 1884; and thirdly, the thorny administrative or constitutional problem.

Lord Glanville, Secretary of State for
the Colonies, c. 1886

THE SOCIAL PROBLEM

From early in the nineteenth century there were many changes in policy that would affect the West Indian colonies. Slavery was clearly at variance with the American Declaration of Independence. Between 1777 and 1804, all the states north of Maryland had abolished slavery. The Constitutional Convention of 1783, as a sop to the four states of the South in order to preserve the union, agreed to the option of abolition after twenty years, a decision that had disastrous consequences. The British abolished the slave trade in British ships in 1807 and abolished slavery throughout the British Empire in 1834, some sixty-two years after Lord Mansfield had declared that slavery was unknown in the laws of England. The emancipation of the slaves brought down the curtain on the drama that began to unfold with the American Declaration of Independence and ushered in a new era of human rights.

The abolition of slavery forcibly introduced the fresh notion of human rights into the colonial equation; thereafter the Colonial Office tended to pay more attention to the goings on in the Legislatures of the former slave colonies. To address the social problem with the mass of people poor, landless, and uneducated, the imperial government in this period assisted the primary schools by making small grants. There were genuine differences between the demographics of the white colonies and those of the other colonies. The problem in Tobago was very real and arose from the colonisation process that established Tobago as a slave colony, with the majority of the population former slaves. While some of the slaves had come from Barbados where they were to some extent acculturated, the conditions under which all the slaves lived originally were not conducive to community life nor was there any formal education. This situation changed dramatically with the abolition of slavery that abolished the status of the slaves and endowed them with normal human rights. Then ensued an honest attempt to Anglicise the local community in which the freeborn British subjects were in the minority: to establish the English language, British law, and the Anglican Church. Despite the nobility of these goals the native or non-white population remained estranged aliens in their own country, and more and more it became obvious that the practice was openly discriminatory, incipient racism. The facts cannot be starker than those provided by the history of the so-called white countries of the British Commonwealth. Racism was the basis of legitimising Britain's late entry into the exploration of America.

THE RACE ISSUE

Underlying the administrative and constitutional problems in Tobago was an unofficial policy of racism that was emerging in the expanding British Empire. No honest history of the British Empire can disregard the role of racism in establishing the colonies scattered over the globe, and this can be seen in the developments of India and Australia as much as it was evident in the British West Indies. While such a policy did not originate in the British Parliament, the boffins at the Colonial Office were certainly aware of it. Racism was one of the problems that would bedevil the governments of the region well into the next century and would come to a head in British colonies in Rhodesia and South Africa.

The question had come to the forefront after the Haitian Revolution, with the prospect for the first time in modern history of white men being ruled by black men. The policy of racism, although veiled, meant that at the end of the nineteenth century, the "white" colonies were moving towards responsible government, whereas in the others as was pointed out they were governed almost without their consent and controlled from London. It was only in 1896 that Dominica became the first of the former slave colonies to have a Legislature controlled by a majority of blacks. This policy affected the course of development in Tobago and was an essential consideration in any decision taken to change the constitution in Tobago.

> "The Spanish sought to integrate the Indians into a miscegenated society, albeit at the lowest possible social level, and the French attempted to 'Frenchify' their indigenes. The English, after decades of moralizing,

sought only to exclude the Indians or, where expedient to annihilate them."[93]

THE FACT OF WEST INDIAN RACISM

Racism in Tobago and the British West Indies as far as we can judge was an adjunct of the Negro slave trade which in the period 1670 to 1807 was dominated by British merchants.

> *"English merchants entered the slave trade relatively late, but by 1650 were regular participants in it. Two decades later they had probably become the leading carriers of slaves, delivering to America each year possibly more slaves than both the Portuguese and the Dutch, who had previously dominated the trade. Having established their dominance by 1670, the English remained the major shippers of slaves from Africa to America until 1807, when Parliament outlawed British participation in slave-carrying. Overall, it appears that in the one and a half centuries before 1807 the British shipped as many slaves to America as all other slave carrying nations put together. In 1670-1807, therefore, the British were the pre-eminent slave traders of the western hemisphere."[94]*

THE SOCIOLOGY OF RACISM

The racism inherent in slavery did not end with emancipation. It is safe to surmise that in the absence of specific legislation guaranteeing and enforcing the rights of the former slaves, racism would have prevailed. While it has been found that the degree of cruelty or liberality in slavery systems depends upon the favourable

---

[93] Pagden, Anthony, *The Struggle for Legitimacy and the Image of the Empire in the Atlantic to c. 1700,* in Canny, Nichols (Ed.), *Oxford History of the British Empire Vol. I,* Oxford: Oxford University Press, 1997, p. 37.

[94] Richardson, Davis, *The British Empire and the Atlantic Slave Trade, 1660-1807,* in Marshall, P. J., (Ed.), *The Oxford History of the British Empire Vol. II: The Eighteenth Century,* Oxford: Oxford University Press, 1998, p. 440.

or unfavourable influence of religion and law, that influence was found to be less decisive than the expectations that prevailed in practice in the societies. Indeed, whether one starts from the *Seite Partidas* of Spain, the *Code Noir* of France, or the Barbados Slave Code, the treatment of the slaves regressed, in the sense used by Galton, towards a common standard observable throughout the world, giving rise to and sustained by a theory of race.

Racism is a complex matter that combines the biological concept of race with the sociological concept of ethnicity. It depends upon and also influences interaction in everyday life and determines class stratification and social relations. An example of one such influence arises from the demographic balance between blacks and whites. For example, in a colony with a high ratio of whites to blacks, it is likely that the upper and middle classes are dominated by whites. By contrast, where the ratio of whites to blacks was lower, the middle class was more likely to be coloured. A second such influence arises from the nature of the economy. For example in Barbados, where land was expensive and labour cheap, it was more likely that the blacks would remain as wage earners and more difficult for them to become proprietors than in Trinidad, where land was cheap and labour expensive. Like crime, racism is a societal problem originating in deviant behaviour that is harmful to the society that generates it.

The distinction between peoples of varying colours is found throughout the Caribbean. Even in the Dutch-, French-, Portuguese-, and Spanish-speaking colonies where attitudes to slavery were markedly different from that of the English-speaking world, the similar phenomenon of racism is observed.[95]

Quite apart from the social factors that engender racism, there is the intellectual theory of race that supports it. In 1849, Thomas Carlyle had published his *Occasional Discourse on the Nigger Question,* advocating the restoration of slavery.

---

[95] Hoetink, H, *Caribbean Race Relations*, Oxford: Oxford University Press,1967, pp. 35-55.

"Although Carlyle was especially vituperative in his assault on blacks, his ideas were broadly representative of British intellectual opinion of peoples of African descent and their capacities."[96]

English racism got a boost after the publication of Darwin's *Origin of Species* in 1859. James Anthony Froude, professor of modern history at Oxford, was the prince of British racism. Despite the strong intellectual support for racism, there is nothing to show that it was adopted as a colonial policy. Racism is a form of prejudice that reflects different cultural norms.

It is tempting to undervalue the effect that British policy had on race relations in the West Indies. But one notable fact is that race prejudice persisted and was more marked in the countries of Bermuda, the Bahamas, and Barbados, which retained their own assemblies and never became Crown colonies like most of the other British West Indian colonies.

But such racism as existed, like Picton's colour bar in Trinidad was unofficial. While Picton did convey his intentions to the Colonial Office, we have no evidence that he was censored or, if censored, that he acted on such censure.

"West Indian slave society further compromised Picton's moral fibre. On his own testimony he had left Britain 'with a strong predisposition against the slave system', but a residence of nine years in the West Indies had produced a complete change in his beliefs. The reason is not difficult to discover. Economic advantage had mollified his previous aversion to slavery. To an anonymous correspondent he confided that his own investments in slaves and sugar plantations had been greatly rewarding. An initial investment of £17,000 raised largely through credit had yielded a gross capital value of all his holdings

---

[96] Palmer, Colin A., *Eric Williams & the Making of the Modern Caribbean*, Kingston, Jamaica: Ian Rundle Publishers, 2006, p.18.

> *of £50,000 by 1802. His enterprise had not only yielded*
> *satisfactory profits, it had induced him in the process*
> *to underwrite all that he had formerly regarded as*
> *questionable in West Indian society. His attitude to slaves*
> *and slavery, the free coloureds and their rights, came to*
> *be determined less by the maxims of the administrator*
> *and more by the standards of the businessman and the*
> *slave owner. Picton solved the problem of temptation by*
> *yielding completely to it."*[97]

Capitalism had triumphed over slavery.

In the prolonged debate over the Trinidad Constitution during the early nineteenth century, the race issue was somewhat of a dilemma. On the one hand the relatively large numbers of free coloureds and blacks that owned property meant that if the constitution was framed in traditional terms, the rulers would be coloured men. This was essentially Froude's argument seventy years later. And Froude's feelings were that it would not be acceptable to freeborn Englishmen to be ruled by coloured men. On the other hand the colonial administration was fully aware of the cruelty inflicted on the slaves by the minority white governments that ruled the British West Indies. In the new age such a system was clearly unacceptable. The winds of change were blowing in a particular direction that led to the abolition of the slave trade, the amelioration of the condition for the slaves, and ultimately to the emancipation of the slaves and a growing recognition of human rights that embraced all men, women, and children.

THE ECONOMIC CHALLENGE

The abolition of the slave trade transformed the so-called triangular trade into bilateral trade between Britain and the countries across the Atlantic.

---

[97] Millette, Dr. James, *Society and Politics in Colonial Trinidad*, Port-of-Spain, Trinidad: Omega Bookshops Ltd., 1985, p. 170.

Although slavery was abolished throughout the empire, it continued to flourish elsewhere, as did the slave trade in the southern United States, Cuba, and Brazil, whereby the economics of the sugar industry had a devastating effect on the competitiveness of British West Indian industry.

The abolition of slavery had, as the planters had anticipated, a deleterious effect on the economy of Tobago. Apart from cutting off its principal source of labour, the practice of slave poaching that emerged meant that slaves within the British West Indies were migrating towards those colonies that paid higher wages. The pay in Tobago was amongst the lowest in the region, and Tobago was thus a net loser to countries like Trinidad and British Guiana.

The dominant classes in those colonies moved to limit the electoral franchise at the same time they sought to transfer the burden of taxation onto the growing numbers of the lower classes by raising the tariffs on imports of essential goods.

The abolition of slavery presented a number of economic challenges for the colonial administration. The first was the matter of compensation, for the loss of property in the slaves was dealt with by the imperial government; the second was the shortage of labour likely to arise from the freedom of the slaves; the third was the loss of competitiveness to other producers that relied either on slave labour or on improved production methods; the fourth was the decline of productivity and production and loss of tariffs from sugar imports that would arise if the slaves were not adequately compensated. Apart from those there were more general considerations: the prevailing economic doctrine had shifted from mercantilism to laissez-faire.

IMMIGRATION

The expansion of the empire together with the curtailment of the slave trade led to a great deal of migration. On the one hand there was migration from Britain and Europe to the colonies as managers, administrators, and pioneers, and on the other indentured labourers migrated from Africa, India, China, and the Pacific Islands, the latter principally to Australia and Fiji.[98] Tobago, nonetheless, did not benefit from this policy as much as did British Guiana, Trinidad, Jamaica, and some other British West Indian Islands: unlike St. Lucia and Grenada, the island did not have the benefit of an imperial guaranteed loan to assist in the immigration of labour from India. Tobago passed a number of laws and accommodated liberated Africans from St. Helena and Sierra Leone. That source of labour was cut off in November 1861 when the Duke of Newcastle, then Secretary of State for the Colonies, ordered that the colonies pay the cost of immigration, where before the costs were met by the imperial government.[99] Inevitably the poor state of the finances in the colony precluded it from meeting the costs of immigration, and this added to the economic decline of Tobago during the second half of the nineteenth century.

CHALLENGES: ADMINISTRATION

The suggestions from Herbert Taylor Ussher, Colonel Crossman, Augustus Gore, and Sir William Robinson confirmed the general findings of Merivale in respect of colonial administrations a generation before, and all pointed towards the need to reduce the cost of administration in Tobago. These men had had much experience in dealing with the administrative problems of a number of colonies in the region. Ussher had served as governor of the Gold Coast before coming to Tobago and returned to the Gold Coast for a second stint after leaving Tobago; his advice suggests that he had some knowledge of the administrative problems of Australia and South Africa. Gore had served as assistant government secretary in Berbice and as colonial secretary to Barbados before becoming lieutenant governor of Tobago. He later became governor of St. Vincent. Colonel Crossman had studied administrative problems in

---

[98]   Northrup, David, *Migration from Africa, Asia and the South Pacific*, in Porter, Andrew (Ed.), *The Oxford History of the British Empire Vol. III: The Nineteenth Century*, Oxford: Oxford University Press, 1999, p. 89.

[99]   Douglas Archibald, Rupert, *Tobago: Melancholy Isle, Vol. III, 1807-1898*, Port-of-Spain, Trinidad: Westindiana, 2003, p. 170.

Jamaica, Grenada, St. Vincent, St. Lucia, Tobago, and the Leeward Islands. Sir William Robinson was a member of the Slave Trade Commission in 1869, was governor of the Bahama Isles from 1874 to 1880, was governor of the Windward Islands that included Tobago from 1881 to 1884, was governor of Barbados 1884 to 1885, and was governor of Trinidad from 1885 to 1889. There was, therefore, a wealth of evidence and informed opinions that supported the need for administrative reform in Tobago.

The Colonial Office was inevitably concerned about the cost of administration in the colonies and its burden on the British Treasury. Concerted efforts were made to reduce these costs in the Victorian age of fiscal prudence.

At the level of the administration these problems were played out as a conflict between the executive (the government-appointed officials) and the representative Assembly (largely the spokesmen for the dominant class). In Tobago in particular, the Colonial Office, cognizant of this issue, made several attempts to resolve the matter through a number of constitutional changes. Despite a slew of administrative reforms that included reducing the size of its Assembly, abolishing the local Privy Council, creating an Executive Committee, modifying the franchise so as to increase the number of voters, and changing its constitution to make Tobago a Crown colony, the island was bogged down with a shortage of capital, low economic growth, and insufficient revenues for the administration to be viable. In 1878, in relation to the establishment of a telegraphic link to Tobago, the idea of the annexation of Tobago to Trinidad was noted. For some considerable time, therefore, the Colonial Office had been agonising over the constitutional arrangements for Tobago and to that end had received a number of suggestions from officials familiar with the region.

ADMINISTRATIVE CONTROL

The imperial power was faced with the administrative problem of controlling its representatives located in the colonies far from the centre of power in an age when communication was quite primitive.

Spain at a very early stage in its colonisation of the New World had recognised this problem of controlling the conquistadores. In exercising great moral concern over the fate of the Amerindians, the Spanish intellectuals recommended the *encomienda*[100] and the *Requerimiento*[101], and ironically, when those did not work, they resorted to Negro slavery.

Coming to the New World after the Spaniards, the British, without the systematic approach of the Spaniards, experienced their own problems of control. The North American colonies eventually rejected some aspects of imperial control—taxation, religion, the institution of slavery—and opted for independence. In the West Indian colonies, where *Campbell vs Hall* had raised the issue of imperial control, the colonies would have liked to exercise that option but clearly did not have the military resources to do so. (The United States could not have achieved their independence at that time without the assistance of Britain's archenemy, France.) The loss of the American Colonies naturally triggered a change in the imperial policy towards the West Indian colonies. The Colonial Office was the interface between the imperial Parliament and the government in the colonies and thus was directly responsible. The Crown colony system was one such change implemented to restore the executive authority in the colonies to the Crown and its appointees.

THE DECISION

A decisive moment came after the Tobago economy virtually collapsed in 1884. Early in 1886, the governor-in-chief of the Windward Islands, Mr Walter J. Sendall (later Sir Walter J. Sendall),

---

[100] The *encomienda* was the system in which the Amerindians were compelled to work on behalf of the Spanish colonists in exchange for small wages, instruction in the Christian faith and the protection of the Castilian Crown.

[101] Bartholomé de las Casas protested the injustice done to the Amerindians by the encomienda. In 1513 a jurist of Ferdinand issued the *Requerimiento* that on the basis of the Papal Donation, stipulated the obligation of all Amerindians to pay homage to the agents of the Crown and to obey their orders.

wrote to the secretary of state, expressing the view that Tobago could be more economically and efficiently administered if it were a dependency of Trinidad. He further indicated that the administrator of Tobago, Mr Robert B. Llewelyn, was of the same opinion.

The Colonial Office had been aware of the movement to annex Tobago to Trinidad ever since the observation of Lieutenant-Governor Ussher in 1872 and the stream of similar recommendations that followed. A Colonial Office minute of 1878, concerned about the lack of infrastructure in Tobago, stated:

> *"It would be a good thing, if some day Tobago is annexed by Trinidad, then electric communication will be established."*[102]

When, therefore, the suggestion came from Mr Sendall to effect the annexation, he was knocking on an open door.

The suggestions for the annexation must have weighed heavily on the mind of the secretary of state, particularly with the prospect of reduced costs of administration. But there is evidence that in electing to annex the island to Trinidad, the Colonial Office must have had thoughts other than the proximity of the two islands.

It is almost certain that the decision to associate Tobago with Trinidad was inspired by the rapid progress being made in Trinidad, particularly under Governor Sir Arthur Hamilton Gordon after 1866. Gordon, stands alongside Chacon and Abercrombie in the pantheon of leaders of modern Trinidad. The son of a British prime minister, he left the Trinidad economy in surplus and was instrumental in extending the network of roads and bridges throughout the island; he was also largely responsible for the distribution of Crown lands, for education reform, and for transforming the economy and society.[103]

---

[102] Cited in Douglas Archibald, Rupert, *Tobago: Melancholy Isle, Vol. III, 1807-1898*, Port-of-Spain, Trinidad: Westindiana, 2003, p. 53.

[103] "In November 1866 one of the most remarkable colonial administrators of the nineteenth century became Governor of Trinidad. At the time no one

In addition the Crown colony system of Trinidad, while lacking the democratic elements of the older colonies, successfully avoided their problem of conflict between the executive and the legislative branches of government. After giving the matter due consideration, therefore, the Secretary of State for the Colonies, Lord Glanville, in mid-1886 wrote to the Trinidad and Tobago governors and suggested to them the possibility of some sort of union between the two islands.[104] In writing to Tobago's governor, he suggested two forms that the union could take. The first was that Tobago be wholly or completely incorporated with the colony of Trinidad, and the second was that the colony of Tobago could become annexed to the colony of Trinidad as a dependency, having a separate treasury and subordinate Legislature and holding to Trinidad the same relation that the Turks Islands then held to Jamaica. He exhorted them to ascertain the opinions and wishes of the inhabitants and to allow a certain time to elapse before introducing the relevant resolutions. The suggestions were duly considered by both Legislatures, and resolutions were made and communicated to the secretary of state.

---

predicted that the administration of Arthur Hamilton Gordon was to be the divide between the post-emancipation years and a period which seems to us to have more in common with the early twentieth century than the economic turmoils of abolition." Wood, Donald, *Trinidad in Transition: The Years after Slavery,* Oxford: Oxford University Press, 1986, p. 265.

[104] The evidence for this comes shortly after the union was consummated in March 1889. In giving his decision in rejecting the Majority Report of the Royal Franchise Commission, Lord Knutsford, then secretary of state for the colonies, wrote, "The unofficial members of the Legislative council have for a long time had greater weight in that body than has been in the case of other Crown Colonies and the island has enjoyed remarkable prosperity which has extended to all classes; which this development has been advanced by the judicial legislation and the liberal expenditure on public works." Despatch from the Secretary of State to the Governor Sir William Robinson, 6 March 1889.

CHAPTER V

Profile of the New Colony

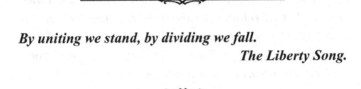

By uniting we stand, by dividing we fall.
                                        The Liberty Song.

A FTER THE RESOLUTIONS OF Legislatures of both colonies had been considered by the Colonial Office, and the Trinidad and Tobago Act of 1887 had been passed by the British Parliament, the Order in Council of 17 November 1888 created the legal basis for the new colony of Trinidad and Tobago to take effect from 1 January 1889.

The minutes of the Legislative Council of Trinidad for 17 December 1888 noted the following:

> *"His Excellency announced that the union of Trinidad and Tobago would take effect from 1st January, 1889 and that the Order in Council on the subject, which was laid on the Table, would be published."*

The Order in Council is reproduced in full in Appendix I below.

Early in February 1889, the governor issued a proclamation to inform the public of his authority to carry out in Tobago the administrative function as he did in Trinidad.

With that order, Tobago severed its ancient ties with the Windward Islands that had begun in 1763. At the union the population of Tobago was approximately 18,000 and that of Trinidad 200,000.

PROCLAMATION

Whereas by the Royal Order in Council uniting the Colonies of Trinidad and Tobago, bearing the date 17th day of November, 1888, Clause 29, it was ordered that from and after the 1st day of January, 1889, the Laws of Trinidad in relation to the subjects specified in the said Clause should be in force in Tobago, and the Laws therefore in force in Tobago in relation to the same subjects shall thereupon cease to be in force;

And whereas by the said Clause it was further ordered that where by the Laws of Trinidad to which the said Clause applied it is provided that any act, duty or thing shall be performed or done, and whether or not at any or within specified time or at any specified place by any Officer or person in the public service in Trinidad, the Governor might from time to time if he should think fit to do so by Proclamation, declare by what Officer or person and at or within what time and at what place any such act, duty or thing should be performed or done in Tobago, and that every such declaration should have the same legal force and effect as if it had been contained in the Law to which it applies;

Now therefore, I William Robinson, Governor aforesaid, do hereby proclaim and declare that the Officers and persons entrusted with the administration within the Island of Tobago by the Laws specified in the said Clause, or having any duties to perform thereunder, shall within the said Island of Tobago perform and do all such acts, duties or things, and shall enjoy all such powers as by the said Laws are enjoyed and conferred upon the Officers

and Persons entrusted with the administration of the said
Laws within the said Island of Trinidad

> *Given under my Hand and Seal of the*
> *Colony, at Government House, in the*
> *town of Port-of-Spain, this 7ʰ day of*
> *February, 1889.*
> *By His Excellency's Command,*
>
> *Henry Fowler,*
> *Colonial Secretary.*

One of the earliest amendments to the Order in Council increased by two the number of members of the Legislative Council: the commissioner of Tobago and the receiver-general joined the list of official members.

EXTRACT FROM THE MINUTES OF THE PROCEEDINGS OF THE LEGISLATIVE COUNCIL OF TRINIDAD AND TOBAGO, 1 APRIL 1889

> *The Colonial Secretary announced that under the Royal Instructions reconstituting the Legislative Council, the Receiver-General of Trinidad and the Commissioner of Tobago were added to the list of official Members.*
>
> *Mr Hamilton, who was in attendance, was sworn and took his seat as Receiver-General.*
>
> *His Excellency committed to the Council a Despatch from the Secretary of State in reference to the Report of the Franchise Commission which was received and also the Additional Instructions re-constituting the Legislative Council.*

Sir William Robinson,
First Governor of Trinidad and Tobago

THE TERRITORY

Tobago, as it had experienced before, became part of larger political entity at the same time that its own physical and human resources were dwarfed by those of Trinidad. The new colony had a population of 200,000 to which Tobago added 18,000. Located to the northeast of Venezuela and separated from it by the Gulf of Paria, Trinidad had a land area of 4,828 square kilometres of the unitary state's total of 5,128 square kilometres. Its geographical coordinates were approximately at Latitude 10° North and Longitude 61° West; this location places it at the southernmost extremity of the Atlantic hurricane belt, where it is relatively sheltered from the violent storms that perennially wreak havoc throughout the West Indian Islands; its physical features, flora, and fauna are similar to that of the South American continent.

> *"In the vast colonial empire of Great Britain there does not exist an Island as valuable for its extent as Trinidad. The fertility of its soil equals, if it does not excel, that of the most productive parts of St. Domingo* [Santo Domingo]*."*[105]

Neglected by the Spaniards who found no gold on the island, Trinidad remained largely undeveloped and untouched by the wars and the economic prosperity that characterised the West Indian islands during the seventeenth and eighteenth centuries. In early 1797, during the Napoleonic war and after Spain shed its neutrality in an alliance with France, British forces then based in Martinique (captured in 1794) captured Trinidad, which was formally ceded to Britain at the Treaty of Amiens in 1802. By the same treaty Martinique was returned to France.

In aggregate the new colony had an enhanced agricultural capability and, more so, marine resources. The suitability of Tobago for the rearing of farm animals augmented the capability of and added diversity to the economic activity that already existed in Trinidad.

THE NAME OF THE NEW COLONY

The Order in Council of 1888 created a new society and a new political arrangement in the form a unitary state with each island enjoying entrenched membership in the new Legislature. The arrangement was naturally skewed because of the huge differences in the resources of the individual islands. Despite this, the language of both the enabling Act of Parliament and the Order in Council made it clear that the political arrangement was that of a unitary state known as Trinidad and Tobago.

---

[105] Joseph, E. L., *History of Trinidad,* London: Cass Library of West Indian Studies, 1971, p. 1.

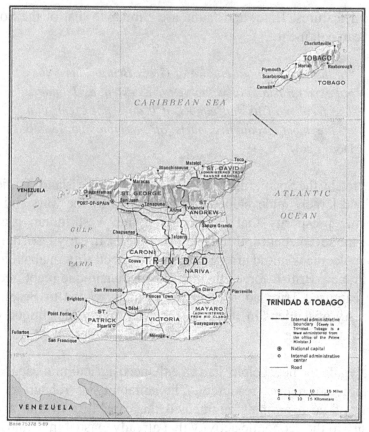

Map of Trinidad and Tobago

Arms of the Colony of Trinidad
and Tobago

This association of one island with another was a new arrangement for the people of Trinidad if not for the people of Tobago. In the case of Tobago, the resident authority was relieved of its responsibility for legislation and justice while retaining some responsibility for administration and finance, as was noted in the resolution of the defunct Legislative Council of Tobago. Following the British tradition that the colonies were the queen's dominions,[106] the enabling Act of Parliament left all of the details and arrangements for the new colony to be determined by Her Majesty, Queen Victoria, in the Order in Council. The name of the new colony was thus established in Clause I of the Order in Council:

> *"From and after the first day of January 1889 (hereinafter referred to as 'the appointed day') the Colony of Trinidad and its Dependencies and the Colony of Tobago shall be united into and constitute one Colony, which shall be called the colony of Trinidad and Tobago, upon the terms and conditions in this Order expressed, and the powers and functions of the Governor-in-Chief of the windward Islands in respect of the Colony of Tobago, and the Administrator of Tobago, shall thereupon cease and determine, and the Executive and Legislative Councils of Tobago shall thereupon cease to exist."*

THE CONSTITUTION

THE EXECUTIVE

The governor of Trinidad became the governor of Trinidad and Tobago. Sir William Robinson thus became the first governor of Trinidad and Tobago. Sir William must be seen as one of the principal architects of the modern West Indies, since while governor-in-chief of the Windward Islands (1880-1885) he had recommended that

---

[106] Marshall, P. J. (Ed.), *The Oxford History of the British Empire Vol. II: The Eighteenth Century*, Oxford: Oxford University Press, 1998, p. 10.

Barbados be separated from the Windward Island group, a move that was put into effect in 1885, the same year he became governor of Trinidad. The appointment of the governor continued to be the responsibility of the British government. The governor, however, was authorised to appoint a number of executive officers that included the attorney general, the solicitor general, the auditor general, the director of public works, the colonial secretary, and the protector of immigrants. In addition the governor appointed the chief justice, the head of the Judiciary, and he also made other appointments to the bench. The governor as chief executive officer presided over an advisory Executive Council. The first attorney general was Stephen Gatty.

THE FINANCIAL BOARD OF TOBAGO

The governor was authorised to appoint a commissioner of Tobago to exercise as necessary the functions of the governor in Tobago except powers of appointing and suspending from office public officers and exercising the prerogative of pardon. Mr Loraine G. Hay was appointed the first commissioner for Tobago.

The Financial Board of Tobago was the one institution established by the union. There has been much ado over the rejection of the proposal for control of the Financial Board by the unofficial members. But the decision was consistent with well-established Parliamentary practice with regard to public funds. Quite apart from the composition of the board, clause XXIII states very explicitly:

> "No Resolution shall be passed, or Regulation adopted, or question allowed for debate, the object of which shall be to dispose of or charge any part of the revenue of Tobago, unless the same be moved, introduced, or proposed by the consent or under the instructions of the Governor."

The refusal to grant control to the unofficials of Tobago was consistent with the Parliamentary convention that public bills be introduced only by Ministers of the Crown. It would have been a travesty of sorts if the Colonial Office allowed the unofficial of the

Legislature, who had no executive authority, to control the public purse. Moreover, it would have perpetuated the old practice whereby the Assembly held sway over the executive in Tobago.

LOCAL GOVERNMENT IN TOBAGO

In accordance with the resolution of the Tobago Legislative Council of January 1887, the Order in Council created a Financial Board of Tobago. This topic dominated the Order in Council, taking up clauses 5 to 26 of the 47 clauses contained therein. The board was authorised to, among other things:

> *"Make Regulations respecting taxation other than duties of customs or duties affecting shipping or excise duty on rum or other spirits, and respecting the collection, receipt, custody, and expenditure of the public revenue of Tobago, and respecting the borrowing of money on the credit of the revenue of Tobago, and respecting markets, cemeteries, public works, roads, the relief of and medical attendance on the poor, the granting of licenses, and purely local character, and by any such regulations to impose penalties by the fine or imprisonment, with or without hard labour, or fine and imprisonment with or without hard labour for the punishment of any breach or contravention of any Regulation of the Board."*

The revenues, expenditures, and debts of the two islands were to be separate and distinct. The Order in Council in fact established local government in Tobago distinct from and subordinate to the authority that exercised power over the colony of Trinidad and Tobago. To Tobago this was new although in the immediate past its administration was subordinate to the government of the Windward Islands based in Grenada.

LOCAL GOVERNMENT IN TRINIDAD

Trinidad at the union had a rudimentary form of local government. This may be seen as a necessary adjunct to the strong central government of the Crown colony system. The system comprised the City Council of Port-of-Spain, the Borough Councils of San Fernando and Arima, and the wards. Despite the fact that the population of Tobago, on account of its history, had more political awareness, among their counterparts in Trinidad there was a substantial minority with long experience in local government. Indeed, the municipal bodies and wards in particular were looked upon as training grounds for participation in the Legislative Council.

THE PORT-OF-SPAIN CITY COUNCIL (1841)

The City Council was a descendant of the Cabildo, a staple of the viceregal government of Spain in the Americas. It was essentially a municipal council and was known to exist in Trinidad since 1625: it was responsible for rates; garbage collection and cleaning of the streets of the city; drainage; cemeteries; security; abattoirs; markets; and street lighting.

THE SAN FERNANDO BOROUGH COUNCIL

Governor Chacon founded the town of San Fernando in 1792. A Town Council was established in 1846, and in 1853 the town was granted the status of borough during the governorship of Lord Harris.

ARIMA BOROUGH COUNCIL (1887)

Arima was granted the status of a borough by Queen Victoria after she was petitioned in her Jubilee year of 1887.

THE WARDS

Ordinance No. 11 of 1847 was the first step taken to organize Trinidad into divisions, counties, districts, and wards for administrative purposes. Ordinance No. 9 of 1849 defined the powers and duties of the wardens. However, the truly defining law of local government in Trinidad was Ordinance No. 13 of 1852 which consolidated a number of earlier pieces of legislation and set a firm basis for local government for the next fifty years. The person responsible for the administration of each ward was a person (the warden) resident within the ward appointed by the governor with broad responsibilities for maintaining the peace, collecting taxes, and supervising local welfare. For example, Clause 8 of the Ordinance states:

> *"And be it enacted, that each Warden shall be charged with making and keeping in repair of the public roads not being royal roads within the Ward, the cost of establishment and maintaining public schools of instruction and the payment of teachers of such schools, the establishment of houses of refuge for the destitute poor incapable of labour, the establishment of dispensaries and the costs of carrying into effect and enforcing sanitary regulations for the preservation of public health within the Ward, the expenses of the burial of paupers and inquests, the costs of printing and advertising of notices and other matters relating to the business of the Ward, and shall also be bound to contribute to the expense of the repairs of the royal roads within the Ward and of the general police force of the Colony."*

But some of the wards displayed the same characteristics of the Tobago Assembly: in some wards no suitable candidates for auditing came forward; in others the rate payers had not bothered to vote; in 1867, Governor Gordon reported that no election had been held in the Chaguaramas Ward since 1859.

THE LEGISLATURE

The governor presided over the deliberations of the Legislative Council where he exercised a casting vote. The Council was comprised of both official members and unofficial members.

The Legislative Council of Trinidad was replaced by the Legislative Council of Trinidad and Tobago.

The Legislature was enjoined from imposing, diminishing, suspending, or abolishing any tax or duty in Tobago other than customs duties and duties on shipping and excise duties on rum and other spirits, or from disposing of or charging any part of the revenue raised in Tobago for any other purpose than for the exclusive public service of Tobago. Notwithstanding that, the Legislature had the power to supersede all matters concerning the regulations of the Financial Board. In general, any ordinance enacted by the Legislature would apply to Tobago unless it was expressed and declared that it should not extend to Tobago. In April of 1889, the colonial secretary announced at a meeting of the Legislative Council that the Royal Instructions reconstituting the Council, the receiver-general, and the commissioner of Tobago were added to the number of ex-officio members. Mr Hamilton was the first receiver-general. The Legislature was unicameral; its enactments were known as Ordinances, and as a Crown colony they could be overruled by Her Majesty in Council. As a Crown colony the Trinidad Legislature had inherited one of the characteristic features of the British Parliament: its strong executive influence. The ex-officio members, contrary to the doctrine of the separation of powers proposed by Charles-Louis de Secondat, Baron de Montesquieu, were all members of the executive appointed by the Crown or governor and thus exerted a powerful influence in both the formulation and the execution of the laws.

THE LAW

Because of the separate legal histories of the two islands, it was enacted that laws in force in Trinidad would be in force in Tobago at the same time that similar laws in Tobago would cease to be in force.

In accordance with Maitland and the Articles of Capitulation, Spanish law was in force in Trinidad in the early nineteenth century. A shortage of persons knowledgeable in Spanish law led to the appointment of George Smith as chief justice, with a mandate to implement Spanish law as was required by the Articles of Capitulation. Within a few months Smith had obtained from the Audencia in Caracas a set of law books on Spanish law with a complement of trained lawyers from the University of Caracas. In addition, the liberation movement by Simon Bolívar saw a number of prominent lawyers flee Venezuela to take up residence in Trinidad. This arrangement, while it complied with the Articles of Capitulation, added to the administrative problems in the polyglot society, and within three decades the decision was taken to establish English as the official language and for English law to supersede Spanish law. In 1879, the Trinidad Judicature Ordinance finally put the law on a firm footing in Trinidad.

Sir John Gorrie, First Chief Justice of
Trinidad and Tobago

THE JUDICIARY

The Supreme Court of Trinidad was replaced by the Supreme Court of Trinidad and Tobago. Sir John Gorrie became the first chief justice of Trinidad and Tobago. The court was required to hold sittings in Tobago at least three times a year for the trial of criminal and civil cases and to hear appeals from the decisions of magistrates under rules issued in accordance with the Trinidad Judicature Ordinance of 1879. Provision was made for the appointment by the governor of a commissioner of the Supreme Court in Tobago. The commissioner, in the absence of a judge of the Supreme Court in Tobago, was empowered to perform the duties of the said judge as prescribed by the rules of the court.

THE SOCIETY

THE PEOPLE

Tobago was less polyglot than Trinidad. The population of Tobago, because it was predominantly of African origin, skewed the population of the new colony slightly towards the African majority. The Royal Cedula of 1783 (the Cedula) had a dramatic effect on the size and composition of the population of Trinidad largely by immigration from the French-speaking West Indian islands.

On the heels of that Cedula, slavery in Trinidad grew rapidly with the majority of slaves by contractual arrangements coming directly from Africa. So moved was the noble Sir Ralph Abercrombie at the sight of the mixed population in Trinidad that he borrowed a line from the Roman poet Vergil in giving a motto to the colony, placed on its flag, badge, and great seal in 1803:

"Miscerique probat populous et foedera Jungi."[107]

In the wake of the conquest of Trinidad in 1806, one year before the British abolition of the slave trade, in a fresh attempt to alleviate the labour shortage, twenty-five Chinese males were brought over from China. By their small numbers they had little effect on the economy or in the society, and they eked out a living by trading in shellfish

---

[107] Vergil, *Aeneid, Book IV,* line 112: "He approves of the mingling of the peoples and their bonds of union." The motto and design of arms of the Colony of Trinidad and Tobago, adopted in 1959 were taken from the Great Seal of Trinidad of 1803.

and charcoal. After the policy of indentureship was adopted in the 1840s, about 2,500 Chinese came to work on the sugar estates, but strictures in the laws of immigration in China somewhat hampered the free flow of immigrants. Adding further to the polyglot nature of the society following emancipation was the migration of indentured labourers from the Portuguese island of Madeira. The high mortality rate of immigrants from Madeira prompted the governor, Lord Harris, to abandon the policy of accepting immigrants from that source. He warmed to the idea of Dr Lushington in following Mauritius and British Guiana in introducing indentured labourers from India.

With indentured labourers coming from India since the 1840s, Trinidad had a substantial number of East Indians that added to a potpourri of dwindling Amerindians; Europeans of Spanish, French, and British origin; slaves; and largely black immigrants from other West Indian islands. With the highest wages in the sugar industry in the British West Indies, Trinidad was like a magnet, attracting workers from the smaller islands displaced by hurricanes or adventurers seeking their fortunes in a land rich with opportunities. Already Trinidad was a highly stratified society by race and colour, and those factors alone would have placed the majority of Tobagonians in the lowest class. But the dire economic circumstances, the low level of skills, and the relatively poor education facilities in Tobago also confirmed that status. The land distribution problem in Trinidad was less acute, and there was an emerging middle class. Social life degenerated rapidly after the British conquest as Chacon's utopian dream faded into obscurity.

> "It is difficult to ascribe to the Cedula of 1783 any other general principle than that of establishing a perfect equality of civil rights between free persons, without reference to their complexion and origin."[108]

With a retrograde leadership in Trinidad under Picton, race relations quickly regressed towards that of the other British West Indian

---

[108] Stephen, Dr. James, Cited by Campbell, Carl, in *Cedulants and Capitulants*, Port-of-Spain, Trinidad: Paria Publishing Co., 1992, p. 218.

islands. Even the new policy that Chief Justice Smith was mandated to implement did not bring the desired result. The failure by both the Spanish and British governments to bring about a more equal society in Trinidad suggests that there were strong social and cultural forces working against those ideals, and racism in the form of a colour bar was the debilitating force, although there were only social restraints as compared with the legal restraints that existed elsewhere. This was confirmed in the 1820s when the imperial government tried to implement measures of ameliorating the condition of the slaves; the reaction from the planters in Trinidad was no different from that of the other West Indian Islands.

RELIGION

Trinidad at the British conquest was essentially a Catholic country, and Catholicism remained the dominant religion at the time of the union. Its Catholicism stemmed from the *Patronato* granted by Rome to the Spanish Crown in 1486 and extended by a number of Papal Bulls to embrace the Indies and included the right and responsibility for evangelising the lands of America.[109] The plight of the natives came to the attention of Isabella when a number of them captured by the conquistadores were sent to Spain and ordered to be sold, as was the custom. The last will of Isabella was fulfilled in a number of missions spread over the island.

> *"Thus, the Queen's first and most important wish . . . was that the Indians should be taught the doctrines of the church and converted."[110]*

> *"Isabella, however, had been deeply interested by the accounts given of the gentle and hospitable character of these islanders, and of their docility. The discovery* [of the Indies] *had been made under her immediate auspices;*

---

[109] Elliott, J. H., *Empires of the Atlantic World: Britain and Spain in America 1492-1830,* New Haven, Conn: Yale University Press, 2007, p. 68.

[110] Las Casas, Bartholomé de, cited in Williams, Dr. E. E., *Documents of West Indian History, Vol. I,* New York, NY: A & B Publishing, 1994, p. 100.

she looked upon these people as under her peculiar care, and she anticipated, with pious enthusiasm, the glory of leading them from darkness into the paths of light. Her compassionate spirit revolted at the idea of treating them as slaves, even though sanctioned by the custom of the time. Within five days after the royal order for the sale, a letter was written by the sovereign to Bishop Fonseca, suspending that order, until they could enquire into the cause for which the Indians had been made prisoners, and consult learned and pious theologians, whether their sale would be justifiable in the eyes of God. Much difference of opinion took place among the divines, on this most important question; the queen eventually decided it according to the dictates of her own pure conscience and charitable heart. She ordered that the Indians should be sent back to their native country, and enjoined that the islanders should be conciliated by the gentlest means, instead of being treated with severity."[111]

After the early conquistadores failed to enslave the native Amerindians, Cortés introduced the *repartimiento* (an allocation of Amerindians to the conquistadores) in the *encomienda* system that was later formalised by Governor Nicolas Ovando in Santo Domingo. In Trinidad, four *encomiendas* were established in San Juan, Caura, Tacarigua, and Arouca. Under the latter in a quasi-feudal arrangement a group of Amerindians were assigned to a colonist to serve and pay tribute while a priest attended to their conversion and spiritual needs. The system of establishing towns as centres of settlement and colonisation throughout the Spanish Empire was made into law by the Ordinances of Phillip II in 1573.

---

[111] Borde, Pierre Gustave Louis, *The History of the Island of Trinidad Under the Spanish Government, First Part (1498-1622)*, Port-of-Spain, Trinidad: Paria Publishing Co. Ltd., 1982, p. 263 (1876).

"The mission was a school of religion, civilization and
political government, though actually the three aspects
were inseparable in the minds of the missionaries."[112]

The mission, to be precise, followed the ordinances of 1567. With
its introduction responsibility shifting from the conquistadores to
the missionaries. There were missions run by the Capuchin monks
at Naparima, Savonetta, Savana Grande (Princes Town), and Arena
(San Rafael).

The Catholicism introduced by the Spaniards was reinforced by
the Royal Cedula of 1783 that was biased in favour of Catholics
wanting to immigrate to Trinidad. This Catholicism had profound
influence in developing civic life in Trinidad before the conquest
and in the politics of the nineteenth century. By contrast, despite the
introduction of Catholicism to Tobago during the French occupation,
religion in Tobago was dominated by the Protestant religions; Islam
and Hinduism had virtually no impact on the island.

The British conquest naturally introduced to Trinidad the Anglican
religion and its associated problems. Unlike in Tobago the Anglican
Church was not established at the conquest in Trinidad; the Articles
of Capitulation, strictly interpreted, together with the fact that the
majority of the inhabitants were Catholics, were not conducive to
such a move. However, by 1831, the Anglican bishop for the region
(The See was known as the Bishopric of Barbados and comprised
the following countries: Barbados, Grenada, St. Vincent, Dominica,
Antigua, Montserrat, St. Christopher, Nevis, the Virgin Islands,
Trinidad, Tobago, St. Lucia, and the Grenadines), based in Barbados,
was an ex-officio member of the Legislative Council of Trinidad.
In 1841, Letters Patent of were issued authorising changes in the
Anglican Church government throughout the West Indies. This
established the Church of England in Trinidad, importing thereby
the religious trouble that England experienced with its Civil War in
the seventeenth century. With the resolute efforts of Woodford and

---

[112]   De Verteuil, Fr. Anthony, *Martyrs and Murderers: Trinidad, 1699*, Port-of-
Spain, Trinidad: Litho Press, 1995, p. 56.

Charles Warner, then solicitor-general, to Anglicise the colony, it was no surprise when the "Ecclesiastical" Ordinance (for the better regulation of the duties of clergy of the United Church of England and Ireland) of 1844 imposed on Trinidad the administrative and legal framework of the Church of England, with the courts empowered to assist in their execution. The religious tranquillity of the colony, enjoyed since 1699, had been disturbed. The Catholics were apprehensive, mindful as they were of the situation in Ireland, where there were churches without congregations and pastors without flocks:

> *"Above all it seemed against all notions of justice that a minority Church should be given the right to expand throughout the colony, and when it asked, to receive Government money for stipends, sextons, buildings and glebe lands, all of which were paid from the taxes of the people, whatever their religion."*[113]

There was a natural conflict between the ruling British elite and the dominant francophone Catholic community. The matter was overcome in due course by accommodation on the part of the authorities and with the disestablishment of the Anglican Church in 1870.

After abolition the steady stream of immigrants from the other West Indian islands added to the growth of Protestantism. Indian indentureship during forty or more years had added new elements of religious diversity, although the introversion of this highly knit community delayed the integration of the principal religions of Hinduism and Islam into the society as a whole. Despite that, Canadian missionaries were instrumental in educating and in small measure converting these immigrants, who were another ethnic group isolated from the mainstream of society in Trinidad.

---

[113] Wood, Donald, *Trinidad in Transition: The Years after Slavery*, (Oxford: Oxford University Press, 1986, p. 195.

The union of Tobago marginally reinforced the strength of Protestantism in Trinidad and Tobago

EDUCATION

Under the Spaniards, the little of the schooling done in Trinidad took place in the missions. The Amerindians were converted and taught the principles of civic life in their own language. The *Code Noir* of 1789 made explicit provision for the education of the slaves. Its very first clause spelled out the obligations of slave owners in the education of slaves, although the emphasis clearly was on religious indoctrination. After the population explosion that ensued from the Cedula, there was an increased demand for education. A number of private schools emerged. They provided primary education to an exclusive set.

In 1825, there were six schools in all of Trinidad. Instruction was at the most elementary level by teachers who were for the most part untrained. Of the six, one was an English boarding school for girls, three were French day schools, one a school administered by the Cabildo for teaching the English language, and the other, an outgrowth remnant of the ancient missions, taught Spanish to Amerindians. All secondary education was acquired by the well-to-do, who sent their children abroad for the most part to France and Britain.

After emancipation the Mico Charity, established by Act of Parliament in Britain in 1835 and based in Jamaica, assisted in the education of the children of the former slaves in Trinidad, as they did in other parts of the British West Indies. The significant contribution of this group was their provision of professionally trained teachers that were in very short supply for running the early schools. The Mico Charity's contribution ended in 1848 and led to the introduction of model schools which were established as practice schools for trainee teachers.

The first secondary school appeared in the 1830s. Although by 1846 there were fifty-four primary schools, the Education Ordinance of 1851 established a system of free and secular schools to be administered by the wards under the watchful eye of a board of education with salaried inspectors. It was no surprise that religious rivalry dogged the education process: the Catholics, Anglicans, and other Christian churches ran over thirty schools, and the Canadian Presbyterian Mission kept seven schools for the children of indentured labourers. All of these schools were privately funded. And primary education was carried out largely in the thirty-seven free primary schools that fell under the jurisdiction of the wards and municipal authorities. The Education Ordinance of 1870 provided state aid to denominational primary schools under very strict conditions.

In the 1870s, with a new policy, state aid was extended to all denominations meeting the required standards and placed secondary education on a sound footing. A competitive scholarship system was immediately introduced for supporting education at the tertiary level. The consequence of this was the training of a suitable cadre of persons for employment in the growing civil service and other professions and an avenue for upward social mobility. The later establishment of secondary schools, discounting the shortcoming of being restricted to relatively few, had given the society a means of social mobility and, together with the expanding economy, produced a reinforcement of the rising middle class. By the end of the century solicitors were being trained in Port-of-Spain. On entry to the union, therefore, Trinidad had acquired the rudiments of a competent class of professionals, and it was no surprise that during the 1890s there would be a constant demand for self-government and greater administrative responsibility. At the same time it offered opportunities, not available hitherto, for higher education to residents in Tobago

THE ARTS AND SCIENCES

The union brought Tobago into a society that enjoyed somewhat more leisure and had a marginally better educated people. Unlike Tobago, the landed coloureds of Trinidad could afford to educate their children in Europe, and by the middle of the nineteenth century the benefits of their efforts were visible in public life. The result of the spread of education was the emergence of another social hierarchy to rival that of the colour bar. This educated elite, predominantly white and French Creole, founded a literary tradition that enriched life in the emerging society. In this vein a literary association was established in 1847, and the Trinidad Public Library was established in 1852. Already in 1824, Dr Jean Baptiste Philippe had penned *A Free Mulatto*,[114] the title given to *An Address to the right Honourable Earl Bathurst [Secretary of State for the Colonies] Relative to the Claims which the Coloured Peoples of Trinidad to the same civil and political privileges with their white fellow-subjects.* In 1838, E. L. Joseph completed his manuscript for **History of Trinidad**. Other written works appearing in this period included Dr L. A. A. De Verteuil's **Trinidad: Its Geography, Natural Resources, Administration, Present Condition and Prospects (1858)**; Dr Antoine Leotaud's **Oiseaux de l'ile de la Trinité (1866);** Michel Maxwell Philip's **Emannuel Apodaca (1854)**; J. J. Thomas's **The Theory and Practice of Creole Grammar (1869)**; and **Froudacity (1889)**. The impact of these pioneers was to place a new emphasis on education as a means of social advancement and its influence can be seen one century later if one goes beyond the confines of the nineteenth century and the world figures of C. L. R. James, Dr Eric Williams, and V. S. Naipaul; we are forced to conclude not only that the institutions of Trinidad were superior to those of Tobago, but that perhaps they were superior to those of the rest of the Caribbean. The most significant cultural development in Trinidad was its Carnival, a festival that among other things reflected the spirit of freedom that followed emancipation in 1834. The enhanced society thus placed the people in Tobago closer to a centre of the arts, and the sciences were also flourishing and a society encouraged social mobility.

POLITICS

The basis of much early political agitation in Trinidad stems from its own Magna Carta: the Royal Cedula of 1783, the *Code Noir,* and the Articles of Capitulation. These documents provide the foundation for nearly all the demands for civil rights and equality that dominated

---

[114] Philippe, Dr. Jean Baptiste, *A Free Mulatto (1824)*, Wellesley, MA: Calaloux Publications, 1996.

the early political issues. Two themes stand out above all others: constitutional reform and demands for equality of human rights. We see a string of political agitators and leaders in Jean Baptiste Philippe; Rev. Francis de Ridder; Thomas Hinde, schoolmaster and member of the Town Council in 1841; Henry Jobity; William Herbert; and Georges Numa Dessources.

No sooner was British rule established than a political rivalry was established in Trinidad. On one side there were the wealthier landowning French- and Spanish-speaking residents, and on the other were the English-speaking merchants and tradesmen. This rivalry was to flourish throughout the nineteenth century in a conscious move to Anglicise the colony (Woodford and Warner) and with the French reviving the indigenous cocoa industry, destroyed by an unknown plant disease in 1727, and the English, with access to British capital, developing sugar and the merchandising of imported goods. The leisure that allowed the arts to flourish in Trinidad also permitted participation in politics, although this was limited to a very small section of the population. As Wood pointed out:

> *"The religious and political controversies . . . meant little to the majority of Negroes, whether they lived in the country or in the growing slums of Port-of-Spain. They had no part in the Government nor had their appetite been whetted for politics. Other than the administration itself there was no organization to represent their interests."[115]*

It is tempting to point out that where the majority of the population is uneducated the political system if aristocratic is inherently very stable. Its stability depends upon the existence of a mass of uneducated people indifferent to or excluded from the political system on the one hand and on the other a benevolent political elite that the mass of the people are prepared to follow. When the elite governs like a philosopher king it reinforces the indifference of the masses that results in a system that is self-sustaining. The Trinidad society

---

[115] Wood, Donald, *Trinidad in Transition: The Years after Slavery,* Oxford: Oxford University Press, 1986, p. 238.

displayed this characteristic throughout the nineteenth century. The government was essentially oligarchic in nature, with the unofficial members dominated by planters. The oligarchic nature of the Crown colony system is seen best by pointing out that after the reform of 1925, only 6 percent of the population was entitled to vote. It was only with the spread of education towards the end of the nineteenth century that expectations changed and the demand for representation by a growing middle class gathered substantial momentum.

The most pressing political problems in the first half of the nineteenth century were the demand for representative government and the matter of colour discrimination. In Tobago the old plantocracy succumbed to the growing political strength of the lower classes, with the breakdown of the society that called out for dire constitutional reform. The principal demands of constitutional reform were met with the establishment of the Legislative Council in 1831. Despite, however, the emancipation of the slaves and before that the amelioration of their conditions, the demands for civil rights were never met because of the persistence of an unofficial bar that pervaded the whole society.

Lord Knutsford's comment in the 1880s indicates that the Legislature of Trinidad was an effective political organ: the burning political issues of religion and education had been resolved but the colony continued to be dogged by two political issues: the lower classes of the society remained largely unrepresented in the Legislature, and the colour bar instituted by Picton was a drag on social and economic development.

THE ECONOMY

The progress made in economic development in Trinidad may be gauged from the report of the Royal West India Commissioners, which found that in 1894, Trinidad, with one third the population of Jamaica, had a much larger export trade. The new arrangement gave Tobago a measure of local government within the framework of the greater responsibility that now lay with the Legislative Council of Trinidad and Tobago. The infrastructure was better developed, which allowed its diverse agricultural production to be transported to market. Governor Gordon extended the road from Arima to Valencia, added an extension to Manzanilla, and thereby provided access to new lands for development and easy access to fishing villages on the east coast of the island.

AGRICULTURE

Silviculture in Trinidad received a huge boost in 1816 when Governor Woodford introduced David Lockhart as director of the Botanical Gardens. Lockhart, a trained botanist visited South America and several West Indian islands and imported many plants for the gardens, which he directed until 1846. His legacy is well known: Crueger's contribution to the flora of the British West Indies; the influence on the Kew Gardens; Charles Kingsley's idyllic description of the forests of Trinidad; and the Imperial College of Tropical Agriculture. Early attempts to manage the agricultural industry saw the formation of an agricultural society. In an era of slavery, however, this group was preoccupied with the question of labour and less with concern for technology. After the Botanical Gardens were established, Lord Harris introduced an annual agricultural show to raise the standards of animal husbandry, awarding prizes for the best kept estate books and essays on sugar cultivation.

In the middle of the nineteenth century, the utilisation of lands in Trinidad for agriculture was as follows: sugar cane (36,739 acres); cocoa and coffee (14,238 acres); ground provision fruits and vegetables (9,914 acres); and pasture (7,356 acres). Sugar production, although above the costs of Cuba, was reorganised through the introduction of a number of central *usines,* with Trinidad pioneering this method of management in the British West Indian colonies. The land reforms and distribution of Governor Gordon introduced a new aspect of sugar production in the form of individual cane farmers delivering their produce to these central factories. While the sugar producers were aware of the new technology used in Louisiana, they did not have the capital for transforming and sought refuge in growing cocoa instead.

Unable to compete with the large capitalised sugar usines, the smaller planters thrived by shifting to cocoa production so as to take advantage of the growing taste for chocolate and cocoa-derived products worldwide. Although indigenous to Trinidad, cocoa production fell dramatically after 1727 after destruction by a plant virus. With the revival of the cocoa industry Trinidad and Grenada, between them, were then the only producers in the British Empire. With the production in Grenada dwarfed by that of Trinidad, the latter enjoyed a virtual monopoly of cocoa in the British market, and this contributed to the growing wealth of the colony.

The workforce in cocoa, bolstered by the immigration of knowledgeable workers from Venezuela—the cocoa *panyols*—rejuvenated the cocoa industry. Aided by the development of roads giving access to markets and the distribution of Crown lands by Governor Gordon, cocoa production flourished to the point when at the end of the nineteenth century, cocoa had surpassed sugar to become the major agricultural export from Trinidad.

The East Indian immigrants had brought with them the culture of growing wet rice, vegetable farming and dairy farming; there was a substantial market for these cash crops in a colony that was growing rapidly.

The union with Trinidad enhanced the potential for raising grazing animals in particular and for agricultural produce in general by providing a large and accessible outlet at the same time that it facilitated the diversification of the agricultural practices in Tobago with enhanced cocoa production.

TRANSPORT AND COMMUNICATIONS

Internally, transportation consisted of navigation on the rivers; the horse-drawn buggy; the horse; mules and donkeys; and bison (the bicycle had not yet arrived in Trinidad). Externally, shipping provided a link with Venezuela. Some sugar estates used private tramways for getting the canes from the fields to the sugar mills.

The simple network of roads laid down in the 1790s by Chacon was extended by Governor Gordon. In September 1871, a telegraph cable linking Trinidad to the outside world was terminated at Macqueripe Bay on the northwest peninsula.

CONCLUSION

To an extent, therefore, the new colony of Trinidad and Tobago inherited some of the problems that had divided Europe after the discovery of America. The conflict between France and Britain was played out in the political battle in the new colony between the English-speaking and the French-speaking residents. For all practical purposes, the Spanish culture that was dominant until the 1770s had waned to the point where there were only small enclaves. In the Christian church, there was a clear dichotomy between the Protestantism of the British immigrants and the former slaves of the other West Indian islands on the one hand and the Catholicism of the earlier immigrants. The Eastern religions of the indentured labourers had little impact on public policy, largely because the group had no representatives in or out of the Legislature. The Canadian mission that looked after the welfare of the indentured East Indians managed some converts to Presbyterianism. At the same time the new humanitarianism generated by the revolutions that took place in Europe, in continental America, and in the Caribbean found its way to Trinidad through its enlightened and frustrated Spanish governor, Don Chacon. The abolition of the slave trade and of slavery itself shifted the development thrust towards economic advances and subsequently to development of the human resources. This was the condition of the new colony at the time of the union.

Charles Kinglsey who was to Trinidad what Daniel Defoe was to Tobago wrote after a visit in 1870 to Trinidad and other islands of the British West Indies:

"... here as in Grenada ... every one he passes looks strong, healthy and well fed. One meets few or none of those figures and faces, small, scrofulous, squinty and *haggard, which disgrace the so-called civilization of a British city. Nowhere in Port-of-Spain will you see such human beings as in certain streets of London, Liverpool or Glasgow. Every one plainly can live and thrive if they choose and very pleasant it is to know that."[116]*

---

[116] Kingsley, Charles, *At Last: A Christmas in the West Indies*, Memphis, Tenn: General Books LLC, 2009, p. 54.

CHAPTER VI

Problems and Progress

History teaches us that men and nations behave
wisely once they have exhausted all other possibilities.
Abba Eban, *Speech in London, 1970*

A
LTHOUGH IT WOULD BE some years before it became apparent, the legislators in Trinidad had a concept of the union that was significantly different from that of the other parties to the decision making process. The invitation from the secretary of state to form the union suggested that Tobago be completely incorporated in the colony of Trinidad or alternatively that it be annexed with a separate treasury and a subordinate Legislature. The resolution of the Legislative Council of Trinidad, accordingly, was for the annexation of Tobago to form part of the colony of Trinidad and for Tobago to maintain a separate treasury. By contrast, the legislators in Tobago held firmly in their resolution that Tobago was to form a united colony with Trinidad, known as Trinidad and Tobago. The Act of Parliament of 1887 and the Order in Council of 1888 were very explicit in confirming the new united colony of Trinidad and Tobago. The difference in interpretation would not emerge until after the relationship between the two islands deteriorated, with the loss of customs duties in Tobago and as members of the Legislature and the Financial Board began to express their feelings frankly and openly about the union. The

difference which was first expressed as a footnote in a report of a select committee led eventually to the new Order in Council of 1898 that would establish the constitutional arrangement of Trinidad with Tobago well into the twentieth century.

THE ADMINISTRATION

The new arrangements meant that although the reconstituted government had responsibility for the laws and the judiciary in Tobago, the development of Tobago continued to be the responsibility of the Financial Board of Tobago. At this stage the government based in Trinidad was responsible for everything in Tobago except those explicitly excluded by the Order in Council. In particular, Tobago was expected to be self-financing. This was obviously an oversight in the decision making process although the difficulty associated with this was alluded to by the dissentient Mr Fenwick of the Trinidad Legislature. The regulations for the new Legislative Council made the Tobago commissioner an ex-officio member of the Legislative Council, and the governor promised to add another unofficial member from Tobago in order to maintain the balance between those two groups. It is not clear what impact this variation of the membership or the new mandate had on the outlook of the Legislature but the existence of the Financial Board in Tobago would have signalled to them that some autonomy was due to Tobago even if only in the terms spelt out in the Order in Council. Few members of the Legislative Council would have been familiar with the history of Tobago. Initially, the two "experts" were the governor and chairman, Sir William Robinson, and Mr Loraine G. Hay, the commissioner for Tobago. Later on Mr George H. McEachrane, who was a livewire on the Financial Board, was made an unofficial member. The governor ought to have had some insight, however, since he was governor-in-chief of the Windward Islands group based in Barbados from 1880 to 1885 and would have had a general notion of the administrative problems of Tobago in that period. There was nothing in the new arrangement to preclude Tobago issues from being raised in the Legislative Council, although the initiative for doing so naturally rested with the Tobago representatives.

Unfortunately the focus of the authorities in Tobago was directed to the matter of revenue as this was its mandate in accordance with the Order in Council. Since Tobago was bankrupt at the time of the union, it meant that the island continued to languish in the prevailing economic circumstances. The constitutional arrangement was quasi-confederational and allowed Tobago complete financial independence. Tobago's economic backwardness with its failed single crop economy is seen in stark contrast with Trinidad, where in addition to sugar production there was diversification into cocoa, coffee, rice, and citrus.

PROBLEMS: 1889-1899

During the decade 1889 to 1899 the union was plagued with four major problems that tended to tear it apart: the problem with the Judiciary, the problem with land distribution, the customs problem, and the constitutional problem of Tobago in relation to the government based in Trinidad and Tobago. The arrangements for the union were grossly inadequate despite the early warning given by Mr Fenwick in his dissenting vote when the matter was debated in the Legislative Council in Trinidad. Although the responsibility for the laws and their execution in Tobago resided in the reconstituted government in Port-of-Spain, the local development of Tobago continued to be the responsibility of the Financial Board of Tobago. This was clear from the board's authority for borrowing money on the credit of Tobago in respect of markets, cemeteries, public works, roads, the relief of and attendance to the poor, the granting of licenses, and matters of a purely local nature. The frustration of the authorities in Tobago generated by the union produced at least three petitions to the Crown seeking relief. The first sought to remove Sir John Gorrie as chief justice; the second prayed for relief for the loss of revenue arising from the new laws concerning customs duties; and the third sought dissolution of the union. In addition there was the burning issue of reform of the policy on land distribution.

THE PROBLEM WITH THE JUDICIARY

Although he lacked the nobility of birth of his fellow Scots, Sir Ralph Abercrombie and Sir Arthur Hamilton, Sir John Gorrie, with the same equanimity as his predecessors, left an indelible mark on the colonial administration of Trinidad and Tobago. Gorrie served as an attorney at the Commission of Enquiry into the Morant Bay riots in Jamaica, served alongside Sir Arthur Hamilton as an administrator in Mauritius and in British dependencies in the Pacific, and served as chief justice of the Leeward Islands before he came to Trinidad as chief justice in 1886. The antipathy of the justice system towards blacks throughout the British West Indies was very much observable in Trinidad in the 1870s. The scourge of Trinidad society was the unofficial colour bar introduced by Picton early in the nineteenth century. The gross injustice that Sir John Gorrie had encountered in Trinidad in 1886 was like a red cape to a raging bull. Having observed at first hand the social conditions under which the poorer classes lived in a number of British dependencies, including Jamaica and the South Seas, he set out on a personal programme of affirmative action to redress the grievances of the poor, upsetting in the process the planter class in Trinidad. After becoming chief justice of Trinidad and Tobago in January 1889, he went immediately to Tobago, where he held court personally. Gorrie's attitude towards the people of Tobago was no different from that of his attitude to the people of Trinidad:

> *"Sir John Gorrie was not merely dealing with a case that had come before the Chief Justice. He was defending the rights of people in Tobago who had never been regarded as having rights at all."*[117]

Since both his procedures and his judgements seemed to favour the landless peasants, he rankled the members of the plantocracy. As a measure of their influence, the estate owners of Tobago persuaded the Legislature to enact Ordinance No. 7 of 1889 to rein in Gorrie

---

[117] Williams, Dr. E. E., *History of the People of Trinidad and Tobago*, New York, NY: A & B Publishing, 1993, p. 127.

by requiring that sittings of the Supreme Court in Tobago be presided over by a puisne judge. Gorrie protested and took up his grievance directly with the secretary of state in England, where he was successful in influencing the authorities at the Colonial Office to disallow the legislation, and he continued to sit on the bench in Tobago. Indeed, the ordinary folk looked forward to his presence with great expectations. Notwithstanding that, the plantocracy tried another tactic in 1890, with the establishment of the Tobago Metairie Commission with S. H. Gatty, the attorney general, as chairman and L. G. Hay, commissioner for Tobago, and R. S. A. Warner, of the Legislative Council, as members. The metayage system had been introduced in 1848 to reduce the cash payments to the peasants. Gorrie naturally had to appear before the commission, where he made some very scathing remarks:

> "Turning to the condition of Tobago, Gorrie noted how impoverished the island was after 50 years of metayage, how wretched its infrastructure and social services; and he asked whether a serious Commission would not have enquired how far the system discouraged agriculture and enterprise generally."[118]

Gorrie was vindicated when the secretary of state, Lord Knutsford, rejected the Report of the Commissioners.

The principal problems requiring judicial action in Tobago were the question of land distribution and the grievances of the peasants. The old problem of the inaccuracy of the size of the land under cultivation in Tobago was aggravated by the abandonment of estates and the use of these estates to settle the payment of taxes. Gorrie also encountered the metayage system of sharecropping that was introduced in 1848 after a devastating hurricane. The system was designed to reduce payments made by proprietors to peasants but left the latter in a state of penury and destitution after the collapse

---

[118] Brereton, Bridget, *Law, Justice, and Empire: The Colonial Career of Sir John Gorrie, 1829-1892*, Kingston, Jamaica: The Press University of the West Indies, 1997, p. 283.

of the sugar industry in 1882. Indeed, much of the litigation was against relatively new proprietors who had acquired the estates after 1882. Holding court *in forma pauperis* and deciding in the majority of cases in favour of the metayers, Gorrie was seen as a champion of the causes of the peasants, who then looked forward to his every visit to Tobago. However, with most of his decisions going against the merchants and planters, the latter soon expressed disaffection not only with the Chief Justice but with the whole concept of the union, which was not operating to their advantage. The discontent in Tobago was manifested in several ways.

THE LAND DISTRIBUTION PROBLEM

With a land area estimated at 74,400 acres the Land Commissioners decided to offer 57,408 for sale as plantations in 1765. Care was taken to reserve land for public use and to keep a reasonable amount for forestry, for conserving rainfall, and for producing timber. In seven annual sales of land between 1765 and 1771, the following acreages were sold: 8,000; 11,090; 14,975; 4,632; 5,183; 9,362; and 8,160. The minimum size of the lots was 200 acres. At those sizes there were less than three hundred landowners in Tobago originally. After the collapse of the sugar industry, not more than 10,000 acres, including that used for ground provisions, were under cultivation. Indeed at least 15,000 acres belonged to distressed proprietors who offered to pay their taxes by abandoning certain lands to the Crown. The mass of the peasantry, however, remained landless and without the vote.

The dire hardship resulting from the collapse of the sugar industry forced the authorities to think about land reform. It is obvious that the metayers suffered the worst fate with the collapse. They had neither land nor capital to tide them over the difficulty. The secretary of state sanctioned proposals for an amendment of the laws dealing with the Crown lands of the colony, and a new code was established in November 1893.

THE PROBLEM OF CUSTOMS DUTY

Considering that Tobago was bankrupt at the time of the union, the decision to establish a separate financial function in Tobago was nothing but a recipe for the disaster that soon followed. The decision makers in Tobago were misguided in the estimates of their revenues, but no doubt they were trying to avoid the higher rates of taxation that prevailed in Trinidad at that time. The taxes on property at the time were 1 shilling to the pound in Tobago and 5 shillings to the pound in Trinidad. Trinidad was at the time embarking on the establishment of the Trinidad Railway, which would bring no tangible revenue to Tobago. The administrators miscalculated both before and after the union the amount of revenue that was due to them from customs duties. The arrangement was that all duties levied in Trinidad on articles imported into Trinidad and transported thence to Tobago was part of the revenue of Tobago. Likewise duties levied on articles imported into Tobago and transferred to Trinidad for consumption was part of the revenue of Trinidad. In addition some of the worst fears, expressed by Mr Fenwick in his dissenting vote in Trinidad, were soon to be realised.

With the provisions of the laws, an increase in the goods imported into Tobago and reconsigned to Trinidad meant a corresponding increase in customs duties remitted to Trinidad from Tobago and vice versa. The authorities did not anticipate individuals coming to Trinidad to shop and taking their personal property back to Tobago in their luggage. Naturally, on these goods no customs duty was repayable to Tobago, but as the secretary of state pointed out the accumulated loss in customs duties over the period 1889-1892 was estimated at £4,926, prompting the administrator in Tobago to write to the Secretary of State for the Colonies in 1894 for relief. In general, the authorities in Tobago thought that no benefits had accrued to Tobago from the union and they were seeking a number of alternative arrangements. The details of the petition, which was rejected by the Colonial Office, are given below.

In October 1893, after Mr Fowler the colonial secretary, had submitted a report on the loss of revenue in Tobago, the secretary of state, Lord

Ripon, directed the governor to lay before the Legislative Council some papers concerning the revenue loss in Tobago. He suggested that a proposal of a yearly allowance be made from the Trinidad Treasury to that of Tobago in compensation for loss of customs duties caused by the union and the consequent diversion of trade. He further suggested that the amount of the allowance should be considered by a select committee and that the commissioner from Tobago should be in attendance. In the debate on the motion to appoint a select committee, the unofficial members for the first time expressed the depth of feeling in Trinidad over the matter. The negative response of some of the members was no surprise considering the contents of their resolution for annexation in early 1887:

> *"Resolved that this Council has no objection to the administrative annexation of Tobago with this Government, Tobago retaining, however, a separate Treasury and separate internal Financial Board on the understanding that such annexation is approved and desired by Her Majesty's Government, and on the further understanding that no pecuniary charge is now or hereafter to be imposed on the Revenue of Trinidad for any service connected with the island of Tobago or the aforesaid annexation for the administrative purposes."*

The acting auditor-general, Mr David B. Horsford, was appointed chairman, and he submitted his report on 30 January 1894.

Hon. William Gordon Gordon

THE CONSTITUTIONAL PROBLEM

As we have seen, the government of Tobago was always problematic. Until 1797, with poor internal and external communications, it was the most southerly of the British islands in the West Indies with its administrative centre in Grenada. In 1834, the administrative centre was shifted to Barbados. The Constitution itself had been modified several times: sometimes to reduce costs and on others for more effective government. More to the point, there was continuous tension between the Executive and the Legislature, and eventually Tobago was made a Crown colony in 1876 with the administrative centre in Grenada. The annexation to Trinidad in 1889 was thus the most recent attempt to bring a viable constitution to Tobago. The period 1889 to 1899 was fraught with problems, and a new solution was sought through the union.

Sir F. Napier Broome,
Governor of Trinidad and Tobago, c. 1894

TOBAGO: A WARD OF TRINIDAD

The search for a viable constitution led to the notion of establishing Tobago as a ward, that is, an administrative unit, as had been established in Trinidad since the 1850s. All members of the Trinidad Legislature were no doubt familiar with this system and its workings. The governor was responsible for the appointment of the warden; the duties of the ex-officio members brought them into operational contact with the wardens, and the unofficial members were familiar with the system if only in knowing the jurisdictional boundaries between the Legislature and those of the local authorities; for example, whereas the royal roads came under the purview of the Legislature, the subsidiary roads were the responsibility of the wards.

Once the idea of making Tobago a ward of the colony of Trinidad and Tobago was leaked to the public, a political dogfight ensued. In December 1893, the first political salvo was fired with a petition with over a thousand signatures by the class of persons opposed to the plantocracy in Tobago. This group included a number of planters from Trinidad who sought to invest in Tobago when the sugar industry collapsed in 1882. While expressing dissatisfaction over the limited provisions in the union, the petitioners prayed in particular for a complete change in the constitutional arrangement, proposing that Tobago be made a ward of Trinidad and for several other administrative changes be made in transport and mail facilities between the two islands.

Another example of the antipathy towards the union by the ruling class came in a resolution at a public meeting in July 1894, when the Hon. G. H. McEachrane, D. McGillivary, J. B. Isaac, and others objected to deepening the relationship with Trinidad.

The genesis of the constitutional problem surrounding the union sprang from two conflicting ideas, at times expressed by the same person. In his proposal to the secretary of state, Mr Sendall, the governor-in-chief of the Windward Islands, suggested that Tobago be administered as if it were a dependency of Trinidad. When the secretary of state put the idea to the Legislative Councils of Tobago and of Trinidad, he provided two alternatives. Firstly, that Tobago be wholly or completely *incorporated into the colony of Trinidad*, and secondly that Tobago be annexed as *a dependency of the colony of Trinidad*, albeit with a separate treasury. The resolution of the Legislative Council of Tobago on 19 January 1887 makes it clear that what was desired was a united colony known as the colony of Trinidad and Tobago.

There is no hint that the arrangement was to be federal in nature, since the new colony was to be governed by one governor and subject to the same code of laws. The resolution of the Legislative Council of Trinidad, in its third incarnation on 8 March 1887, makes indirect reference to the correspondence of the secretary of state, stating that there was no objection to the proposal that included a separate treasury for Tobago, and agreed to have one governor and one code of laws. Curiously, nowhere in the Trinidad resolution is the name of the new colony mentioned. The enabling Act of Parliament of 1887, known as the Trinidad and Tobago Act, established a name that was echoed in the all subsequent legislation. The loss of customs duties in the period immediately following the establishment of the union prompted politicians of both islands to rethink the constitutional arrangement. Perhaps the sorest point of the union in that decade was the matter of Tobago as a ward of Trinidad. The notion of Tobago as a ward owes its birth to a postscript attached in February 1894 by Mr William Gordon-Gordon, a member of the select committee, in its report on compensation to Tobago for the loss of customs duties. This set the ball rolling for a number of events that would provoke a revolt in Tobago but would lead to a final solution to the nagging problem.

In his despatch to the Colonial Office of March 1894, concerning the Report of the Select Committee, the governor attached the following significant note to the report:

> *"I approve of the foregoing Report with the addition of the following words: That if Tobago be converted to a Ward of Trinidad and its affairs managed economically, its position and prospects would be materially altered and it would become a valuable adjunct to Trinidad."*[119]

This idea was so potent that it immediately sparked off an unscheduled debate as to what should be done about the union with Tobago. Thus, while considering the matters of the select committee and the memorial of the Financial Board of Tobago, the secretary of state wrote to the governor on 19 June 1894 and suggested:

> *"Rather than revert to the old system, I should be disposed if local feeling did not stand in the way, to favour the policy advocated by Mr Gordon in his postscript to the Report*

---

[119] *Council Report No. 22 1894 of the Legislative Council of Trinidad and Tobago.*

*of the Committee, namely to complete the union between
the two islands by converting Tobago into a Ward of the
Colony of Trinidad [sic]."[120]*

Later in the year, as word of the proposal to make Tobago a ward of the colony of Trinidad and Tobago was leaked, the antipathy against the union was made manifest in a second petition initiated by the members of the Financial Board. Members already incensed over the intransigence of the Legislature in Trinidad concerning the issue of customs duties balked at the prospect of losing what little autonomy they still possessed. They appeared to have forgotten that the Resolution moved by Mr Henderson on 19 January 1887 was withdrawn after its rejection by the Colonial Office. So once again, on 25 July, a memorial was sent to Her Majesty the Queen. On this occasion the memorialists prayed for customs autonomy for Tobago and for annexation to the Windward Islands. The memorialists included the Honourable George H. McEachrane, D. McGillavary, J. B. Isaac, and other prominent members of the Tobago society.

On 15 August, the Financial Board considered a request from the governor for an opinion on the question of making Tobago a ward of Trinidad. The board resolved as follows:

*"That this Board having considered His Excellency's
Minute 3367/2259 of 1ˢᵗ August, 1894, forwarding copies
of correspondence laid before the Legislative Council
of Trinidad [sic] on the subject of compensation to
Tobago for the loss of Customs duties are of opinion
that the results of the best interests of Tobago since the
annexation to Trinidad in 1889, have been so disastrous
that no practical benefit whatever would accrue by
Tobago becoming a Ward of Trinidad."[121]*

---

[120] Despatch from the Secretary of State for the Colonies, Lord Ripon, to the governor of Trinidad and Tobago, tabled as *Council Paper No. 206 1894 of the Legislative Council of Trinidad and Tobago.*
[121] *Minutes of the Proceedings of the Financial Board of Tobago 15ᵗʰ August 1894.*

That same day a public meeting organised by the activist Reverend Canon E. A. Turpin at the Scottish Kirk made a certain resolution. At the meeting of the Financial Board of Tobago held on 16 August 1894, the Honourable Mr McEachrane handed in the following letter embodying a resolution passed at a public meeting held in Scarborough the previous evening. The commissioner was requested to pass the letter on to His Excellency the Governor, and he agreed to do so.[122]

> *Tobago*
> *August 15th, 1894.*
> *To the Hon'ble*
> *G. H. McEachrane,*
> *Thomas Blakely, Esq.,*
> *Revd. H. A. Todd,*
> *Members of the Financial Board.*
>
> *Gentlemen,*
> *I am directed by the Revd. Canon E. A. Turpin Chairman of a public meeting held in the Scotch Kirk last evening to intimate to you that at a meeting of over 200 Taxpayers the following resolution was unanimously carried:*
> *"That this meeting protests against Tobago being made a Ward of Trinidad or in any way being more closely connected with the Island if Trinidad."*
>
> *I have the honour to be,*
> *Sirs,*
> *Your obedient Servant,*
> *(Sgnd.) Isaac A. Hope*
> *Secretary.*

As would be expected, not everyone in Tobago was against the union. The final salvo was fired in the struggle to dissolve the union was made by the unofficial members of the Financial Board in December

---

[122] Ibid.

1894. In a petition with 200 signatories, the group prayed for dissolution claiming that the union had been disastrous for Tobago with loss of revenue; unwillingness of the Trinidad Legislative Council; the introduction of class prejudice by the judgements in the metayer disputes; the lack of sympathy for their causes; the difference in religion and nationality; and the lack of interest on the part of the governor in the affairs of Tobago. In addition they feared that making Tobago a ward of Trinidad would have the following harmful effects: increased land taxes; the imposition of cumbrous, expensive, and inappropriate laws of Trinidad; the diversion of profits of trade to Trinidad; exposure to a corrupt administration; and finally loss of prestige and identity.

PROBLEMS WITH THE ECONOMY

Tobago's economic backwardness with its failed single crop economy is seen in stark contrast with Trinidad, where in addition to sugar production there was diversification into cocoa, coffee, rice, and citrus. Wages in Trinidad were about 50 percent higher at one shilling a day, compared with 8 pence a day in Tobago.

As Mr Fenwick of the Legislative Council in Trinidad had predicted, the revenue of Tobago was cut drastically with the new customs arrangements. The country continued to languish in the prevailing dire economic circumstances. The collapse of the sugar industry in 1884 had brought a rush of new owners to the failed estates in Tobago. The continuing depression in the sugar industry put pressure on the new owners to pay for the canes ground for the peasants, and in very many instances the peasants' canes were not ground as a means of avoiding the liability of payment. The bottom line was that the workers' canes were not crushed, resulting in huge losses to the peasants. The decision makers in Tobago, essentially the representatives of the merchant and planter class, were misguided in their estimates of the revenue, and Tobago remained impoverished.[123]

---

[123] The impression of the chief justice on his first visit in 1889 to Tobago was: "It was scarcely possible to convey to an English mind the squalor about the Island," cited in Brereton, Bridget, *Law, Justice, and Empire: The Colonial*

The taxes on property at the time were one shilling to the pound in Tobago and five shillings to the pound in Trinidad. Trinidad was at the time embarking on constructing the Trinidad Railway. The administrators miscalculated both before and after the amount of revenue that was due to them from customs duties. Not surprisingly, some of the worst fears expressed by Mr Fenwick in his dissenting vote in Trinidad were soon to be realised. The chief justice had also observed that he did not expect that

> ". . . that prosperity will be brought back to Tobago
> until the Union with Trinidad had been made absolute,
> abandoned estates sold in lots to peasant proprietors and
> men with new ideas entrusted with the Government."[124]

DECISION OF THE COLONIAL OFFICE

In general, the authorities in Tobago thought that no benefits had accrued to Tobago from the union, and they were seeking a number of alternative arrangements. In 1894, a petition was sent to the Crown praying for separation of the island from Trinidad. The petition was rejected, and in May 1895, the secretary of state, Lord Ripon, gave his decision on the matter to the governor. In correspondence remarkable as much for its style as for its logic, the secretary with an assumed humility refuted the claims of the memorialists as he denied their wishes:

> "I have very carefully considered what advice I shall
> tender to Her Majesty concerning the Memorial, of the
> inhabitants of Tobago forwarded in your despatch No.
> 564 of the 7ᵗʰ of December which was duly laid at the foot
> of the Throne.

Career of Sir John Gorrie, 1829-1892, Kingston, Jamaica: The Press University of the West Indies, 1997, p. 271.

[124] Brereton, Bridget, *Law, Justice, and Empire: The Colonial Career of Sir John Gorrie, 1829-1892*, Kingston, Jamaica: The Press University of the West Indies, 1997, p. 283.

You will be good enough to inform the Memorialists that Her Majesty cannot accede to the prayer of the memorial and dissolve the Union between Trinidad and Tobago which took place under an Act of Parliament, and that I have arrived at the conclusion that I should not, at the present time or on the facts before me, be justified in advising the Queen to vary the terms of Her Majesty's Order in Council of 17th November 1888 as regards the question of local control of Customs and Excise.

You will point out to the Memorialists that the memorial is based in part on a misconception of facts. As I indicated in my despatch No. 206 of the 19th June last the loss of actual revenue, to Tobago through the Union with Trinidad has been insignificant. An annual allowance is made to the Government of Tobago as a re-imbursement of Customs duties collected in Trinidad on goods consumed in Tobago. That allowance which was £421 in 1889, amounted to £1,000 in each of the succeeding years, and it appears to me to represent fairly on the whole any claim which might properly be made by the government of Tobago on this account. The purchase of goods at Port-of-Spain by Tobago labourers can deprive Tobago of but little revenue though it does undoubtedly transfer profits from the storekeepers of Scarborough to those at Port-of-Spain; this however cannot be considered a loss to the community at large and does not constitute a sufficient ground for interference. Similarly the loss of revenue owing to the reduction of import duties on certain commodities under the arrangement with the United States of America in 1892 was not an economic loss to the community.

I admit that the experience of Tobago with regard to its administrative connection with Trinidad has not so far been fortunate, but that has been due to exceptional causes now past unalterable, causes which could not be remedied by a change of connection. The real causes of

> *stagnation and loss of revenue lie deeper. They are to be*
> *found in the depression of trade and agriculture which*
> *is not peculiar to Tobago, though it may be felt there at*
> *present with peculiar acuteness. A mere administrative*
> *reform can do little to relieve such a condition of affairs*
> *and I regret that, until a stronger case can be made out,*
> *I must decline to take what seems to me the retrograde*
> *step of advising the Queen to issue an amending Order in*
> *Council enabling the Government of Tobago to impose a*
> *separate Tariff of Customs duties."[125]*

The decision given by the secretary of state brought some relief to the matter of customs duties, while at the same time it brought reason to bear on the broader problem. The decision on the constitutional matter was to retain the status quo, and five years or more would elapse before the solution rejected by the Tobagonians would be implemented as the best viable option for all parties.

When word of the governor's suggestion for the administration of Tobago as a ward was learnt by the Financial Board, all hell broke loose in Tobago. Strong feelings were expressed that if the decision was implemented, the island would lose its identity and would become a dependency of Trinidad, like Monos[126].

PROGRESS

ADMINISTRATION

With two representatives from Tobago sitting on the Legislative Council, it did not take long to get the administrative machinery in Tobago working once again. The initial tendency was to blame

---

[125] Cited in correspondence from the commissioner for Tobago to the members of the Financial Board of Tobago, reproduced in the *Tobago Gazette* of 31 May 1895.

[126] Monos is one of five islets located off the north west peninsula of Trinidad and is recognized as part of the territory of Trinidad. The islet has no independent political institutions.

the annexation for the continued woes experienced in Tobago. As it became evident that the troubles in Tobago were more deep seated, the Financial Board became more objective and realistic about its future, and thereafter much progress was made. Attitudes were somewhat softened after the governor attended a meeting of the Financial Board in Tobago, and the board was invited by the governor to send two members to the meetings of the Legislative Council based in Trinidad. The governor, Sir F. Napier Broome, whose negligence of his duties and love for billiards did not go unnoticed, visited Tobago and addressed members of the Financial Board. In an informal meeting with the Financial Board on 30 April 1895, Governor Sir Napier Broome brought a better understanding of the issues and noted that despite the disadvantageous circumstances, he was pleased to observe the many signs of improvement on the island. He had seen new houses erected or in the process of being erected; the people seemed to be in good health and well fed; and the financial situation was much sounder than it was two or three years before. He reminded members that a system for the distribution of Crown lands had been introduced and that already several hundred acres had been granted. Finally he was delighted that an old debt of £2,000 due to the Crown agents had been settled and was extremely pleased to note the harmonious relations between the members of the board and the commissioner. The arrears of taxes had been collected. Buildings taxes were collected with the assistance of the warden, Mr E. Macdougall; sinecure offices were abolished, saving £784; and the Amending Land and House Tax Regulations of 1894 had had a most salutary effect on revenues.

LAND REFORM

New arrangements were made for the sale of lands, the metayage system was abolished, and the descendants of slaves were able to purchase small plots of land. Rural lands were made available at a fixed price of £1 per acre; a fixed charge of 10 shillings per acre was established in lieu of survey and grant fees. Several hundred acres had been granted with the passage of the Land and House Tax Regulations of 1894, which precluded the possibility of losing large amounts of revenue as in the past when an estate owner only had to hand over some worthless plot in order to get rid of his liability. Land in sizes of up to five acres was allocated to peasant proprietors who were required to plant cocoa, coffee, and other lucrative crops.

THE ECONOMY

Notwithstanding the problems of lost revenue, the economy of Tobago had begun to show signs of improvement, with a silent transformation taking place. By 1894, 52 percent of the exports from Tobago went to Trinidad; this trade included ponies, cattle, sheep, goats, pigs, and chickens. The union with Trinidad had produced a new outlook in Tobago. The old fixation with sugar was gradually receding despite the resistance of a few diehards with vested interests in the industry. With inspiration from the thriving economy in Trinidad, agriculture was being slowly transformed.

By the start of 1895, there was confirmation of the new outlook in Tobago. The system whereby estate owners handed over worthless acres to the state was abolished. Due to the personal supervision of the commissioner, the expenditure on poor relief and hospitals was reduced without impairing the quality of those services. A savings bank, which was long contemplated, was established and on 31 December 1894 had 166 depositors, whose savings amounted to £874. The problem of the deplorable condition of the roads was being tackled. With the assistance of the secretary of state, a loan of £10,000 was secured sought with the assistance of the Secretary of State it was hoped to effect some repairs to public buildings, remake some of the roads, to open three or four new tracks to and through the Crown Lands. By 1897, some progress had been achieved in diversifying agricultural production that then included sugar, coconuts, coffee, cocoa, and other tropical products.

THE JUDICIARY

With the departure of Sir John Gorrie as chief justice, some measure of trust was restored to the members of the plantocracy in Tobago.

At the end of 1898, the Tobago Rules of 1899 were issued. These rules, made under the Judicature Ordinance of 1879, regulated the procedures and practices of the Supreme Court of Tobago in accordance with the Order in Council of 1888.

THE ROYAL COMMISSION 1897

In 1897, the British government appointed the Royal West India Commission to investigate the plight of the sugar industry in the British West Indian colonies. The commissioners were Sir Henry Wylie Norman, a former governor of Jamaica; Sir Edward Grey; and Sir David Barbour. The secretary to the commission was Mr Sydney Oliver. The commissioners took evidence in London from persons with interests in the sugar industry in the West Indies before visiting the territories, where they took further evidence and inspected the facilities involved in sugar production. The report of the commission had a strong influence on resolution of the problems of the union. They visited both Trinidad and Tobago, and the opinion that Tobago should be fully amalgamated with Trinidad was growing into an avalanche. The acting governor of Trinidad and Tobago, Mr C. C. Knollys, familiar as he was with the ward system as operated in Trinidad since 1851, testified before the Royal West India Commission:

> *"I am of opinion that Tobago should be made an integral part of Trinidad. It is hardly more inaccessible [from the centre of administration] than the distant wards of Trinidad, and I think it could be better administered from headquarters. There is temptation to run the administration on lines jealous of the Central government. The various Departments also would have the advantage of the experience of the Trinidad heads of Department, under whom they would be placed. Immigration would*

be allotted to Tobago, Customs restrictions could be abolished and other advantages would ensue."[127]

By then the notion was manifest to the point that it was fully adopted and recommended in the Report of the Commissioners:

"We believe that the carrying out of all the reforms and changes which we have recommended will be facilitated by the complete amalgamation of the two islands of Tobago and Trinidad. Under present conditions, the welfare of Tobago is inseparably connected with that of Trinidad and although the Government of Tobago is very economically administered, it appears unnecessary and may be mischievous to maintain a separate Treasury, a separate account of revenue and expenditure and a separate staff of officials for an island which has a revenue very little in excess of £8,000 a year."[128]

---

[127] *Council Paper No.4 1898 of the Legislative Council of Trinidad and Tobago.*
[128] Report of the Royal West India Commission of 1897, published as *Council Paper No. 153, 1897 of the Legislative Council of Trinidad and Tobago.*

Sir Henry Norman, Chairman Royal West
India Commission 1897

*"We recommend the complete amalgamation of Tobago
and Trinidad, and the abolition of the separate account
of revenue and expenditure. Tobago would then become
a ward, or district, of Trinidad, and the islands would
have a common exchequer. To this measure objections
would, no doubt, be raised locally, though we believe the
majority of inhabitants of Tobago are in favour of it. The
owners of large tracts of land are afraid that financial
amalgamation with Trinidad might lead to the tax on
land being raised to the level of that prevailing in the
latter island. We are unable to see why this result should
necessarily follow, as Tobago, in its present condition,
has a good claim for a separate treatment in this matter.*

The traders seem to fear that amalgamation with Trinidad would reduce their business in connection with the import trade, and possibly with the export trade. This result might follow, but from the point of view of general interest, no sound argument against the amalgamation can be based upon it."[129]

Sir Hubert E. H. Jerningham,
Governor of Trinidad and Tobago, 1897-1900

On 18 April 1898, His Excellency the Governor, Sir Hubert E. H. Jerningham, addressed the Legislative Council of Trinidad and Tobago and read a despatch, dated 22 March 1898, from the secretary of state relative to the proposed complete amalgamation of Tobago with Trinidad. The governor informed the Council that a commission had been issued to enquire into and report upon the proposal.

The commission was duly appointed with William Low, resident commissioner of Tobago, as chairman; Mr George McEachrane,

---

[129]   Ibid.

member for Tobago; Vincent Brown, Q. C., solicitor-general; Mr Hugh Clarence Bourne, auditor general; and Mr Robert H. McCarthy, collector of customs. Not much is known of the outcome of that commission (or if it ever met at all), but later in that year the Privy Council issued a new Order in Council that brought an end to the decade-long constitutional problem.

THE FINAL SOLUTION OF 1898

The creation of a separate treasury in Tobago in 1889 turned out to be a divisive issue that frustrated the progress of the new unified colony. What originated as a footnote to the Report of the Select Committee to determine the loss of customs duties suffered by Tobago between 1889 and 1894 turned out to be the most potent idea to save and advance the union. In proposing that Tobago be made a ward of Trinidad and Tobago, Mr Gordon Gordon solved the conceptual problem that had dogged the administration of the union from its inception. In Trinidad the distinction had long been made between the municipal government and the "national" government. At the conquest, Abercrombie encountered the Cabildo, a municipal council that was a staple of Spanish administration in the New World. With the establishment of the Legislative Council in Trinidad in 1831, the Cabildo with its Spanish laws and language was replaced. It was clear from that time that the municipal authority was subordinate to the national authority.[130]

By contrast, in Tobago, there never was a municipal government different from the national government. Its small size precluded such differentiation, as it probably did in Barbados and elsewhere. There was no question of giving Tobago another layer of government since the island, in the opinion of so many, was already severely over

---

[130] "In 1840 the Council of Government abolished the Cabildo, and replaced it with a town council, modelled on English Municipal bodies. The new town council was to be strictly subordinate to the local [national] government." Brereton, Bridget, *A History of Modern Trinidad 1783-1962,* Kingston, Jamaica: Heinemann, 1981, p. 74.

governed. To some extent the division of the country into parishes was an attempt to give the colony another layer of government, but this initiative collapsed with the disestablishment of the Anglican Church. The notion that the government in Tobago was in some way subordinate to the government based in Trinidad was inconceivable to the administration in Tobago. It is to the eternal credit of Mr Gordon-Gordon, therefore, that the government of Tobago was conceived as a local government within the united colony of Trinidad and Tobago. The conflict inherent in the Order in Council of 1888 was finally resolved in 1898 when Gordon-Gordon's idea was put into effect. There was a remarkable convergence of views on this topic that lurked beneath the turmoil of the first decade of the union. Gorrie's expectations would now be fulfilled and prosperity returned to the island.

The new legislation established the unitary state of Trinidad and Tobago: it cut out the Financial Board and the subdivision of the Supreme Court in Tobago and made Tobago into an administrative division of the united colony of Trinidad and Tobago; it created one Legislature, one treasury, one Judiciary and one set of laws for the government of Trinidad and Tobago. The principal clause of the Order is here reproduced:

THE ORDER IN COUNCIL 1898

> Whereas by an Order of Her Majesty in Council, bearing date the *seventeenth day of November, 1888 (herein-after called the principal Order), the Colony of Trinidad and its dependencies, and the Colony of Tobago, were, from and after the First day of January 1889 (in the said Order referred to as "the appointed day"), united into one Colony;*
>
> *And whereas by Our Order in Our Privy Council, bearing date the 6th day of April 1889, we did amend the 13th Clause in the principal Order:*

And whereas it is expedient to revoke the principal Order, except Clauses 1, 2, and 37 thereof, and to revoke the Order in Council of the Sixth day of April 1889:

Now, THEREFORE, in pursuance of the powers in US vested by the Trinidad and Tobago Act, 1887, it is hereby ordered by Her Majesty, by and with the advice of Her Privy Council, as follows:

- *The whole of the principal Order, except Clauses 1 2, and 37, and the Order in Council of the Sixth day of April 1889, are hereby revoked, but such revocation shall not affect the validity, or invalidity, or effect of anything done or suffered before the date of the coming into force of this Order.*
- *On and after the date [1ˢᵗ January 1898] of the coming into force of this Order, the Island of Tobago shall be a Ward of the Colony of Trinidad and Tobago; and the revenue, expenditure and debt of Tobago shall be merged to form part of the revenue, expenditure, and debt of the united Colony, and the debt due from Tobago to Trinidad shall be cancelled.*
- *Save as in and by this Order expressly otherwise directed the Laws of Trinidad in force on the date of the coming onto force of this Order shall be in force in Tobago, and the Laws theretofore in force in Tobago, so far as they differ from the Law in force in Trinidad, shall thereupon cease to be in force. Provided that this Clause shall not affect the validity, invalidity, or effect of anything done or suffered before the coming into effect of this Order, or any right, title, obligation, or liability acquired or incurred before that date.*
- *All future Ordinances enacted by the Legislature of the colony shall extend to Tobago, provided that the Legislature of the colony may at any time within the several Acts, Ordinances, and Regulations of Tobago enumerated in the Schedule hereto, and of any other and further matters and things in respect of which*

it may be deemed necessary to enact such special and local Ordinances or Regulations applicable to Tobago as distinguished from the rest of the Colony.

- *The Acts, Ordinances, and Regulations of Tobago enumerated in the Schedule hereto shall, until repealed or amended by the Legislature of the colony, continue locally in force in Tobago, but such Acts, Ordinances, and Regulations shall in every case be construed as amended by and read together with this Order; and in particular wherever in such Acts, Ordinances, and Regulations any duty is imposed upon or power conferred upon any special officer or person, such duty or power shall be performed or exercised by such person or persons as the Governor may from tome o time by Proclamation appoint for the purpose.*

- *Until the Legislature of the Colony shall otherwise provide, the following provisions shall take effect in Tobago, that is to say:*

- *Any land tax payable in respect of lands in Tobago shall be levied at such rate as to the Governor in Council shall seem fit notwithstanding that any similar tax is levied throughout the rest of the colony at a higher rate.*

- *The license fees authorized by "The License Regulation, 1898," shall continue to be collected and paid in Tobago as heretofore in lieu of any license fees in force in the rest of the Colony, save and except that no license fees shall be payable for the keeping of horses, geldings, mules, mares and asses.*

- *The license fees for spirit licenses now payable in Tobago shall continue to be collected and paid as heretofore, the Trinidad Ordinance No. 2 of 1881 to the contrary notwithstanding.*

- *There shall not be charged upon produce which have been raised or manufactured in Tobago, and shall be shipped from Tobago to ports or places beyond the limits of the Colony, any taxes, rates, or charges for raising funds in aid if immigration.*

Such of the powers and duties heretofore exercised and performed by the Commissioner of the Supreme Court of Tobago, and by the Deputy Marshal of Tobago, as it shall seem expedient to continue shall be exercised and performed by any such person or persons by the rules of the supreme Court, to be framed under the Trinidad Judicature Ordinance, 1879, shall be prescribed and determined.

This Order shall come into force from and after a date to be proclaimed in Our Colony of Trinidad and Tobago by Our Governor and Commander in Chief of Our said Colony.

W. FITZROY

SCHEDULE

- The Stamp Ordinance, No. 19 of 1879.
- The Vaccination Ordinance, 1882, No. 2 of 1882.
- The Medical Aid Ordinance, 1882, No. 6 of 1882.
- The Turtle Preservation Ordinance, 1885, No. 2 of 1885.
- The Wild Birds Protection Ordinance, 1885, No. 8 of 1885.
- The Anglican Church Inc. Trustees Ordinance, 1887, No. 7 of 1887.
- The License Regulation, 1893, No. 2 of 1893, as amended by the Amending Licenses Regulation, 1893, No. 6 of 1893.
- The Destitute Persons Relief Regulation, 1893, No. 10 of 1893.
- The Liquor License Ordinance, 1883, No. 2 of 1883, as amended by the Amending Licenses Regulation, 1893, No. 6 of 1893.
- An Act relating to lands in this Island commonly called the Three Chains, 28 Vict. Cap. 2 as amended by Regulation No. 5 of 1894.

- The Road Regulation, 1894, No. 3 of 1894, as amended by the Road Amendment Regulation 1894, No. 6 of 1894.

In merging the two legal systems, special provision was made for the preservation of the Three Chains Act, the Medical Ordinance of 1882, the Turtle Preservation Ordinance of 1885, the Anglican Church Inc. Trustees Ordinance of 1887, and the Destitute Persons Relief Regulation of 1893.

When the dust had finally settled in Tobago by 1900, the metayage system was abolished; the distribution of Crown lands had alleviated the insecurity of the landless; the descendants of the slaves were able to purchase small plots for cultivation; and the economy was diversified from sugar into food crops, cocoa, livestock, and exports to Trinidad so that with the passage of time, in stark contrast to the merchants and planters, the peasants began to view the unification as acting in their favour. Most significantly, the development of Tobago became inextricably linked to the development of Trinidad.

CHAPTER VII

Historians and the Union

---❖---

While the facts of history may exist in their own right, they come to use and notice through the mind of the historian who selects, interprets, and uses them.
G. R. Elton, *The Practice of History.*

---❖---

THE POLITICS OF FAILURE

"The nature of the breakdown of civilizations can be summed up in three points: a failure of creative power in the minority, an answering withdrawal of mimesis on the part of the majority and a consequent loss of social unity in the society as a whole."[131]

TOBAGO, WHEN IT CAME to the union with Trinidad in 1889, was a failed political society. It is clear that there was little unity in the society as a whole at that time. Toynbee's objective criteria for the breakdown of civilizations, were clearly discernible: the ruling class had no solution to the problems of the society, as they were in pursuit of their own interests and did not serve as a model for the majority. But this was the case in many of

---

[131]   Sommervell, D. C., in Toynbee, Arnold, *A Study of History, Abridgement of Volumes I-VI,* Oxford: Oxford University Press, 1987, p. 246,.

the former slave colonies in the West Indies at that time, and this factor on its own is insufficient to explain the breakdown in the society. For example in neighbouring Barbados, where there was a history of institutionalised racial discrimination and clearly no social unity, there was a social compact that, on the one hand, preserved the ancient constitution and avoided Crown colony status, and on the other, because of the long history of slavery and the adaptation of the majority of the population, the creative leadership continued to serve as a model for the society.

At its creation as a political society under British colonisation, Tobago was transformed from a pristine island sparsely populated by two Amerindian tribes into a sugar producing slave society.

> *"The competing empires of Europe had beaten fiercely on these islands, repeopled after the aborigines had gone, turned into sugar islands, places of the lash, where fortunes could be made, sugar the new gold. And at the end, after slavery and sugar, Europe had left behind nothing that could be called a civilization."[132]*

Naipaul's view is that of a twenty-first-century commentator on the legacy of the European incursion into the Caribbean. Naipaul is by no means a historian, but his view even if biased coincides with the conclusion of several noted historians. Such a broad indictment glosses over the minor successes of Bermuda, the Bahamas, Barbados, and Cuba as it does over the spectacular failures of Turks and Caicos and of Tobago. But none of the historians treat the systemic political problems that ultimately forced Tobago into the union with Trinidad

One of the earliest enactments of the Tobago Assembly was "an Act for declaring slaves to be real property." Slavery by then had been firmly establishment in the British West Indies. The Barbados Slave Act of 1661, modified in 1676, 1682, and 1688, had served as a model for similar legislation in Jamaica, Antigua, and South

---

[132] Naipaul, V. S., *A Writer's People*, London: Picador, 2007, p. 24.

Carolina. The landowners of Tobago and their agents, few in number, were British and were the unquestioned rulers; the rest of the population were, for the most part, slaves, landless, and by law the chattels of the landowners; they had virtually no human rights. Moreover, by 1763 the native Amerindians had either emigrated to Dominica or Trinidad or otherwise became extinct; in any case they disappeared from the pages of history of Tobago after the colonisation. Schematically, therefore, at the start of its British colonisation Tobago was a slave society which functioned relatively well during the heyday of slavery.

> *"The year 1771 may be considered as the era of Colonisation Completed; and of Tobago becoming truly (I wish I might add permanently) British, in its people, in the privileges, in its laws, in its administration of executive authority, of legislation, and of justice, and in the security of persons and properties then given."*[133]

However, when participation by the British in the slave trade was abolished in 1807, changing thereby the economics of the supply of slave labour, the relationship between the slaves and their masters deteriorated. The restriction in the supply of slaves, together with the demands for labour in the newer British colonies like British Guiana and Trinidad after the Napoleonic wars, forced the slave owners to make greater demands on the slaves to increase their output and to resort to mechanisation to enhance the productivity of the industry. Contemporaneously, the British government had initiated a number of measures to ameliorate the harsh conditions under which the slaves lived. These moves were resisted by the plantocracy, who hardened their attitude towards the slaves, and in consequence the relationship with the slaves deteriorated further. In this period the planters petitioned the Crown, protesting the new measures, and went so far as to seek the removal of the governor

---

[133] From the *Journals* of Young, Bart., William, governor-in-chief of Tobago between 1807 and 1815. Cited in Douglas Archibald, Rupert, *Tobago: Melancholy Isle, Vol. I, 1498-1771*, Port-of-Spain, Trinidad: Westindiana, 1987, p. 124.

and chief executive, who supported the measures; this action was a precursor of the long and silent constitutional struggle between the Legislature and the executive in Tobago that led eventually to the collapse of civil society.

Emancipation in 1834 granted rights to the slaves, and with it the social relations on the island changed dramatically. The fragile social compact on which the society was built was destroyed, and the society never really adjusted to that change. The slaves were able then to form stable conjugal relationships whereas before, as the property of the planters, they were liable to be randomly moved or sold. However, fifty years later when the new chief justice paid a visit to Tobago, he was awed by the squalor of the physical environment and more so by the justice that was meted out to the peasants. Gorrie had been to a number of other British colonies before coming to Trinidad and thus had a fair measure of the conditions that existed in Tobago. Gorrie, having investigated the Morant Bay riots in Jamaica, quickly detected the antipathy between the plantocracy and the mass of the population that was at the root of the breakdown of the society in Tobago. The political system failed for a number of reasons because the franchise, restricted as it was, gave no voice to the majority of the citizens, and moreover, the rulers were overtly hostile to the wishes of the masses, even if the economic situation was a very difficult one to manage.

PROBLEMS OF POLITICAL DEVELOPMENT

With this fundamental weakness in the societal structure, it was no surprise to find on analysis that Tobago displayed many of the classical symptoms of crises of political development: crises of identity; of legitimacy; of participation of penetration; and of distribution.[134] Examined in this light we find an identity crisis brought about by the emancipation of the slaves. The historic event changed the

---

[134] Binder, Leonard et al., *Studies in Political Development 7: Crises and Sequences in Political Development,* Princeton, NJ: Princeton University Press, 1971.

structure of the society by removing much of the authority of the ruling plantocracy over the peasants. Until then the authority was based on ownership, as the peasants were the chattels of the planters.

The effect of emancipation was traumatic, although the planters were aware that it was imminent. The purposiveness of the society that existed while the slaves were the chattels of the plantocracy was lost; the slaves with their new liberty withdrew the females and children from the labour force. This move indicated very clearly that there was no clear consensus on nation building; it was an unambiguous pointer to the **identity** crisis. The slaves who had few rights and no property lacked the economic perspective of the rulers. In the age of colonialism, the identity of the government was always a political issue. This was a characteristic whether the native population was decimated, as in the Americas and Australasia, or whether the colonists were settlers from the mother country, as in Barbados and South Africa. In the slave societies of the Caribbean where the slaves were in the majority, the social structure and in particular the class structure was such that there could be no effective national identity. Another indicator of the identity crisis in Tobago was the failure of the established church to take root in Tobago; a few years after disestablishment, the census of 1881 showed that Anglicans comprised a mere 15% of the population. This failure, however, was not peculiar to Tobago as indeed it was throughout the empire, with few exceptions, and eventually resulted in its disestablishment.

The **legitimacy** crisis did not exist in Tobago at its colonisation. There is no question that slavery was legitimate then, as it was allowed by European law for centuries. The loss of legitimacy was precipitated by the new thinking on human rights, the American Revolution, the French Revolution, the Haitian Revolution, abolition of the slave trade, and emancipation of the slaves. Those changes in conjunction with the introduction of formal education brought about a widening of perception on the part of the majority of the people that was manifested in terms of new demands and in resistance to authority in the form of an increasing number of riots and an increase in political activity. At the crux of the problem of legitimacy are the issues of capacity and equality that despite agreement on a national identity preclude some groups from supporting the national agenda. A legitimacy crisis is usually resolved by constitutional change or some form of institutional innovation. The search for a proper constitution during the period 1838 to 1888 underscores the existence of the **legitimacy** crisis in Tobago. The question of the legitimacy of the colonial assemblies in the West Indies was recognised by the British authorities at the time of the abolition of the slave trade and influenced the decision that made Trinidad a Crown colony.

The **participation** crisis was obvious from the limited nature of the franchise. The Franchise Act of 1871, which extended the vote to all landowners with an annual rental value of £5, was one of several steps taken to engender the participation in the political process, but the number of such landowners remained relatively small. Moreover, the attitude of the courts towards the peasants was such as to deny them a sense of justice, as Gorrie found to his dismay.

It would be difficult to say that Tobago suffered from a **penetration** crisis of political development. The small size of the colony allowed the measures of the government to encompass the whole community. There was no question of territorial separation.

The **distribution** crisis was evident from the elitist character of the society; particularly in the area of land ownership. There was a mitigation of this problem with the former slaves finding various forms of tenancy and ownership. The monoculture of sugar was also another indicator of the distribution crisis. Certain jobs and professions were shared *en famille*, thus adding to the problems of distribution.

But the societal structure alone was not the only contributor to the political failure in Tobago. The major contributor was the constitutional conflict that persisted between the Executive and the Legislature. That problem, however, was solved nominally when the Crown colony system was introduced in 1876.

THE HISTORIANS

The historians for the most part have not dealt adequately with the reasons for the formation of the unions. Almost all of them, writing in a tone that was understandably anticolonial, failed to confront the systemic issues that brought Tobago to the point of collapse. The anticolonial view, strongly critical of the Crown colony system, largely ignored the early nineteenth-century opinion that the West Indian assemblies were inherently irresponsible. In 1797, the West Indian assemblies were the subject of a bitter denunciation by Abercrombie, the commander of British forces in the Caribbean during the Napoleonic wars:

> "It was a most outspoken denunciation of the West Indian system of government. It expressed not simply the view of a frustrated and disgusted commander, but the attitude of an age. The feeling that West Indian Assemblies were inherently irresponsible was widespread in ministerial circles. But the Assemblies were sheltered by the constitutional usages of centuries; they had rights and they had powerful defenders."[135]

The conclusion that the assemblies were irresponsible came at a time when the abolition of the slave trade was being contemplated, and these thoughts were crystalised in the Crown colony system.

The union itself is so important in the constitutional history of Trinidad and Tobago that two things stand out: firstly, the very short shrift given to the topic by historians, with the possible exceptions of Dr Williams, who devoted a full chapter to the subject, and Craig-James, who drawing on access to a wide range of diplomatic papers provided much insight on the development of Tobago society during the nineteenth century. Secondly, despite these works, there is the huge void in the public domain about the topic.

---

[135]   Millette, Dr. James, *Society and Politics in Colonial Trinidad*, Port-of-Spain, Trinidad: Omega Bookshops Ltd., 1985, p. 101.

Thus, while historians accurately recorded the events that took place in Tobago and even examined the relationship between the rulers and the masses, there was little evaluation of the effectiveness of its political institutions and no assessment of the viability of Tobago as an island colony. No commentator sensed the urgent need for constitutional change, despite the warnings of a stream of administrators. The most striking thing about all of the histories is the failure to highlight the fact that Tobago as a political community was a failed enterprise. With the exception of Dr Williams, the historians viewed the political system from the position of the colonisers, that is they judged the system on the basis of that imposed on the colonial population rather than that desired by them.

OTTLEY

C. R. Ottley did little more than lament the fact that the union took place. His narrative description, while it accurately recorded the indifference of the legislators and the decline of the Legislature, did not bring judgement to bear on the nature of the decision, but he was prepared to evaluate its effects. It seems clear that whatever the merits of the decision, expectations were high as to the outcome of the union, and the latter was unsatisfactory.

> *"This measure however did not produce the desired effect, for the colony continued its downward march, with the result that with effect from January 1899, Tobago, with head downcast and spirit completely broken, accepted the derogatory and humiliating position of a Ward of Trinidad, an unwanted ward—a very unwanted ward."[136]*

Ottley obviously recognised the failure of the political system in Tobago but did not acknowledge that the union provided Tobago with a change of constitution necessary to end the continuing class conflict and the persistent breakdown in the separation of powers between the executive and legislative arm of the government.

---

[136] Ottley, C. R., *The Story of Tobago*, Port-of-Spain, Trinidad: Longmans Caribbean 1973, p. 95.

Mr C. R. Ottley, Historian

DOUGLAS ARCHIBALD

"The union with Trinidad, under the special conditions contained in the resolution of 28 January, 1887, in no way caused any great improvement in the grave social and economic problems that continued to beset the Island. Finally, after ten years of uncertainty and increasing frustration among all classes, by an Order in Council, Tobago became a ward of the colony of Trinidad and Tobago, on 1ˢᵗ January 1899, under the governorship of Sir Hubert Jerningham, K.C.M.G.

"From neutrality in 1763, Tobago had passed through one hundred and thirty-five years of turmoil and war, natural disasters, the agonies of slavery and the empty promises of an emancipation, to eventually lose its identity and enter into a state of enforced obscurity, as the ward of another island, Trinidad, that was completely alien in character."[137]

---

[137] Douglas Archibald, Rupert, *Tobago: Melancholy Isle, Vol. III, 1807-1898*, Port-of-Spain, Trinidad: Westindiana, 2003, pp. 204, 205.

While passing judgement on the effect of the decision to form the union, Douglas Archibald made no evaluation of the decision itself. On the effects, his opinion that there was increasing frustration among all classes seemed to be at variance with the facts as found by the Norman Commission. Like Ottley he gave a very good description of the history of the island; he was extremely potent about the explorers and navigators who made early attempts at colonisation but made no assessment of the effectiveness of its principal institutions.

ROBINSON

Robinson, like all the historians of the union, did not acknowledge that Tobago at the union was a failed political colony. Of all the historians he was most judgemental of the decision to form the union. To be fair, he thought that the union was a sensible and obvious step. He did this, however, without acknowledging the failure of the political system in Tobago. He felt instinctively that the system was inadequate, but because he did not identify the source of the failure, he could not give a proper prescription for the remedy. His judgement, however, was not based on the conditions that led to the union but on ideas generated in the Caribbean after the union, that the one crop economies and separation were harmful to development and that integration and diversification were essential for economic growth. Robinson, nonetheless, had his own thoughts as to how the union should have been consummated:

> *"What was needed was an integration based on equality and animated by the philosophy of the greatest good for the greatest number. Such an economic system supported by a similarly directed political system, is the only enduring arrangement for economic and political union."[138]*

Stated as an ideal, Robinson could hardly be faulted except for the vague notion of equality which he failed to explain. However, his

---

[138]   Robinson, A. N. R., *The Mechanics of Independence*, Cambridge, MA and London: MIT Press, 1971, p. 22.

meaning became somewhat clearer as he commented on the progress of the union:

> *"A sensible and obvious step thus gave rise to misgivings that proved not altogether justifiable, as the history of the union demonstrated. **What was to have been a union of equality** degenerated into one of public inequality, one of the superior and the inferior, one of territory and dependency, and Trinidad's feeling's seeped into both official and unofficial attitudes towards the union."[139]*

Mr A. N. R. Robinson, President and
Prime Minister of the Republic and Historian

It emerges that Robinson was not concerned merely with the equality of citizens under the law but with some nebulous notion that the two former colonies should be treated equally after the union. To be precise, Robinson seemed to be saying that the government of the colony ought to have treated the two islands equally. It is a common failing of demagogues to treat as equals things that are unequal, and Robinson's statement was an apt manifestation of that error. This was one of the most astonishing statements made by any historian about the union. It comes as a surprise since none of the reports of

---

[139] Ibid., p. 24.

the British Parliament; of the Colonial Office; of the Tobago House of Assembly; or of the Legislative Council of Trinidad suggested an equal relationship. Neither the Norman Commission nor the generation of administrators of Tobago that preceded the union thought or expressed the view that the union was one in which there would be an equality relationship. Quite contrary to Robinson, commentators pointed to the unequal relationship inherent in such a union: the huge difference in human and physical resources; the differences in economic performance; and most important of all the increase in responsibility on the Legislature based in Trinidad for the government of the united colony. While Robinson acknowledged the need for the union of 1889 and its institutions, he glossed over its merits or demerits and did not see the inherent weakness. He approved of the "broad" franchise on which the commissioners of the financial board were elected. The Norman Commission of 1897 thought that having a separate treasury in Tobago was almost mischievous, but Robinson, a former Minister of finance writing ninety years after Mr Fenwick pointed out the lack of wisdom in such a move, could see nothing wrong with this even in the face of a bankrupt economy. It is clear that Robinson did not see Tobago as a failed society but rather as one colony seeking to enhance its future by negotiating and uniting with another colony.

Professor Bridget Brereton

Brereton

Professor Brereton[140] admitted that Tobago was virtually bankrupt, its economic situation hopeless, its government top heavy, and its constitution farcical. To dismiss the problem as constitutional, as she did, while it is accurate, avoids the discussion of the real political problems that are at the root of the society or what new constitutional arrangements were required to put Tobago on a firm footing. Indeed while the constitution may be faulted for systemic reasons, it also collapsed because of the internal dissention between the executive and the legislative branches. The union with Trinidad was obviously a new constitutional arrangement. The Trinidad government, albeit with better resources but with looser constitutional arrangements, had succeeded in integrating a more diverse population while promoting economic development and general welfare.

Brereton attributed the decision to form the union to the need for London to save money and to improve the quality of administration in Tobago. Whilst those observations were undoubtedly true, the problems were far deeper. There was a societal problem. There was no social compact, as indeed there was very little social intercourse between the rulers and the peasants, and to that extent the colonisation process had failed. Where before emancipation there were few riots, there were an increasing number of riots over small matters: the Land Tax riots, the Mason Hall Dog Tax riots, and the Belmanna riots, all in a colony of less than 18,000. What was true of Tobago was true of most of the British West Indian slave societies, as the West India Commission of 1897 recognised. Brereton's view that London brought about the change must be balanced by the fact that such change initiated by the imperial government was not always politically feasible. Barbados, despite the Letters Patent issued for that purpose, did not become a Crown colony in the 1880s on account of an understanding between the rulers and the ruled in which promises were made to the latter in order to preserve their ancient political institutions. The Barbados government of that

---

[140] Brereton, Bridget, *A History of Modern Trinidad 1783-1962*, Kingston, Jamaica: Heinemann, 1981.

period did not have the legitimacy problem that existed in Tobago. The West India Commission of 1897 all but stated that these were failed colonies in recognising that the failure was the natural result of the policies pursued. In the heyday of slavery, the islands were very profitable, but once the question of human rights entered the equation, the whole basis of life in the colonies collapsed.

CRAIG-JAMES

Craig-James came closest to identifying the root of the political problem that led to the union, although that clearly was not her aim. She of all the historians emphasised the evolution of social relationships in what was an artificial society and did a very good job at it. Her work captured, like no other, the strained relationship between the administration in Tobago and the pundits at the Colonial Office. She showed with much documentary information the development of a rudimentary social structure into three well-defined strata—dominant, middle, and lower—in the period between emancipation and the consummation of the union. More than that, she gave the best account of the political history of the colony in the period and noted the conflicts between the Assembly and the executive authority and the various attempts, including the changes to the constitution, to resolve those conflicts.

The second pillar on which she constructed her hypothesis for the economic failure was the near monopoly of the source and deployment of capital in Tobago. This skewed distribution of resources was a barrier to the welfare of the people dependent upon imports to fill the gap in the economy arising from a specialisation in the production of sugar for export.

Supporting the theory of the breakdown in Tobago, she chronicled several of the conflicts that existed between the executive and the Legislature, although she fell short of identifying explicitly this constitutional weakness as being at the root of the political failure in Tobago. This political problem of conflict between the executive and the Legislature was certainly not unknown to British parliamentarians. Moreover, Madison, in expounding on Montesquieu's doctrine of the separation of powers while explaining the new American Constitution to the American people, had warned that *the Legislature by virtue of the reach and scope of its legislation on the one hand and its power of the purse on the other, has the tendency to encroach on the two other branches.*

Craig-James held the view that Tobago was economically unviable. Moreover, she had pointed out the conflicts between the legislative and executive branches of its government. Despite these views, however, Craig-James nowhere endorsed the decision to form the union as in the best interest of the people of Tobago. But the irony of that tale is that it misses the big picture and does not connect the absence of social relations between the peasants and more importantly between the rulers and the masses as a great drawback on the political community. But again while focusing on that aspect of the colony, she avoided looking at the institutional problems associated with the viability of the colony: its security, the welfare of the people, and the constitutional arrangements. In the end her judgement on the union was that the people of Tobago were hard done by the union, by being contrary to the wishes of the majority of the people, and based very clearly on consequences and disappointments which she documented at length, she implicitly disapproved of the union. She dismissed as flippancy the suggestion from Sir William Robinson that the people of Tobago be relocated in Moruga in Trinidad. But historically the situation in these islands can lead to desperation: after the hurricanes of 1813 and 1815 the Turks and Caicos islands were virtually abandoned.

PREMDAS

The commentary by Premdas was the one most relevant to the nature of the union. Premdas's concern was not so much about the decision to form the union as it was about the modern secessionist movement in Tobago. In doing so, however, he could not avoid completely taking into account the history of the union. Whether it was deliberate or in error, he succeeded in turning the historical justification for the union on its head. Citing a number of sources, he noted that one of the several reasons for secession was that *"the separatist group conceives of itself to be in an* **unsatisfactory dependent status,** *an essentially economic factor."[141]*

It is difficult to refute this argument fully without delving into the history of Tobago since the union, but no one familiar with that history can cite a period when Tobago as a separate entity was not, to a large extent, dependent on Trinidad for its economic survival. And it is certain that in the period leading up to the union Tobago was very dependent upon Trinidad for its economic survival as a colony. That much was evident to the Norman Commission. That relationship was, indeed, one of the principal reasons for bringing about the union and was not unrelated to the difference in sizes of the two former colonies viewed as separate entities. But independence was not the crucial factor in Premdas's argument. Premdas himself pointed out that Barbuda chose to leave a West Indian grouping and to become a British colony. In the phrase "unsatisfactory dependent status" his key word was, therefore, unsatisfactory, which placed the matter squarely in the political domain. This statement seemed rash, for it suggested that the viability of the unitary state depended upon whether or not one of the components of the union viewed the economic status as satisfactory. Even if it were true that an independent Tobago had what it thought was a more satisfactory economic status, there would be several other important considerations including those of security and the burden of administrative costs that would ensue as a result of the separation.

WILLIAMS

The treatment of the topic by Dr Williams deserves special consideration. Williams, contrary to Robinson, did not see the union as one of equality between the two former colonies. He evidently thought that Trinidad bore greater responsibilities and ought to have been compensated for assuming the responsibilities of the mother

---

[141] Williams, Colin, *National Separatism,* cited in Premdas, Ralph R., *Secession and Self-Determination in the Caribbean: Nevis and Tobago,* Port-of-Spain, Trinidad: UWI School of Continuing Studies, 1998, p. 100.

country for Tobago. There is much, however, that is unsatisfactory in his historical account. His first error was to depict Michel Maxwell Philip as an Englishman.[142] Whatever doubts exist about his birth, C. L. R. James described Michel Maxwell Philip this way:

> *"Handsome as creoles have been . . . born at Cooper Grange Estate, Naparima in South Trinidad and the offspring of a white owner and a coloured woman on the estate."[143]*

Maxwell Philip was related to Dr Jean Baptiste Philippe, the author of a petition to Lord Bathurst, then Secretary of State for the Colonies. Dr St. Luce Philippe, brother of Jean Baptiste, was a member of the first Legislative Council of Trinidad. The family came to Trinidad from Grenada after the Cedula of population. Williams's error could easily be excused as a mistake of fact on the part of a great historian. But one of the thrusts of Dr Williams's argument was that the British government was trying to ram the union down the throats of the people of Trinidad and Tobago, and in depicting Maxwell Philip as an Englishman and member of the colonial Legislature, he was bolstering that argument. This was Williams in his anti-colonial mode. It was, indeed, an egregious error as Michel Maxwell Philip was the very antithesis of what Williams made him out to be. He was, as the record shows, an undoubted patriot and as a long-serving solicitor general was allowed to move the resolution since it was he, who whilst acting as attorney general, as he frequently did, had introduced the first draft of the resolution to the Legislative Council. Williams's depiction is also most ironical for Maxwell Philip was denied the plum position of attorney general despite being eminently

---

[142] With reference to the debate on annexation in the Legislative Council of Trinidad in 1887, Williams noted, "On that day the Solicitor-General, Mr Maxwell Philip, an Englishman moved the following motion." Williams, Dr. E. E., *History of the People of Trinidad and Tobago,* New York, NY: A & B Publishing, 1993, p. 142.

[143] James, C. L. R., *Michel Maxwell Philip: 1829-1888,* in Sander, Rheinhard, W. (Ed.), *From Trinidad: An Anthology of Early West Indian Writing,* London: Hodder and Stoughton, 1978, p. 253.

qualified for the job, merely because he was a coloured man in an age when there existed an unofficial colour bar.

Secondly, Williams got caught up in the age-old debate about the Wilberforce movement and the economic decline of the sugar industry as the cause of the abolition of slavery. It is astonishing that Williams, the astute historian, failed to acknowledge the fundamental change in human rights that was the outcome of the American Declaration of Independence, the French Revolution, and the Haitian Revolution. Compared to the social forces released by those huge movements, Wilberforce was a mere irritant to Pitt the Younger, the prime minister, as the British Parliament grew gradually to accept the new doctrine of humanitarianism. Williams, therefore, rejected the argument of the British government wanted to impose Crown colony government as a means of getting around the tyrannical nature of the West Indian elected assemblies—in effect white oligarchies—and argued instead that the Crown colony government was imposed on grounds of racism. Williams was delivering a lecture at the University of Essex in 1969 when he quoted Froude:

> *"The relative numbers of the two races being what they are, responsible Government in Trinidad means government by a black parliament and a black ministry . . . and English Governor-General will be found presiding over a black Council, delivering the speeches made for him by a black Prime Minister; and how long could this endure? No English gentleman would consent to occupy such an absurd situation."*

Although Froude, an eminent British historian, was well known as a racist to Trinidad society, he cannot be blamed for the policies of the British government. Indeed, both James Stephen and Lord Goderich of the Colonial Office had expressed their disgust over a system of government where the whites were in the minority and exercised power over the majority, who were blacks and slaves. Similar views were expressed by Governor Drysdale in Tobago and by Sir John Gorrie, the first chief justice of Trinidad and Tobago. The Crown colony system, while it admittedly deprived the majority of blacks of the democratic rights of self-government, was meant to protect those very blacks from the excesses of a tyrannical and hostile white minorities who held substantial proprietary interests in the colonies while holding sinecures in the legislative assemblies of these colonies. If, indeed, the imperial government harboured racist sentiments, they were clearly superseded by the duty to ensure the welfare of the people in the colonies.

Thirdly, Williams was against the union on grounds of abdication of responsibility or of administrative neglect by the mother country. This argument is essentially anachronistic. The modern concept of state intervention for economic and political development, implied by Williams, did not exist at that time. The prevailing doctrine was one of laissez-faire, especially since the colonies were essentially the king's property in an age when Parliament still paid great respect to the royal prerogative. The colonies were developed by franchises granted by the king (and in the case of India, by special companies). It was, of course, the duty of Parliament to defend the king's colonies against foreign aggression, and this resulted in the long delay in recognising the independence of the United States of America. It was only at the end of the nineteenth century, with the imminent decline of the sugar industry and dire social consequences that it spelt for the West Indies, that the Royal Commission acknowledged the responsibility of Britain for the development of the West Indies. Put simply, while the economic tide was rising the question of state intervention did not matter. The ideas of socialism, although formulated in the nineteenth century by Fourier, Saint-Simon, Marx, and others, did not become fashionable until the early part of the twentieth century, at which time it tended to displace the earlier doctrine of laissez-faire. (Williams makes the point that the intervention was necessary to consolidate the empire at a time when the United States and Germany were becoming dominant players in world trade.) The outcome of the new policy was the Colonial Development and Welfare Organisation which was only given birth after the Second World War on the recommendation of the Moyne Commission.

Fourthly, Williams argued that Tobago was forced to unite with Trinidad after a failed attempt to foist the colony on Barbados. That argument masked the tortuous path that Tobago followed from the time it was first ceded to Britain in 1763 to the union with Trinidad in 1889. This instability of Tobago points less to the neglect of the colonial powers than it does to the long-term viability of the island.

Fifthly, Dr Williams's treatment of the speech by the learned attorney general of Trinidad and of the unofficial members of the Council in the debate on annexation was unwholesome. Granted that Mr Gatty's speech was somewhat eccentric, it in no way reflected the general tone of the Council or the governor or the secretary of state. The latter's only known stricture was that the Crown could not let the unofficials control the Council. As was noted, the unofficials had made a sterling contribution in the Legislature of Trinidad; in some instances they outnumbered the ex-officio members and were only limited by the restriction to impose taxation and by the casting vote of the governor. In any event, and as Williams noted, the resolution came under heavy fire from the unofficials; the voting showed that there was one abstention in Dr de Boissiere and one vote against by Mr Fenwick. That meant that six of eight of the unofficials voted in favour of the resolution. Quite contrary to what Williams suggested about the Council, its performance was in some way exemplary if not quite outstanding, and this was acknowledged by the secretary in his response to the Report of the Franchise Commission the following year. Despite the eccentric opinion of Mr Gatty, his judgement appears to have been quite sound. As chairman of the Franchise Commission, he dissented from the opinion contained in the report of the commission and submitted his own minority report. Moreover, his recommendations were accepted by the Colonial Office rather than those of the majority report.

Sixthly, the secretary of state, Lord Glanville, by letter of 1886, directed that the resolutions of the Legislative Councils concerning the union ought to have taken place only after the people of both colonies had been consulted. There clearly was no intention to ram anything down the throats of the members of the Council or of the people of Trinidad and Tobago.

Seventhly, Dr Williams implied that Trinidad ought to have been compensated by the British government for taking on the responsibility for the future development of Tobago. Indeed, the West India Commission of 1897 recommended that the imperial government provide funds for infrastructure development and for education and no doubt if Tobago were a separate colony at that time it would have benefited from such a programme. But in alliance with Trinidad with an economy in surplus the funding for development in Trinidad and Tobago was not necessary.

Finally, despite the nit-picking, Dr Williams, like so many other commentators since, had no suggestion as to what should have been done or how the matter should have been treated. The only reasonable conclusion that one can draw is that he thought the government ought have funded the development of Tobago until such time as the island became self-sustaining.

CONCLUSION

The success or failure of the union ought not to be judged alone by the measures implemented by the reinvigorated Legislative Council of Trinidad and Tobago. The unitary state was still a British colony, and to that extent its fortune would remain dependent on British policy. In the same way that exogenous factors led to the collapse of the Tobago economy during the nineteenth century, we ought to expect that exogenous factors would influence the progress of the union during the twentieth century. One such factor was undoubtedly the change in colonial policy that was taking place at the time of the union.

One gets the impression that all the administrators recognised that there was a need, given the condition of the colony in 1888, for something to be done about Tobago, and in particular some sort of union with Trinidad was desirable. Of all the historians, Robinson had a clear notion of what form the union ought to have taken, while others were content to merely comment on the nature of the union as it was created or on the way it functioned. Robinson's idea of equality between the two colonies is in stark contradiction to the recommendations of the experienced administrators of Tobago and of the West India Commission of 1897 and to that which was implemented. All the recommendations acknowledged that the people and institutions of Trinidad would play a dominant role in the union.

The analysis of the circumstances surrounding the union by the historians is uniformly disappointing. Not a single one of Ottley, Williams, Douglas Archibald, Brereton, Premdas, or Craig-James gave credit to the stream of colonial administrators, who, confronted with the practical problems of the day in governing Tobago, proposed what was evident to a Dutch observer in 1667, viz., that the close geographical ties should form the basis of a closer union. The information that indicated that Tobago was in pressing need of reform was overwhelming. The conscientious efforts of a whole generation of colonial administrators seemed to have been largely ignored. Drysdale, Ussher, Gore, Robinson, and Sendall all expressed deep concern over the welfare and future of Tobago. The Crossman Commission and the Royal West India Commission (1897) both suggested that the situation in Tobago needed urgent reform. No historian saw the union as a result of the natural growth in relationship between the two islands during the course of the nineteenth century. Instead, the act of union was seen as another act of colonial oppression. A close study of the history of the island in the thirty years prior to the union reveals that the ancient government had virtually collapsed and the society was in disarray

Dr Eric. E. Williams, Prime Minister of
Trinidad and Tobago (1962-1981) and Historian

CHAPTER VIII

Tobago's Superior Institutions

*There is no law devised by man which is perfect and
there is no power which cannot be abused.*
Dr Patrick Solomon, Sunday Express[144]

WILLIAMS'S ARGUMENT

TODAY, DESPITE THE LONG association of the two islands, popular myths persist about the nature of the union and of how the individual islands were affected by the association. These persistent myths come to the fore on every occasion that questions arise about the constitutional relationship between Trinidad and Tobago. One such myth, the source of much acrimony, is that Tobago lost its ancient and superior institutions when it was annexed to Trinidad. This particular myth owes much to Dr Williams. When writing on the history of colonialism in Tobago during the nineteenth century, he opined:

> *"Tobago was superior to its sister colony in Trinidad because as one of the older British colonies, it enjoyed representative institutions. It had its own bicameral*

---

[144] Dr Patrick Solomon was a former deputy to Dr E. E. Williams and the quotation is taken from a Trinidad and Tobago newspaper, the *Sunday Express* of 8th July, 1989.

legislature with its own Governor and Commander-in-Chief."[145]

This myth would have deserved greater credibility had Williams not contradicted himself since he, elsewhere, ridiculed the system in Tobago as:

"the absurdity of self-governing institutions in an island of some 12,000 people."[146]

"But the representative system was a farce. The franchise in Tobago was the prerogative of a mere handful of people."[147]

Those three statements taken together imply that the system of government in Trinidad during the period under consideration was an even greater absurdity than what existed in Tobago. Despite avowing Tobago's superior institutions, he devoted chapter 7 of *History of the People of Trinidad and Tobago* to "Trinidad as a Model Slave Colony." The title and theme of the chapter suggest that Trinidad was to serve as a model colony for Tobago and, indeed, for the rest of the British West Indies. That policy position taken by the imperial government was, to some extent, inconsistent with the assertion of the superiority of the Tobago institutions. In expounding that position, Williams was uncharacteristically ambivalent on a matter of such importance. Williams's assertion was not always shared by others. For example, James V. Drysdale, lieutenant governor between 1857 and 1864, left some scathing remarks about the Tobago Constitution:

"The true basis of all Representative Government must be Representation, but Representation insofar as it concerns the people of Tobago, is a mere fallacy, twelve at least

---

[145] Williams, Dr. E. E., *History of the People of Trinidad and Tobago,* New York, NY: A & B Publishing, 1993, p. 136.

[146] Ibid., p. 122.

[147] Ibid., p. 131.

> *of the whole sixteen Members of the Assembly being the*
> *nominees of a single individual."[148]*

A similar view was expressed by C. R. Ottley, the author of a brief narrative history of Tobago:

> *"To say that Tobago's ancient system of Government*
> *patterned though it was on that of the United Kingdom,*
> *having a lower House of Assembly and the Legislative*
> *Council (House of Lords), constituted a democracy*
> *would be entirely fallacious. It was in fact an autocracy*
> *in which some fifty or so planters elected sixteen of their*
> *members every three years to represent their interests,*
> *and to battle the Colonial Office when necessary for the*
> *preservation of their economic and social rights."[149]*

Also disagreeing with Williams to some extent was Henry Isles Woodcock, a former chief justice of Tobago. His disagreement was not only with the Tobago Constitution itself but with the laws that he was required to administer over the period 1862 to 1867:

> *"The laws of Tobago are more crude and insensible*
> *than those of any civilized country with which I am*
> *acquainted."[150]*

Based on the opinions of Drysdale, Woodcock, Ottley, and Williams himself, it would be difficult to concede the notion that Tobago had superior political institutions. But perhaps a more objective approach is required if the subject is to be dealt with adequately.

---

[148] Craig-James, Dr. Susan E., *The Changing Society of Tobago 1838-1938, Vol. I, 1838-1900*, Port-of-Spain, Trinidad: Paria Publishing, 2008, p. 234.

[149] Ottley, C. R., *The Story of Tobago*, Port-of-Spain, Trinidad: Longmans Caribbean 1973, p. 82.

[150] Woodcock, Henry Isles, *A History of Tobago*, London: Frank Cass, Library of West Indian Studies, 1971, p.178.

THE AIMS OF UTOPIAS

The idea of the suitability of constitutions is something that attracts all politically minded persons, and in this respect Dr Williams was no exception. Plato's *Republic*, St. Augustine's *City of God*, Hobbes's *Leviathan*, Sir Thomas More's *Utopia*, and Bolingbroke's *Patriot King*, to mention a few, are all examples of ideal constitutions. They typically attempt to give timeless definitions to the aims and problems of government, the authority of the state, and the rights of citizens. The problems have been elaborated upon by numerous philosophers, historians, and politicians alike. S. B. Chrimes, a British historian, in giving the English solution to the eternal problems of government, stated:

> "The fundamental problems of government, like most of the really basic problems of human existence, do not change. They remain essentially the same in all ages and all places. Since the remote, prehistoric times when men first sought to improve their hard lot by establishing civil government of some kind—how, when, or where, no one can say—the fundamental problems involved must have been present, however dimly realized, as they are still present today. These problems, then as now, are essentially how to reconcile apparently opposite aims and ideals. How to reconcile, without constant resort to force, law with liberty, progress with stability, the State and the individual; how to bind the government in power to law of some kind; how to reconcile government, strong enough to be effective, with the consent of at least the majority of the governed: these are the fundamental problems, always existent, always in the nature of things demanding solution."[151]

Perhaps a terser statement based on oriental philosophy was given by the American economist and political scientist W. W. Rostow:

---

[151] Chrimes, S. B., *English Constitutional History*, (Oxford: Oxford University Press, 1971, p. 1.

> *"Whether in an African tribe ruled by custom and the elders or a Greek city state, whether in Nixon's America or Mao's China, men look to government to find an acceptably balanced way to do these three things: protect them from others; provide acceptable standards of welfare; settle quarrels among themselves, peacefully, on terms judged equitable, holding the community together."*[152]

Viscount Bolingbroke, translating Cicero, stated:

> *"The good of the people is the ultimate and true end of government . . . the greatest good of a people is their liberty."*[153]

THE PROBLEM WITH POLITICAL IDEALS

Because of his prominence as a historian and more so as a prime minister of Trinidad and Tobago, Williams's statement ought not to be dismissed lightly. But comparing institutions, and passing judgements on them as Williams did, is always fraught with dangers. To begin with we have to be mindful if not wary of the many failed utopias conjured up by philosophers in the past. Many ideal institutions fail *ab initio* because they are not rightly suited to the purpose or people they are intended to serve. We have much evidence of this from the many political conflicts and the many instances of tyranny of the twentieth and twenty-first centuries. Montesquieu, however, was the first to hint of this danger that was so eloquently expounded by Sir Isaiah Berlin:

> *"When the great French Revolution failed to make men happy and virtuous overnight, some of its adherents*

---

[152] Rostow, W. W., *Politics and the Stages of Growth*, Cambridge University Press, 1971, p. 11.

[153] Bolingbroke, Henry St. John, Viscount, cited in Armitage, David (Ed.), *Bolingbroke: Political Writings*, Cambridge: Cambridge University Press, 1997, p. 244.

claimed either that the new principles had not been properly understood, or had been inefficiently applied, or that not these, but some other principles, were the true key to the solution of the problems; that, for example, the purely political solution of the Jacobins had fatally oversimplified matters and that social and economic causes should have been duly taken into greater consideration. When in 1848-49 these factors had been taken into account and the results had proved disappointing, the believers in a scientific solution declared that something also had been left out—say the war between the classes, or the Comtian principles of evolution, or some other essential factor. It is against the "terrible simplifiers" of this type, whose intellectual lucidity and moral purity at heart seemed to make them all the readier to sacrifice mankind again and again in the name of vast abstractions upon altars served by imaginary sciences of human behaviour, that Montesquieu's cautious empiricism, his distrust of laws of universal application, and his acute sense of the limits of human powers, stand up so well. . . . In making laws, one must, above all, have a sense, which only experience or history can sharpen, of what goes with what; for the rapports of laws with human nature and human institutions in their interplay with human consciousness are immensely complex, and these cannot be computed by simple and tidy systems: timeless rules, rigidly imposed will always end in blood."[154]

If we are to make a proper judgement of Williams's statement we may take two approaches: the first a subjective view, by merely looking at the letter of the law that established the institutions, and the second an objective approach, to see how the institutions functioned in practice.

---

[154] Berlin, Sir Isaiah, *Against the Current—Essays in the History of Ideas,* Oxford: Oxford University Press, 1981, p. 160.

THE SUBJECTIVE APPROACH

In comparing the political institutions of the two colonies it is perhaps best to consider two time periods: the first from 1763 to 1831 and the second from 1831 to 1888. It is clear that the major contrast in the constitutions of the two colonies changed with the introduction of a Legislative Council in Trinidad in 1831. The subjective evaluation ought to pass judgement on the suitability of the constitution for the society it is intended to serve.

1763 TO 1831

In this period, the European wars fought in the Caribbean made the security of the colonies a strong priority; with slavery prevalent throughout the region, there was little concern for the welfare of the majority of the populace, the majority of whom had no civil rights; the system of justice clearly did not suit the majority of the people.

If we take a purely subjective approach to compare the political institutions of the two colonies in this period, the Tobago institutions were markedly well defined and superior to those of Trinidad.

THE TOBAGO INSTITUTIONS (1763-1831)

THE REPRESENTATIVE PROCESS

The Tobago Constitution has its origin in the Proclamation of George III of 1763, and the law making authority of the governor general, Robert Melville, is clearly traceable from that source. From the very beginning, the Tobago legislature was bicameral and had an elective element. We may assume that this was the basis on which Dr Williams attributed superiority to the Tobago institutions, since the elective element made it directly representative.

The elective element has its undoubted advantages in bringing local issues to the attention of the deliberative body (Parliament), and those members of the society entitled to vote enjoy direct participation in the democratic process. We observe, however, that not all legislatures determine membership on a purely elective basis; some deliberative bodies include a non-elective element, giving recognition to the fact that the elective element is not an end in itself but merely a means to the end. For example, Canada, whose government has the admiration of many people worldwide, has a Senate in which all the members are appointed by the governor general on the advice of the prime minister. In India, the House of Representatives has two members nominated by the president to represent special interests.

Secondly, while in the primitive condition of the state, an elected representative serves as an ambassador or attorney of his constituency; as the state grows, local issues become embedded in or side-lined by broader national issues (or in extreme cases may be rejected as limited resources and agreed priorities may determine). Moreover, the Parliament itself becomes a forum that specialises in law making, policy formulation, and governance, matters in which the interests of constituents tend to be peripheral. In these latter circumstances it is the wisdom of the representative rather than the views of his constituents that matter most, and ultimately it must be this way if the representative is to enjoy freedom of speech in his deliberations.

The Tobago franchise, nonetheless, catered to a somewhat limited electorate and a still more restricted membership. C. R. Ottley's scathing remarks properly highlight the exclusiveness of the entire process, with the mass of the population completely left out of the system. At the union Tobago, like Trinidad, was a Crown colony and had no elective element.

The Tobago Constitution of 1763, with its bicameral legislature and limited franchise, was in keeping with those of other British colonies at that time. The loss of the island to France for brief periods did not significantly alter the constitution, as the Articles of capitulation confirmed. In 1763 the number of native Amerindians in Tobago had dwindled to a trickle. The constitution with its accompanying programme for the distribution of Crown lands was designed for pioneers on a desert island. More to the point, at the time of its colonisation slavery was acceptable to the colonists; and, indeed, the third act passed by the Tobago Legislature was "An Act for the Good order and Government of Slaves." This type of constitution was found to be so repulsive that it had given rise to a humanitarian movement and to a new doctrine of universal human rights. Perhaps the most damning criticism of this type of constitution in relation to the slave colony came from Sir James Stephen Under-Secretary Stephen, a distinguished official of the Colonial Office:

> *"Popular franchises in the hands of the Masters of a great body of Slaves were the worst instruments of tyranny which were ever yet forged for the oppression of mankind."*[155]

Stephen's comment came after observing the inhumane results of the regular franchises in the West Indies and serves as a grim reminder of Montesquieu's warning that timeless rules rigidly applied will always end in blood.

The franchises for the representative assembles were so restrictive that all control rested in the hands of the slave masters with the dire consequences that followed. While Williams pointed out, and rightly so, the independence of the older assemblies in refuting the impositions of the imperial government, he glossed over the simple fact that in the majority of cases what the assemblies were striving for was not in the best interests of the majority of the people.

THE LEGAL AND JUDICIAL SYSTEM

From 1763, in the absence of statutes, the common law of England was assumed to prevail and by mid-eighteenth century Tobago had a full slate of courts. In 1856 Tobago was added to the circuit of the Court of Appeal of the Windward Islands.

---

[155] Cited in, Williams, Dr. E. E., *History of the People of Trinidad and Tobago*, New York, NY: A & B Publishing, 1993, p. 67.

The Trinidad Institutions (1625-1831)

The Representative Process

At the time of the union the Trinidad Legislature had no elective element. Although he gave no explanation for his assertion in his book, we get an indirect glimpse of Williams's thoughts on the subject from a speech made earlier at a political meeting in 1955:

> *"Crown Colony government . . . may indeed be the best thing for the people, but a wrong decision made by the people is better a thousand times than the most correct decision made for them; and who in Trinidad and Tobago will have the temerity to say that Crown Colony decisions were correct in theory and the best thing for the people in practice?"[156]*

The Legal and Judicial System

The legal and judicial system in Trinidad before 1777 fell under the jurisdiction of the Audencia of Santa Fe de Bogatá in Colombia, established in 1547 and one of several created by Spain during the sixteenth century throughout the Americas. In 1777, a captaincy-general was created in Caracas, Venezuela, under the Audencia at Santo Domingo and included Trinidad and a number of other territories in a new administrative division. In 1786, a new Audencia was created in Caracas with jurisdiction over all territories falling under the ambit of the captaincy-general. The Audencia was a high court, staffed with doctors of law that heard appeals from the courts of first instance in Trinidad. In 1794, Chacon established a *consulado* or commercial court which was a departure from strict Spanish law.

---

[156] Williams, Dr. E. E., *The Case for Party Politics in Trinidad and Tobago,* in Sutton, Dr. Paul K., Compiler, *Forged From the Love of Liberty: Selected Speeches of Dr. Eric Williams,* Port-of-Spain, Trinidad: Longmans Caribbean, 1981, p.108.

THE EXECUTIVE

Under the Spaniards the governor functioned as a viceroy and had plenipotentiary powers. The principal institution was the Cabildo an urban based council. This changed little in the period after the British conquest, with the Crown maintaining for various reasons (particularly the weakened authority of the executive by the assemblies of the older West Indian colonies) tight control over the Executive Council of Advice comprised of four members.

1831 TO 1888

In this second period, Tobago was in a permanent state of institutional change: bicameral Legislature, unicameral Legislature, Crown colony.

IN TRINIDAD STABILITY

Over the next fifty years there were modifications and additions: the Protector of Immigrants replaced the Protector of Slaves; the auditor general replaced the collector of customs; the director of public works and the solicitor general were added with a corresponding increase in the number of unofficials. During a brief period of intense Anglicisation, the bishop of Barbados sat as an official member.

THE APPROPRIATENESS (THE JUDGEMENT)

To be palatable, Williams's claim that they were representative must be taken with a huge grain of salt. The franchises that existed then were little different from that which prevailed in Athens some 2,300 years before. The slaves who made up the majority of the population had no vote, women were almost totally excluded, and men were limited severely by their incomes or ability to pay taxes. Tobago in 1790 was essentially an African population and fundamentally a slave society.[157]

---

[157] Williams, Dr. E. E., *History of the People of Trinidad and Tobago*, New York, NY: A & B Publishing, 1993, p. 58.

By contrast with Tobago, the Trinidad Constitution was more problematic and more laboured in its formation. It was established after the American, French, and Haitian revolutions, and after the slave trade had been abolished, that is, in a period when the concept of human rights was undergoing fundamental change. The British authorities found themselves on the horns of a dilemma when faced with the task of producing a new constitution for Trinidad in the early 1800s. In addition to the matter of the slaves, the complex and polyglot society that the British met in Trinidad at the conquest required special treatment. This has not gone without notice. After early quandaries over its constitution,[158] the Articles of Capitulation provided for the retention of Spanish laws; the culture and language were predominantly French at a time when Britain was at war with Napoleon. The society was, nonetheless, highly stratified by colour with the governor and whites at the top and a continuous gradation to the darkest of the blacks at the bottom.

> *"You will immortalize yourself if you will frame a constitution for Trinidad—it has baffled all your predecessors who have uniformly left it as they found it governed by Spanish law and petitioning for English. Trinidad is like a subject in an anatomy school or rather a poor patient in a country hospital and on whom all sorts of surgical experiments are tried to be given up if they fail and to be practiced on others if they succeed. Stephen is the operator and there are occasional consultations with Doctor Wilberforce and Zachary Macaulay on the state of the patient's health and the progress of the experiment. The poor patient has to go through some very severe operations; she is now actually bound down for a most painful one, a registration of slaves with severe penalties*

---

[158] "The second issue was even more serious. Its relevance was much more immediate than *Campbell vs. Hall* had been. It made Trinidad a key factor in one of the great debates of the time, perhaps of all time, and brought together in the most direct manner the two different but connected topics of constitutional change and experimentation." Millette, Dr. James, *Society and Politics in Colonial Trinidad*, Port-of-Spain, Trinidad: Omega Bookshops Ltd., 1985, p.77.

> *on those who fail to observe the regulations of an Order*
> *in Council prescribed by Dr Stephen."[159]*

Using Bolingbroke's yardstick we may omit the effects of either constitution before emancipation. The question of liberty as we know it was not applicable.

In the case of Trinidad, this is a simple task. Early in 1889, the Royal Franchise Commission submitted its report on a limited franchise for the Trinidad Legislature. The report dealt specifically with the appropriateness of the Trinidad Legislature and more or less defended the status quo in rejecting proposals for the introduction of an elective element at that time. By contrast the Tobago Legislature had been whittled down from its original state because it was inappropriate, and even Dr Williams in his sombre moments called it farcical and absurd.

Nevertheless, an ideal constitution never did anyone any good. Aristotle, when he was establishing political science some 2,500 years ago, studied 157 constitutions and concluded that no matter what form the constitution takes, we may still have bad government. For example, Barbados, with one of the oldest parliaments in the world, is well known for its iniquitous Barbados Slave Code that served as a model for slavery in the British North American colonies. Again, the United Stated of America, despite the exalted rhetoric of its constitution, was amongst the last, eighty years after the Declaration of Independence in which slavery was denounced, to abolish the slave trade and then only after the country was divided by a Civil War over the slaves who in one part of the country enjoyed, if that is the right word, no civil rights. Williams, who studied politics at Oxford, was aware of that notion of Aristotle, and that probably explains why he settled the dilemma in a rhetorical question. But the decision to impose an institution upon a people or to adopt a particular form of

---

[159] Peel, Sir Robert, cited in Millette, Dr. James, *Society and Politics in Colonial Trinidad*, Port-of-Spain, Trinidad: Omega Bookshops Ltd., 1985, p. 65 footnote.

constitution is an act that has practical consequences and cannot be settled in the abstract.

Williams was not merely comparing the constitutions of the two colonies. He was in fact passing judgement, and it is regrettable that he did not bring his formidable intellect to bear on the problem. Perhaps the best way to judge an institution is by its results in relation to its objectives. This matter was settled decisively by Plato in Book IV of *The Republic* when deliberating about the nature of justice. Plato had begun by arguing that

> *"of all the things of a man's soul which he has within him, justice is the greatest good and injustice the greatest evil."*

He further argued that justice is to be seen in the state more easily than in the individual and concluded that through temperance (i.e., the function of the judiciary); courage (i.e., the function of the executive); and wisdom (i.e., the function of a deliberative Assembly), the ideal of justice was achieved by the state. What was true in Plato's day is probably true for all time; that is to say, justice is the residual virtue that retains a balance between temperance, courage, and wisdom. Therefore, if we are to make comparative judgements of constitutions, it is not sufficient to make structural comparisons like Wheare or his refinement in Wolf-Phillips, but we must then apply those structures to the societies they are intended to serve and examine how well justice has been served.

IN TOBAGO INSTABILITY

The franchise in Tobago was the prerogative of a mere handful of people. The result of this new Representation of the People Bill (1860) was that the number of voters increased from 102 to 215. At the ensuing elections, 91 voted, and the representatives for St. John and Plymouth were returned by the vote of one voter in each district.[160]

---

[160] Williams, Dr. E. E., *History of the People of Trinidad and Tobago,* Brooklyn, New York: A & B Publishing, 1993, p. 132.

Fortunately appropriateness is a factor that can be achieved by modifying a constitution, and these changes over time are a good indicator of its suitability.

Williams was making a cursory comparison of the Crown colony system with full internal self-government. He did not deny the possibly superior virtue of the Crown colony system on this occasion, although he held that self-government is a thousand times better even if it makes wrong decisions. In avoiding an explanation for the basis of this judgement, Williams dismissed it in a rhetorical question, but it seems obvious that he was relying on the doctrine of self-determination. But in comparing the constitutions of Trinidad and Tobago, the principle of self-determination did not arise or at best was a marginal issue, since they were both Crown colonies.

Cognizance must be given to the fact that at the union the laws of Trinidad, for the most part, formed the core of the new laws of Trinidad and Tobago. This may be interpreted to mean that the Trinidad laws were more suitable than those of Tobago for the administration of the new unitary state. The Legislature in Trinidad was partially shielded from the problems of local government, as these were delegated to the municipalities. The Legislative Council would then fix its attention to national issues.

THE JUDGEMENT

Using Rostow's criteria for judging institutions, we note that in both cases priority was given to the institutions set out to ensure the security of the colony; it would be pedantic to argue that in either case the institutions were designed to promote the welfare of the people; the means of resolving issues was marginally better in Trinidad— before emancipation—, where Spanish law had made concessions for the trial of slaves unknown under the British administration.

The Objective Approach

Heeding the warning of Montesquieu, the objective approach must take into account, as best as possible, the appropriateness of the institutions to the people and place at the particular time.

The objectivity of the institutions may be judged by examining their aims and objectives. The statements by politician Viscount Bolingbroke, historian S. B. Chrimes, and economist W. W. Rostow provide convenient yardsticks by which we may measure the effectiveness of the institutions.

By many of the criteria set by Chrimes, the institutions of both Tobago and Trinidad fall short. Of neither colony could it be said that the government had the consent of the majority. Of course, Chrimes was writing in 1947, when the adult franchise was almost a universal right, whereas in the period under consideration few women had the vote in any part of the world. Nor could it be said that the government of either colony was concerned with reconciling opposite aims and interests, and these may be debatable. But in reconciling law with liberty and the state with the individual, the constitution is very far from the criteria.

Institutions Compared in Practice

1. The security that prevailed before emancipation collapsed when the slaves were freed. The government, dominated by members of the plantocracy, was permanently at loggerheads with the mass of the population. Their domination of the Legislature severely hampered the work of the executive.
2. On the welfare test, the government was a dismal failure. Several commentators had noted that Tobago was the most backward of the West Indian islands.
3. On the Rostow's test of resolving disputes and dispensing justice, the system was a marked failure.

The very second act of the Legislature of Tobago after 1763 set out to define slaves as property. In Trinidad the situation was not much different except that under Spanish law, manumission was easier to achieve, and the *Code Noir* enshrined a number of rights which the slaves in Tobago did not enjoy. If, however, we split hairs over this matter the evidence comes down in favour of the Trinidad institutions. For example, despite the elective element in the Tobago Legislature, the members inevitably acted in their own interests rather than the interest of the population as a whole. Firstly, in 1823, when the imperial government was trying to ameliorate the conditions of the slaves in Tobago, based on the somewhat better conditions in Trinidad, there was indignant protest from the Tobago Assembly:

> *"The British proposal that the slave should be allowed resort to the law courts for redress was rejected by the Tobago Assembly as tantamount to immediate freedom for the slaves."*[161]

By contrast it seemed that in Trinidad as far back as 1790 the slaves had the right to appeal, in major cases, to the Audencia in Caracas.[162] Secondly, the Tobago Legislature welcomed the change to Crown colony government because the members of the ruling plantocracy saw it as a means of curbing the power of the lower classes. Thirdly:

> *"In many parts of the West Indies in the 1830's, for example, it became virtually impossible in jury trials to obtain conviction of whites for crimes against blacks. Law, traditional property rights, individual civil rights, and ethical convictions were all in dispute."*[163]

This was the condition that Gorrie encountered on his first visit to Tobago in 1889, forcing him to adopt a policy that amounted to

---

[161] Williams, Dr. E. E., *History of the People of Trinidad and Tobago,* New York, NY: A & B Publishing, 1993, p. 130.

[162] Millette, Dr. James, *Society and Politics in Colonial Trinidad,* Port-of-Spain, Trinidad: Omega Bookshops Ltd., 1985, p. 22.

[163] Porter, Andrew, *Trusteeship and Humanitarianism,* in Porter, Andrew (Ed.), *The Oxford History of the British Empire Vol. III: The Nineteenth Century,* Oxford: Oxford University Press, 1999, p. 200.

222

affirmative action. The authorities failed to discern and to respond to the new tide in the affairs of men that was washing away the old civilisation and ushering in the new. The situation in Trinidad was, if anything, only marginally better for Gorrie had invoked the wrath of the legal community in either country

Fourthly, the legislators in Tobago resented the annexation of 1889 because it brought losses to their own interests, while the common man gained from the lower prices available from shopping in Trinidad.

By contrast the Trinidad Legislature had dealt effectively with the religious and educational problems that threatened to consume the society and had developed a credible programme of economic development. The verdict of the Colonial Office of the government in Trinidad in 1889 in response to the report of the Royal Franchise Commission was quite positive. In the words of Lord Knutsford:

> *"The unofficial members of the Legislative Council of Trinidad have for a long time had greater weight in that body than has been the case in other Crown Colonies and the island has enjoyed remarkable prosperity which has extended to all classes; while this development has been advanced by the judicious legislation and by a liberal expenditure on public works."*[164]

If we are to judge by Rostow's criterion of welfare, the Trinidad institution was far superior to that of Tobago

Fifthly, from a practical viewpoint, the Order in Council of 1888 was of such a nature as to bring the laws of Tobago up to date with those of Trinidad. This hardly suggests that the laws of Tobago were superior to those of Trinidad; the better thing to have done in that circumstance was to bring the laws of Trinidad in line with the laws of Tobago, which had a longer history under British rule. The

---

[164] *Minutes of the Proceedings of the Legislative Council of Trinidad, 19th December 1888.*

concrete evidence for a superiority of the Tobago institutions must reside in the period before Tobago became a Crown colony in 1876 before the bicameral Legislature of which Dr Williams wrote was abolished. The reasoning is sound in general, but in the context of the colonial era, it fails for two reasons.

The simple truth ignored is that despite the lofty ideals of a constitution, we may yet have bad governments or deviations from the ideals as Aristotle had pointed out: deviations from the ideal monarchy lead to tyranny; deviations from the ideal aristocracy lead to oligarchy; and deviations from the ideal democracy (called polity by Aristotle) lead to demagoguery. Put in simple terms, a monarchy is perverse if the monarch is corrupt; an aristocracy is perverse, if the executive is corrupt and a democracy is perverse if the society is corrupt.

TRINIDAD'S INSTITUTIONS IN PRACTICE, 1876-1888

In any case, the people of Trinidad had enjoyed local or municipal government in a tradition that dated back to Spanish colonialism. Crown colony government had given Trinidad a strong central executive, something that was clearly absent from the government in Tobago. In addition, in keeping with the best principles of management there was a second layer of government in the evolving municipalities and in the ward system. Obviously, the administrative requirement in Tobago was quite small and to some extent did not warrant a second tier. Indeed, the internal communications were so poor that some delegation of duties would have resulted in greater benefits to the society. But when one compares the effectiveness of the councils or of the rights of the citizens, all the evidence suggests that the performance of the Legislature in Trinidad was superior to that of its sister council in Tobago. In fact, when the status of Tobago was reduced to that of a Crown colony, the move was warmly welcomed by the merchant and planter class as a means of denying the emerging lower classes access to the democratic institutions.

The Legislature in Tobago, although representative in form, was dysfunctional: it was oppressive to the slaves, and it was reactionary to the attempts by the imperial government to ameliorate the condition of the slaves in the period before abolition. At that time, because of the *Code Noir* and the Articles of Capitulation, the slaves and free coloureds in Trinidad enjoyed rights that were certainly not enjoyed in Tobago **before 1797.**

THE CONTEXT OF CONSTITUTION MAKING

HUMAN RIGHTS VS SELF-DETERMINATION

The Crown Colony government that evolved in Trinidad at the end of the Napoleonic wars marked the emergence and crystallisation of the new concept of universal human rights that had relegated the older rights to self-determination and civil rights to a subordinate position in public affairs and in the evolving international law. In 1772, in *R vs Knowles, ex parte Somerset* (Somerset's Case), Lord Mansfield determined that the slave, James Somerset, could not be held against his will in England and ordered that he be released by his owner, Charles Steuart, a visiting Bostonian who had him imprisoned on a ship captained by Knowles after the slave had run away and was recaptured. Lord Mansfield's judgement was one of a litany of declarations of human rights in that era: Jefferson's draft of the Declaration of Independence; Tom Paine's *Common Sense* and *The Rights of Man*; the *Liberté, Égalité, Fraternité* of the French Revolution; and the Haitian Revolution. These events took place with a span of thirty years and created a new concept of human rights that did not exist when Columbus set out from Europe in 1492. When the time came to provide the people of Trinidad with a constitution after 1797, the British government could not proceed by way of a traditional Assembly. In fact the conditions in Trinidad sparked a great debate that led to the decision to establish a Crown colony in Trinidad. We may in retrospect regard the imposition as an intervention to secure the rights of the subject peoples. It is remarkable that as democracy was being spread to new countries and after the United Nations was introduced in 1946, the incidence of intervention on humanitarian grounds became a common remedy to tyrannical governments worldwide. Seen in this light the

Crown colony system was superior where it sought to displace a representative system that was substantially inhumane.

The dichotomy between human rights and the right to self-determination, which troubled Williams, is not an easy one to resolve since self-determination may work against the achievement of human rights. We see examples of the dilemma posed by these choices in the British Prime Minister Canning and in the Trinidad and Tobago prime minister. Canning in 1824 yielded to the self-determination of the Jamaican parliament rather than agree to the amelioration of the condition of the slaves in that country, although such a remedy had been adopted in Trinidad. Dr Williams who was fiercely anti-colonial in his outlook, leaned naturally on the side of self-determination but mindful of the abject condition of the slaves throughout the West Indies he could con bring himself to answer one way or the other. He must have been aware of the significance of the argument in determining the course of constitutional development in Trinidad, in ameliorating the condition of the slaves in Trinidad based on the *Code Noir* that Abercrombie met at the conquest,

But the most compelling evidence of the working of the constitutions is given by the behaviour of the people. The historical records show that runaway slaves were going from Tobago to Trinidad and not otherwise. While there may be several reasons for that we cannot overlook the harsh treatment meted out to such slaves. Pitt in the celebrated debate pointed out that in the West Indies a slave was put to death after running away for the first time. By contrast after 1773 when such slaves arrived in Trinidad from Tobago and most likely from elsewhere, in accordance with the Spanish law they were not to be treated as slaves and were to be given employment on maintaining the royal roads.

CONCLUSION

We may conclude therefore that even if the representative Assembly was a superior institution to the Crown colony system, it did not deliver justice for the majority of the people. Plato thought that the proper object of civil life was justice. This elusive quality varies in time and place, and in the case of the West Indian slave societies during the early nineteenth century, the sense of justice was out of step with the rest of the civilised world.

Comparing the political institutions of two countries has its challenges, particularly when there are marked differences in size, resources and history between the two. Notwithstanding that, if we ignore the abstract arguments and take an objective approach the judgement is clearly in favour of the Trinidad institutions as compared with those in Tobago at the time of the union. The words of Lord Knutsford on behalf of the Trinidad Legislature are decisive. Their true potency is revealed when we consider that in delivering that judgement, Lord Knutsford was arguing against granting a limited elective franchise to the Trinidad Legislature, which in 1889 was a wholly nominated body. If, therefore, Williams was correct about Tobago's superior institutions, then there is very little by fact or opinion to support it. Although democratic in theory, the franchise was very restrictive and resulted in so little participation as to make a mockery of the term "democracy." The strength of the argument rests solely on abstract considerations of the Tobago Constitution. The argument ignores the suitability of the constitution for the society it was intended to serve. Williams's claim is so preposterous that he contradicts himself. The system he praises as superior in one place he denounces as farcical in another. But to be fair to Williams, the purpose of his principal argument was to establish the right of the colonial assemblies to stand up to the imperial government. That matter was resolved in 1774 in the decision of *Campbell vs Hall*. The effect of the legal opinion was that by granting representative government to a colony, the Crown had divested itself of further legislative authority over that colony.

Williams dismissed in a rhetorical question the contentious issue of the bad governance of the assemblies as mentioned above. It appears, therefore, that Williams was prepared to accept the wrong decisions of the self-governing assemblies as part of their responsibility to self-determination. Twentieth-century international law has made the question of the Crown colony system almost academic. The formation of the United Nations and the adoption of the Universal Declaration of Human Rights have made intervention in the affairs of sovereign countries on humanitarian grounds almost commonplace. The right to self-determination is not the absolute value that existed with the United Dutch Provinces, which fought for their independence from Spain in 1581.

But here the great historian in making his comparison overlooked the relative superiority of the functioning of the Trinidad legislature and society.

Trinidad had a long tradition of municipal government dating from the period of Spanish rule. The Spaniards had a well-developed system for municipal government throughout the colonies. The economy was flourishing with surpluses. The Royal West India Commission of 1897 noted that Trinidad, with one third the population of Jamaica, had a larger export trade. The Trinidad infrastructure was far better developed. Trinidad, in a very early stage, adopted the postage stamp: the Lady Macleod. It also joined the telegraphic union of Panama and had a regular steamship service.

The arts were flourishing. If we go beyond the confines of the nineteenth century and the of world figures in C. L.R. James, Dr Eric Williams, and V. S. Naipaul, we are forced to conclude not only that the institutions of Trinidad were superior to those of Tobago, but that perhaps they were superior to those of the rest of the Caribbean. Williams's statement about the Tobago institutions, although erroneous, points to the need for mature consideration whenever constitutions are made.

Contrary to the claim of Dr Williams, it is undeniable that the Crown colony system of Trinidad with all its iniquities did much better in meeting the accepted goals of government than the allegedly superior system that existed in Tobago. This in itself does not mean that Trinidad's institutions were superior or that Tobago's institutions were inferior. What it does is recall Montesquieu's warning of the perils that await us in judging constitutions in the abstract.

Clearly, in comparing the institutions of the two colonies Trinidad and Tobago, an objective approach is required. The British, with their wealth of administrative experience throughout the Empire since 1812, had garnered what was required in these circumstances:

> *"any 'analogy' with the Westminster model was 'formal and nominal rather than real.' Local forms 'must be matters of compromise and of adaptation to the peculiar conditions, character, wants and resources of the place.' Moreover, even 'the closest parallelism in forms' would 'often involve the widest deviation in substance.' As a commission of inquiry in Malta sensibly remarked: 'To graduate our ideas of the perfection of Government by the resemblance which it bears towards our own, is a mode of reasoning as unjust, as it is erroneous; but it is an error into which Englishmen are too apt to fall.'"*[165]

It is tempting to compare the constitutions throughout the British Commonwealth with that of the United Kingdom from which most of them are derived. But the British Constitution is propped up with one feature that precludes mimesis: the monarchy. Despite the regicide, the Queen-in-Parliament, the loss of several prerogatives, and above all the growth of republicanism, the Crown continues to be an important pillar of the British Constitution. And what it retains and promotes is the sense of honour that pervades the various branches of the state. Despite enjoying life membership of the Legislative Council of Tobago, there were frequent absences from its meetings and likewise members were delinquent in attending meetings in other places. This led to the constitutional amendment replacing the bicameral system with a single chamber.

The problems of political development that prevailed in Tobago were not unknown in Trinidad, although their effect on the society was

---

[165] Stephen, Dr. James, cited by Burroughs, Peter, *Imperial Institutions and the Government of Empire,* in Porter, Andrew (Ed.), *The Oxford History of the British Empire Vol. III: The Nineteenth Century,* Oxford: Oxford University Press, 1999, p. 175.

not quite as acute. For example, there clearly was a participation crisis as witnessed by the stream of demands during the 1890s for reform of the franchise. Moreover, the identity problem in Trinidad, if anything, was more severe than it was in Tobago. But the Trinidad constitution had a strong executive that was a characteristic of Crown colony government. The conflicts between executive and Legislature were minimal with the ex-officio members having a built-in majority in the Legislature.

An institution may fail for one of three reasons: firstly, the institution is inadequately structured for the purpose it is intended to serve; secondly, the men who operate the institutions may fall short of what is required of them; and thirdly, the concept of the institution itself may be impracticable. In the case of Tobago, the power of the Legislature was clearly too much for the executive and served to frustrate the efforts of the latter. The percipient Madison, one of the founding fathers of the United States, had warned in his *Federal Papers* of the natural tendency for the legislative branch to overpower all others. He thus became a strong advocate of the doctrine of the separation of powers. The imperial government tried to resolve the matter but only with recourse to the less democratic system of Crown Colony government, in effect making the Legislature subordinate to the Executive. This decision removed the inherent conflict between the two branches of government, but Tobago continued to languish economically. In the end it was decided that the concept of a self-governing Tobago was not viable, and the option for union with Trinidad was taken up.

CHAPTER IX

Myths of the Union

Quae volumus, ea credimus libenter. (We readily believe what we wish to be true)
Julius Caesar, *De Bello Civili*, Bk. II.

T ODAY, DESPITE THE LONG association of the two islands, popular myths linger on about the nature of the union. These persistent myths come to the fore on every occasion that questions arise about the constitutional relationship between Trinidad and Tobago. The principal myths may be listed as follows: Tobago, at the time of the union, was of great strategic and economic importance to the powers of Europe; Tobago, because of the annexation, lost its superior political institutions; the union was forced upon the people of Trinidad and Tobago; the act of annexation was unpopular; Tobago was made a ward of Trinidad; and the union had a federal constitution. The myth of superior institutions has been adequately treated in the previous chapter and will not be examined here. These myths are as much the result of misinformation as they are of misguided opinion. If any conclusion can be drawn, it is that there is a continuing need for political education in Trinidad and Tobago that includes the history of the constitution.

THE MYTH OF STRATEGIC AND ECONOMIC IMPORTANCE

This myth, propagated by Premdas, surrounds the economic and strategic importance of Tobago to the powers of Europe. The statement, although it enjoys widespread belief, particularly in Tobago, is largely false and is most likely part of the legacy of Daniel Defoe.

ECONOMIC IMPORTANCE

The idea of economic importance belongs to the eighteenth century and not to the nineteenth, as Premdas has asserted. It probably arises from the fact that at the time of cession to the British in 1763, Tobago was French and the French West Indian colonies of Haiti, Martinique, and Guadeloupe were amongst the richest countries in the world. Quebec and Louisiana were among the territories ceded by France in exchange for these West Indian islands. At no time of its history could the production of Tobago be compared with that of Cuba, Haiti, or any of the sugar producing colonies of the Caribbean. The limiting factors were the acreage under cultivation, the limited labour force, and the poor infrastructure.

The rapid economic decline after the end of the Napoleonic wars also undermines the myth of the economic importance of Tobago during the nineteenth century. Moreover, Tobago lost its economic importance completely when the sugar industry declined.

The myth of the economic importance of the island is more baffling and perhaps the more difficult to sustain. Robinson noted:

> "Yet as late as 1862 the island rivaled St. Kitts for the first place in sugar production in the West Indies. Statistics for the early nineteenth century disclose that in 1839, whereas imports were £113,371, exports amounted to £183,566, a trade surplus of over £70,000."

Robinson did not go as far as Premdas in claiming economic importance but pointed to some bright spots in the colony's performance, which was gloomy during most of the nineteenth century.

Indeed, Tobago was amongst the least developed of the West Indian islands, and this was not consistent with its economic importance. It is more likely that Tobago was considered an economic liability by the imperial government late in the nineteenth century, a notion than easily finds favour with the historians. The British government refused in 1875 to pay the subsidy to increase the number of visits of the liner delivering mail to the island. Nor could Tobago afford to pay the subscription fee for providing the telegraphic link to the outside world.

STRATEGIC IMPORTANCE OF NEUTRALITY: THE FRANCO/ DUTCH WAR OF 1676

With regard to strategic importance, the statement is largely false. Firstly, as is evident from its history of colonisation, Tobago was considered a neutral island for most of the period 1684 to 1763. Confounding this notion of strategic importance was the greater controversy as to whether Tobago was a neutral island or not. This neutrality spans the period 1678 to 1763. The origin of the neutrality remains obscure, but most sources suggest that in 1748, at the Treaty of Aix-la-Chapelle, both France and Britain agreed to the neutrality of the island. Contradicting Premdas on the security of Tobago was Douglas Archibald, whose account is more credible. It is clear that if Tobago was considered a neutral island then it would be of strategic importance to no one.

During all of the nineteenth century, except for the period 1803 to 1804 when it was occupied by the French, Tobago was a British possession.

At no time in this period was the island threatened with invasion by an alien power, and the security arrangements on the island were downgraded, with some responsibility for the security of the island shifted to Barbados. Its period of insecurity belonged to the seventeenth and eighteenth centuries. Quite contrary to the claim made by Premdas, the island was treated with such scant regard for its security that it changed possession no fewer than thirty-three times in the period 1580 to 1814. The frequency with which possession of the island changed in that period indicates, if anything, the low priority given to its defence. If we revert to the early seventeenth century, we see that the island was of little or no strategic importance to the major powers of Europe:

> *"Throughout the many years of the Courland interest in Tobago, its settlement there, while it existed, was never really disputed by the Spaniards, French, Dutch or British, except on one occasion when it was subordinated by the Dutch for a few years. Preoccupied elsewhere, it is possible that the major European countries accepted that tiny Courland amounted to nothing in the power struggle in Europe and so could harm no one, and that its claim to any portion of the New World could be brushed aside and obliterated whenever the need arose."[166]*

Despite the building of forts by the Dutch, the French, and the British, the island changed hands so frequently that despite the disputed neutrality during the period, we can attach no strategic importance to the island. At one period the island was occupied as a trading post for slaves by the Latvians, who were hardly what one would call a European power at any time since 1492.

The evidence during the nineteenth century clearly shows that there was a downgrading of the security arrangements for the island. The demobilisation of the 6th West India Regiment in 1818, the deactivation of Fort King George in 1854, and the necessity of summoning a warship from Grenada in order to put down the Belmanna riots in 1876 all point to the downgrading of the military facility in Tobago. In January 1854, Fort King George was deactivated on the understanding that ships of war would be constantly located within call of Barbados. From the point of view of internal security,

---

[166] Douglas Archibald, Rupert, *Tobago: Melancholy Isle, Vol. I, 1498-1771*, Port-of-Spain, Trinidad: Westindiana, 1987, p. 28.

the police force was augmented and laws were passed to authorise the formation of a volunteer armed militia.

Except for the period 1783 to 1833, when the island was governed directly by France or Britain, the most senior person on the island was the lieutenant governor, who held no commission, but the governor general held a general commission of vice admiral that extended over all the islands in the group.

IMPORTANCE OF LOCATION

Concerning the strategic importance of Tobago, Premdas was only partially correct, for the records show two such occasions for brief periods. The first occurred after the third Anglo/Dutch war in 1676 in which the English navy was humbled by its Dutch counterpart. The triumphant Dutch navy consolidated its position in the Caribbean by attacking and capturing the French possessions of Marie Galante and Cayenne. The French navy led by Vice Admiral Le Comte d'Estrées retaliated swiftly and recovered both Cayenne and Marie Galante by the end of 1676 before attacking the Dutch in their stronghold located at Rockley Bay in Tobago in February 1677. The Dutch had other possessions in the Caribbean that included Curacao, Saba, and St. Eustatius but on learning of the plans for the French expedition decided to concentrate their forces in Tobago. After a month of fighting the battle ended in a stalemate, although the Dutch were devastated. However, the French again led by d'Estrées returned in full force in December 1677 and by the end of the year had overwhelmed the Dutch.

The second occurred a century later during the American War of Independence, France was an ally of the fledgling United States. Spain was neutral in that war. After capturing Tobago and receiving it by cession at the Treaty of Paris in 1783, one of the French negotiators, the Marquis of Bouille, made a case for the importance of Tobago to the French military:

"[He] *made a most interesting report to his government of the importance of Tobago as a military and naval*

235

> *station, and which was supposed to have influenced*
> *the government of France in so earnestly making its*
> *acquisition a condition in the Treaty.*"[167]

The French experiences in these battles for Tobago must have left them with the sense that Tobago was of some military importance. Tobago was then the most southerly of the British islands and, with the exception of Barbados, the most to windward. The importance alluded to by Bouille was short-lived as the British recaptured the island in 1793, and with the capitulation of Trinidad in 1797, Tobago lost whatever importance it may have held. The well wooded and watered Spanish Trinidad with its close proximity to the South American continent, and to Venezuela in particular, together with the safe anchorage at Chaguaramas alone would have made Trinidad the more important strategic choice. But, in addition, Trinidad had had long diplomatic, cultural, and social ties with Venezuela, going back to the days of Spanish colonialism. It is reasonable to guess that even if Trinidad were not British, then British Guiana would have upstaged Tobago in strategic importance to Britain.

It is obvious that the strategic importance of the island followed the same pattern of its economic importance and declined steadily during the nineteenth century. During the seventeenth century if the island were of strategic importance to any country of Europe, it would have been Spain or the Netherlands, because of the proximity of the island to Trinidad and Venezuela (Colombia), then Spanish possessions, and the Guianas, then a Dutch possession.

THE MYTH THAT THE ANNEXATION WAS FORCED ON THE PEOPLE

The myth persists that the union was forced. This may be attributed to a number of historians, including Williams, Brereton, Premdas, and Robinson. The latter did not go so far as to state that the union

---

[167] *Young's Journal*, cited in Woodcock, Henry Isles, *A History of Tobago*, Frank Cass Library of West Indian Studies, 1971, p. 191.

was forced, but nevertheless, he misstated the process by which the union came about. Williams's thoughts:

"The initiative for the union of Trinidad and Tobago came neither from Tobago nor from Trinidad but from the Secretary of State for the Colonies."[168]

"Thus were Trinidad and Tobago united, by the insistence of the British Government, into what could only be called a confederation."[169]

Brereton wrote:

"This was not the result of agitation for union by the people of either island, or even by the powerful interest groups; it was by imperial fiat, the outcome of Britain's anxiety to shuffle off the responsibility for an impoverished little country by tacking it on to a more prosperous one."[170]

Premdas added:[171]

"The Tobagonian plantocracy objected strenuously to this forced [my emphasis] merger, but could not dispute the decision because of the bankrupt state of the island's economy."

---

[168] Williams, Dr. E. E., *History of the People of Trinidad and Tobago*, New York, NY: A & B Publishing, 1993, p. 139.
[169] Ibid., p. 147.
[170] Brereton, Bridget, *A History of Modern Trinidad 1783-1962*, Port-of-Spain, Trinidad: Heinemann, 1981, p. 153.
[171] Premdas, Ralph R., *Secession and Self-Determination in the Caribbean: Nevis and Tobago*, Port-of-Spain, Trinidad: UWI School of Continuing Studies, p. 104.

Robinson's idea was:[172]

> *"In a memorandum to the secretary of state for the colonies dated November 1, 1873, Augustus Gore, the governor of Tobago, observed quite candidly that there was no need for Tobago to maintain a separate government from that of Trinidad."*

> *"In 1883 the British government appointed a commission of inquiry to make recommendations for the improvement of the economic structure of Grenada, St. Vincent, St. Lucia and Tobago. The commission supported Gore's proposal, and Parliament empowered Queen Victoria to declare the union by an Order-in-Council."*

As Jefferson[173] observed so poignantly, it is very difficult to pinpoint the origin of an idea. But as early as 1667 a Dutch commentator had noted the possibility of a union of Trinidad and Tobago. Doubtless, that idea would have occurred most likely to anyone familiar with the geography of both countries. This became increasingly so, as it did to several administrators with experience in the West Indies in the thirty years or so before the union was consummated. In reviewing the decision process, we are certain that almost all the historians were wrong about the origin of the idea. But Robinson was wrong to suggest the idea originated with Governor Gore. Gore was merely one of many holding the opinion, and the initiative did come from Mr Sendall. Moreover the date of 1873 Robinson quoted is certainly incorrect, for Gore was governor between 1877 and 1880.

To get the origin of the idea for the union wrong is one thing, but to say that the decision was forced was even more erroneous. To begin with the decision, as we have seen, was taken only after consultation with the people of Trinidad and Tobago. As we have

---

[172] Robinson, A. N. R., *The Mechanics of Independence*, Cambridge, MA and London: MIT Press, 1971, pp.21, 22.

[173] "Ideas are, of all things in nature, the least capable of confinement or of exclusive appropriation."

shown above, the idea originated from persons knowledgeable about the administration in Tobago, including a number of its governors. The decision was taken unanimously by the Legislative Council of Tobago after consultation with the people of Tobago.

The union can be said to have been forced only insofar as the executive authority for making the decision resided in Britain and not in Trinidad or Tobago. But in their condemnation of the decision, these historians collectively dismiss the advice of a generation of governors and administrators about the fate of Tobago. Yet, despite Jefferson's stricture on the origin of ideas, it is almost certain that the proximate cause of the administrative initiative for the union came in 1886, from Mr Walter J. Sendall, then governor-in-chief of the Windward Islands to which Tobago belonged. This is seen, indirectly, from a despatch from Secretary of State Lord Glanville to the governor of Trinidad and published as Council Paper No. 5, 1887 of the Legislative Council of Tobago.

No. 5   **Council Paper**   **1887**

Despatch from the Secretary of State Requesting Consideration of Proposal of Annexation of Tobago

Downing Street,
21st July 1886.

I have the honour to inform you that the Governor-in-Chief of the Windward Islands has expressed his opinion, in which the Administrator of Tobago concurs, that the Colony of Tobago would be economically and efficiently administered if it were a dependency of Trinidad. This suggestion appears to me to be worthy of careful consideration, and unless you see any insuperable objection to it, I request that you will place yourself in communication with Mr Sendall on the subject, and that if you agree with him as to the expediency of making Tobago a dependency of Trinidad, you will be good enough to formulate, in conjunction with him, and with

the assistance of Mr Llewelyn, Administrator of Tobago,
the details of an arrangement which you can both
recommend for that purpose.

I have the honour to be,
Sir, ...
Your most obedient, humble servant.
Glanville.

That correspondence illustrates that not only did the initiative come from the governor responsible for Tobago but that he had discussed the matter with the most senior official resident in Tobago and had had his agreement, before putting the proposal to the Colonial Office. On that score both Dr Williams and Mr Robinson were wrong in claiming that the initiative came from the Colonial Office. In addition Mr Robinson seemed to have confused the recommendations of the Crossman Commission of 1883 to reorganise the Windward Islands as a new Crown colony based in Barbados with the idea of the union of Trinidad and Tobago. As is well known, that move was scuttled when the Bajans objected and the British consented to retain their ancient Legislature of Barbados and to separate them for the Windward Island group.

Furthermore, we can only accept that the union was forced if there were methods available more appropriate than that pursued. If we compare the making of the Trinidad and Tobago union with that of the United Kingdom of 1707, we find that the one element missing was a treaty signed by the members of a commission comprised of members of both colonies. With both the colonies being Crown Colonies, that process could only have been completed with a commission arriving at an agreement to be approved by the Crown.

We can speculate that if such a commission had been established, it certainly would have fleshed out some of the matters merely touched on by the Order in Council, but the proceedings would have been so lopsided in terms of the resources available to each of the two participants that the result could hardly have been much different from what actually took place. Indeed, after the teething problems experienced with the Order in Council of 1888, Governor Jerningham in 1898 established a commission comprised of members from Tobago and from Trinidad. The commission sanctioned the amalgamation of Tobago as a ward of the colony of Trinidad and Tobago. In any event there can be no doubt that, in the absence of such a formal treaty, Tobago as a society was the principal beneficiary in the period immediately following the event. It must be said, however, that the importers as a group were big losers and could hardly have come about more democratically given the state of political development that existed in both colonies at the time of the union. The procedure required the most senior officials, that is, the governor of Trinidad, the governor-in-chief of the Windward Islands, and the administrator of Tobago, to meet and to agree on a course of action.

In addition the opinions of the inhabitants were to be ascertained before resolutions were moved in the respective Legislative Councils. Using Brereton's argument we note that the union between England (and Wales) and Scotland was not the result of agitation by the people of either country. Quite to the contrary, the Scots rioted over the decision, and the treaty document signed in Scotland had to be given armed escort to England. What should surprise us in such political matters is if the decision turned out to be unanimous. That the union of 1707 and the union of 1888 met with some dissent is not sufficient to dismiss the validity or the legitimacy of the decision. The procedure on reflection was quite similar to that followed to bring about the Acts of Union that united England and Scotland in 1707. Moreover, the procedure was seeking to impose the strong central executive over Trinidad and Tobago that the Acts of Union had imposed on the United Kingdom. Although the Legislature of that colony had lost its elective element we know that rudimentary political opinion existed in Tobago. The Belmanna riots were an indication that political awareness existed among the lower classes, particularly so amongst the immigrants from Barbados, where despite the harsh and oppressive conditions the slaves were brutally aware of the democratic processes. The later memorials of the 1890s also suggested that there was some political cohesion amongst the ruling classes. But whatever political differences existed about the annexation at the time of decision making were subjugated in the unanimous vote in Tobago that supported the resolution for annexation. The decision to establish the union was taken only after the resolutions by the Legislative Councils, as the example of Barbados had shown a negative resolution would, most likely, have hampered the implementation of the political change.

THE MYTH THAT THE DECISION WAS UNPOPULAR

In regards to this myth, what can certainly be said is that the decision lacked popular support, but this is a far cry from stating that it was unpopular and must be taken with a huge pinch of salt.

To begin with, this myth is directly contradicted by the resolutions of both Legislative Councils. In the case of Tobago, the vote was unanimous. In the case of Trinidad, the vote was twelve *for* and one *against*, with one abstention. This clearly shows that amongst the legislators the move was not unpopular. Since both colonies were Crown colonies, it is difficult to judge the popular sentiment from the votes of their representatives in the Legislature. The attitudes, however, of both Legislatures showed a degree of apprehension over the outcome of the union. In the case of Trinidad, the Legislature wanted to be indemnified against pecuniary losses; in the case of Tobago, in a subsequent resolution the Legislature wanted to be able to return to the status quo ante in the event the union turned out to be unfavourable. There were no real means of measuring public opinion as we know it today in those times. It is true that the opinions expressed in the daily newspapers in Trinidad at the time indicate disagreement with the decision, but this must be balanced with contemporary evidence that there was widespread ignorance and political indifference to these matters among a huge sector of the population. The report of the Royal Franchise Commission of March 1889 showed that there was very little support for the petition seeking to reform the electoral process in Trinidad. Moreover, it was evident that those who did sign the petition had little knowledge of the matter at hand. Lord Knutsford, in rejecting the report, wrote inter alia:

"The petition which gave rise to the appointment of the Commission was promoted by a very small number of persons and it is very doubtful whether the great bulk of the signatories understood the contents. The question appears moreover, to have been regarded with absolute indifference by the great majority of the more influential classes in the Colony and the proprietors of the country districts have no adequate conception of the meaning and objects of popular election and representation."

The remarks of the secretary of state were based on the Report of the Franchise Commission, and if true there was certainly no popular opinion in Trinidad opposed to the union.

In the period leading up to the union Tobago was a Crown Colony and had no elected representatives. When it did have an elected Assembly, the number of persons meeting the requirements to be electors did not exceed 150. Sir John Gorrie, the first chief justice of Trinidad and Tobago, said,

"Many black Tobagonians view, contrary to that of most of the islands merchants and planters that the unification was likely to serve their interests."[174]

The Royal West India Commission of 1897 reported of the amalgamation as a Ward of Trinidad and Tobago:

"We believe that the majority of inhabitants of Tobago are in favour of it."[175]

Moreover, the strenuous objection by the members of the plantocracy cited by Premdas came only after the union was consummated in

[174] Brereton, Bridget, *Law, Justice, and Empire: The Colonial Career of Sir John Gorrie, 1829-1892*, Kingston, Jamaica: University of the West Indies Press, 1997, p. 285.
[175] Report of the Royal West India Commission of 1897, published as *Council Paper No. 153, 1897 of the Legislative Council of Trinidad and Tobago*.

1889 and after the merchant class suffered unanticipated losses from a reduction in their sales.

The same is true of Williams's critique. In pointing to the objections, he does not state at what point they arose, but it is obvious from the sources he cites that he was referring to objections made after 1889. The beneficiaries of these losses were the merchants in Trinidad and the ordinary folk of Tobago, who found it more convenient to travel to Trinidad to make certain purchases after the union came into effect. The ruling class was more concerned with its own survival and status than for the plight of the ordinary folk of Tobago. So that while the union was to the detriment of the ruling class, it was to the benefit of the majority of the people of Tobago; this much was acknowledged by the secretary of state in his response to the memorialists in 1895. In any event Premdas's criticism acknowledges the ambivalence of the ruling class towards the decision due to the bankrupt state of the Tobago economy.

THE MYTH THAT TOBAGO WAS MADE A WARD OF TRINIDAD

This myth is well founded and derives from the correspondence of the secretary of state, from the ambiguity in the minds of the legislators in Trinidad, and more so from errors in the records surrounding the annexation. Notwithstanding the facts, the disparity in sizes of the two colonies gives rise to the perception and expression that Tobago was a ward of Trinidad.

A careful reading of the resolution of the Legislative Council of Trinidad of 1887 reveals the ambiguity over the issue of whether or not Tobago ought to be added to or absorbed by Trinidad. This view is corroborated by Sir William Robinson, the governor of Trinidad, who suggested that Tobago should be absorbed in Trinidad. The note by Mr Gordon-Gordon also adds to the myth. The correspondence of Governor Sir F. Napier Broome refers to Tobago as a ward of Trinidad. The Order in Council was printed in 1898 as Council Paper No. 4 of the Legislative Council of Trinidad and Tobago. The myth has been perpetuated by many historians including Douglas

Archibald and Pemdas. But there is no doubt that the Order in Council of 1898 made Tobago a ward of the Trinidad and Tobago.

We see the myth taking root in the correspondence from Secretary of State Lord Glanville to Mr Sendall, the governor-in-chief of the Windward Islands in 1887. His suggestion that Tobago be administered as a dependency of Trinidad would have appealed to anyone familiar with the affairs of the two colonies. But the myth owes its longevity partly to beliefs held by the legislators in Trinidad at the time of the union. The resolution of the Legislative Council of 8 March 1887 said inter alia:

> *"Whereas Her Majesty's government have* [sic] *expressed the opinion after consideration of the condition and prospects of the colony of Tobago, and having regard to its geographical proximity to, and means of communication with this Colony, that it is expedient that the Colony of Tobago should be **annexed and form part of the Colony of Trinidad** [my emphasis]: Resolved that this Council has no objection to the administrative annexation of Tobago with this Government."*

The language of the resolution makes it clear that whatever other thoughts the members may have had, they were in favour of Tobago forming part of the colony of Trinidad, and this was a view representative of the legislators of Trinidad; it is no surprise therefore that the myth existed of Tobago being a ward of Trinidad. The Trinidad legislators were, no doubt, familiar with the Ordinances of the 1840s that created the ward system in Trinidad as part of the system of local government.

A similar opinion had been expressed earlier by the governor of Trinidad, Sir William Robinson:[176]

---

[176] Craig-James, Dr. Susan E., *The Changing Society of Tobago 1838-1938, Vol. I, 1838-1900,* Port-of-Spain, Trinidad: Paria Publishing, 2008, p. 292.

"Tobago should in my opinion, be incorporated with Trinidad and thus become part and parcel of that Colony."

While many persons held the view that Tobago should be a ward of Trinidad, the myth deepened when the suggestion entered the official record in the postscript of Mr Gordon-Gordon to the Report of the Select Committee of February 1894, where he used the words "Ward of Trinidad." These very words were used by the governor of Trinidad, Sir Napier Broome, in writing to the secretary of state, and the same were used by the secretary of state in writing to the authorities in Tobago that resulted in the furore of 1894. This was noticeably at variance with the resolution by the Legislative Council of Tobago of 19 January 1887, and different from what was approved by the imperial Parliament and the Order in Council of 1888. The difference would have been noticeable even to a casual observer. The matter was resolved in the Order in Council of 1898 that made it clear that Tobago was a ward of the colony of Trinidad and Tobago. Despite the proposal recorded by Sir F. Napier Broome in 1894 to make Tobago a ward of Trinidad, such a proposal was never entertained, and the Order in Council of 1898 unambiguously made Tobago a ward of the Trinidad and Tobago. At that time the administrative system of wards had been firmly established in Trinidad and was precisely what was required in Tobago, given the circumstances that precipitated the union. There is, however, a genuine historical basis for the persistence of the view expressed by Premdas. In a number of documents of 1894, the term "Ward of Trinidad" occurs: in the Report of the Select Committee to consider compensation for loss of customs duties where it originated; in the governor's report of the Select Committee to the secretary of state; in the secretary of state's suggestion to the governor as an alternative to Tobago reverting to an association with the Windward Islands; in the governor's correspondence to the Financial Board in Tobago; and in the subheading of Council Paper No. 177 of 1898 of the Legislative Council of Trinidad and Tobago, where it erroneously printed:

"The Secretary of State's despatch and Royal Order in Council constituting Tobago a Ward of Trinidad."

The subheading was obviously in error since both the accompanying despatch from the secretary of state and Clause 2 of the Order in Council state:

"Tobago shall be a Ward of the Colony of Trinidad and Tobago."

Nevertheless, the myth persists with the assistance of some of our historians. If this signifies anything, it is a reflection of the Tolstoyan[177] neglect of our history. For example, Rupert Douglas Archibald[178] writes on one page:

"Tobago became a ward of the Colony of Trinidad and Tobago."

And on the very next he writes:

"Tobago [would] lose its identity and enter into a state of enforced obscurity, as the ward of another Island, Trinidad."

It seems as though the historian himself was not sure of the status of Tobago, although lurking somewhere in his mind was the idea that Tobago was a ward of Trinidad. As the author of one of the more popular histories of Tobago, Douglas Archibald has contributed greatly to the myth. But he was not alone in that regard. Premdas, whose concern was less with history than it was with the political relationship between Trinidad and Tobago, says the same thing:

"The final and most humiliating blow came when Tobago was made a ward of Trinidad."[179]

---

[177] Tolstoy, Count Leo, "History is like a blind man telling a tale that no one listens to."

[178] Douglas Archibald, Rupert, *Tobago: Melancholy Isle, Vol. I, 1498-1771*, Port-of-Spain, Trinidad: Westindiana, 1987, pp. 204, 205.

[179] Premdas, Ralph R., *Secession and Self-Determination in the Caribbean: Nevis and Tobago*, Port-of-Spain, Trinidad: UWI School of Continuing Studies, 1998, p. 141.

But the myth itself is contradicted by the documents of the union. The first is that the Act of Parliament that enable the creation of the union is cited as the Trinidad and Tobago Act. Moreover, in all the subsequent documents, the unitary colony (state) is referred to as Trinidad and Tobago and never as Trinidad, if indeed, Tobago was to be incorporated as a ward of Trinidad.

THE MYTH OF THE FEDERAL CONSTITUTION

Much of the confusion over the status of Tobago stems from a misunderstanding of the nature of the union. At the root of this myth is the question: does the constitutional arrangement between Trinidad and Tobago create a unitary state or a federal state? The idea has been firmly implanted that the arrangement was a confederation.[180]

> *"Thus were Trinidad and Tobago united, by the insistence of the British Government, into what could only be called a confederation."*

As close as it comes to describing the arrangement of 1889, however, the definition of confederation does not quite meet the bill. The term "confederation," strictly speaking, is used to describe *"an association of sovereign member states that by treaty have delegated certain of their competencies to common institutions in order to coordinate their policies in a number of areas without constituting a new state on top of the member states."* The classic example is the Confederation of the United States that declared their independence from Britain in 1776. (That arrangement was short-lived and was replaced by the federal Constitution adopted in 1789.) The countries of the Caribbean Community (CARICOM) may be considered a confederation.

The idea has also been implanted that the union of Trinidad and Tobago was a federation. Professor Bridget Brereton, writing in

---

[180]   Williams, Dr. E. E., *History of the People of Trinidad and Tobago,* New York, NY: A & B Publishing, 1993, p. 147.

her authoritative work,[181] stated, *"1889: Tobago linked in a federal union."*

Of course the term "federal" may imply that the arrangement was a confederation, but we interpret the term here in the strict sense. If we accept Professor Wheare's definition, the annexation was clearly not a federal union.[182] Such an arrangement would have necessitated the existence of three Legislatures: a Legislature of Trinidad, a Legislature of Tobago, and a Legislature of Trinidad and Tobago. Clearly, at no stage of the decision making process did such a notion arise. It would have been, therefore, a political quantum leap for Tobago, for Trinidad and Tobago to be made a federal colony in the strict sense in 1889, even if the huge disparities in population and economic strength that existed between the two colonies were ignored. The intention ab initio in bringing about the union of Trinidad and Tobago was to create a unitary state or unitary colony, as was appropriate at the time. The model of a unitary state with a strong central executive was one that evolved out of the Tudor dynasty in England, as was applied to all the colonies of the emerging British Empire. The prime example was the Acts of Union of 1707 that created the United Kingdom. The aim of creating a unitary state is manifested in the Trinidad and Tobago Act of 1887; in the Resolutions of the Legislative Councils of Tobago and of Trinidad in 1887, and in the Order in Council issued by the Privy Council in 1888.

This is not to say that the distinction between a federal state and a unitary state is always clear cut. Indeed, such a distinction may

---

[181] Brereton, Bridget, *A History of Modern Trinidad 1783-1962*, Port-of-Spain, Trinidad: Heinemann, 1981, p. 251.

[182] "In a **federal** Constitution the powers of the government are divided between a government for the whole country and government for parts of the country in a way that each government is legally independent within its own sphere. . . . In a **unitary** Constitution on the other hand, the legislature of the whole country is the supreme law-making body in the whole country. It may permit other legislatures to exist and to exercise their powers, but it has the right, in law, to overrule them; they are subordinate to them." Wheare, K. C., *Modern Constitutions*, Oxford: Oxford University Press, 1969, p. 19.

be sometimes quite obscure. Such was the case of the Dominion of Canada, created by the British North America Act of 1867. That law, modelled as it was on the authority that the British government exercised over the colonies, gave so much power to the central government. It was only with the passage of time, with the growth of provincial rights, and through judicial interpretation that the constitution became truly federal. In any case if one had to seek a model for the union, apart from the arrangement between Jamaica and the Turks Islands, the only other example was the Act of Union of 1707.

In 1763, Tobago was part of the government of Grenada, with the governor general based in Grenada; from 1833, it was part of the Windward Islands group, with the governor general based in Barbados; in 1885, when Barbados left the group, it remained part of the Windward Islands Group, with its governor-in-chief based in Grenada. Moreover, when the union took place, there was no lieutenant governor of Tobago and the highest ranked official was the administrator, indicating the true political status of the island at that time. Clause XX of the Order in Council pointed the Financial Board in the direction of local government, and but for a few exceptions under clause XXVII, the Legislature of Trinidad and Tobago had the power to make laws for Tobago and to void legislation passed by the board in Tobago.

Any doubts about the nature of the union of Trinidad and Tobago may be dispelled by referring to the Acts of Union of 1707 that united the Kingdoms of England and Scotland. As was well documented, when the Tudor line ended at the death of Elizabeth in 1603, James VI of Scotland became James I of England, but it was only when the Stuart line itself was threatened with extinction in 1707 that the two kingdoms became united in a unitary state. The motivation for the union stemmed from the need to get the people of Scotland to agree to the Hanoverian succession already determined by the Act of Settlement of 1701 in England, and the outcome was the fulfilment of the dream of James I of England and James VI of Scotland.

Even if the legal instruments do not make clear the true nature of the union, we must conclude that the intention was to establish a unitary state that the colony became after 1898.

THE TRUE NATURE OF THE UNION

There ought to be no doubt about the nature of the union between Trinidad and Tobago. Nowhere throughout the British Empire in 1888 was there a constitution that was not modelled on the British Constitution. The prevailing British model for government at the time may be seen in the Constitution of the United Kingdom, the British North America Act of 1867, and the self-governing West Indian Islands. The unitary model for Trinidad and Tobago was of the same ilk. The federal structure of the governments of Canada and Australia were to be adopted much later. Indeed, the enabling Act of Parliament of 1887 states explicitly that the intention was to unite the two former colonies into one colony, and the nature of its constitution was to be inferred from the ensuing Order in Council.

Few administrators, then or now, could be taken aback by the action of the Order in Council of 1888 to abolish the extant Executive and Legislative Council of Tobago in creating the new colony. It was manifest from the existence of the municipal council and the system of wards that "local government" was a way of life in Trinidad at the union. Section XX of the Order in Council of 1888 clearly defined the "local government" function of the Financial Board in Tobago within the unified colony of Trinidad and Tobago. The ambiguity, if any, of the Order in Council of 1888 was resolved in 1898 by making Tobago a ward of Trinidad and Tobago, preserving the "local government" function at the same time that it abolished the Financial Board that was the source of so much confusion in the period 1889 to 1894.

These popular myths, some of them contradictory (for example, that on the one hand Trinidad and Tobago had a federal constitution, and on the other that Tobago was a ward of Trinidad) are at the root of the constitutional matters that now exist over the Tobago issue. They point to a huge gap in the area of political education in Trinidad and Tobago, particularly with regard to our history. They are grim reminders of the days when the Crown colony system allowed minimal participation of the mass of the people in the political life of the country.

The union created a new entity, and thereby Tobago lost its identity, as did Trinidad. With the majority of the resources, Trinidad would of necessity lose less than Tobago, and even if people worldwide find it convenient to refer to the new colony as "Trinidad," the latter would never more be the same as it was before the union. The name "Trinidad and Tobago" preserves for posterity the separate histories of the two islands, although there were alternatives where identities were preserved, like the United Kingdom comprising England and Wales and Scotland, or like Spain, where the identities of Aragon and Castile were lost.

What was certainly lost was the mystique, created in 1719 by Daniel Defoe, about the idyllic isle in the Caribbean.

EPILOGUE

---

*In history one must be on one's guard against seeing
the obvious and missing the significant.*

H.D. Kitto, *The Greeks*

OVERVIEW

AT THE TIME OF the union in 1888, the world differed considerably from 1763, when George III of Britain created the four governments known as Quebec, East Florida, West Florida, and Grenada. By 1888, Quebec had become part of the confederation of Canada, and East Florida and West Florida were fully integrated into the federal government of the United States of America. In the Caribbean, the countries that comprised Grenada, also known as the South Charibee group, went their separate ways. In 1770, Dominica was separated from the group and became a district seignory, and after 1805 it was governed as a British colony in its own right. In 1896, it was made a Crown colony. Grenada, St. Vincent, and Tobago, despite their vicissitudes, remained in a political union until 1888, and they were all Crown colonies at that date, with an administration based in Grenada. Within that group, however, Tobago continued on its tortured path with its government downgraded, notwithstanding all the developments of the nineteenth century.

253

The insecurity that dogged the territories of the Caribbean region during the seventeenth and eighteenth centuries evaporated after the Congress of Vienna in 1815, and development consisted principally of two things: firstly, the humanising of those societies by transforming the slaves from chattels into citizens with civil rights, and secondly, the introduction of new technology into the sugar industry. The spread of mechanisation with its greater productivity lent an economic argument to the abolition of slavery, and the latter was in turn a major factor in the collapse of the sugar industry in the West Indies. Driving a nail in the coffin of the sugar industry was the development of beets in Europe as an alternative to sugar cane as a source of sucrose. These factors ultimately brought into question the viability of a number of colonies and pointed to, even if it did not lead to, a change in British colonial policy.

The sugar industry of Tobago ground to a halt in 1882; nonetheless, by then the problems of Tobago were more than economic in nature. Despite the best efforts of the imperial government through administrative and constitutional reforms, Tobago remained a failure as an independent political community. Unlike most of the other islands, where there was a communal life of sorts, with a substantial number of free individuals, Tobago was only minimally changed from a slave colony comprised of slaves and slave owners. After emancipation, the intransigence of the plantocracy remained a huge barrier to the development of a political community. The driving force for change on the island was as much the initiative of the churches and individual philanthropists as it was of the colonial government. At the approach to the end of the nineteenth century, it became increasingly obvious to the colonial governments that Tobago required a new solution. Changes in the constitution failed to resolve the fundamental problem of the separation of powers between the executive and the Legislature. But the conflict loomed large to the point where labourers and mechanics were petitioning the Crown in support of the executive and decrying the members of the Assembly.

At this stage, the situation was so desperate that depopulation was considered. But the course taken in 1887 was to establish a union with Trinidad. In arriving at the final arrangement for the union, it was clearly demonstrated that the peasants had no voice in the Legislature of the colony: whereas the peasantry was petitioning the Crown for closer union with Trinidad, the plantocracy was petitioning the Crown for separation from Trinidad.

THE PROCESS OF ESTABLISHING THE UNION

Creating the union was always a challenging task, given that there was relatively little political intercourse or formal relations between the two Crown colonies.[183] In retrospect it seems that despite the anticolonial rhetoric of the historians, not much more could have been done to improve the process of bringing about the union. While there were earlier precedents in the Laws in Wales Acts 1535-1542 and the Crown Act of Ireland of 1542, for comparison we may take as a benchmark the case of the union of 1707 between Scotland and England—then two self-governing states. The process entailed essentially four elements: firstly, the Union with Scotland Act passed in the English Parliament in 1706; secondly, the Union with England Act passed in the Scottish Parliament in 1707; thirdly, the signing of the Treaty of Union (which contained twenty-five articles, was negotiated by a team comprised of commissioners from both countries, and was ratified by their respective parliaments before the passage of the Acts of Union); and fourthly, the treaty provided among other things for the creation of a Parliament of Great Britain based on the English bicameral system at the Westminster Palace and with membership of each country specified.

The proposal in 1886 from the secretary of state to the governor-in-chief of Tobago suggested the Turks and Caicos Islands vis-à-vis Jamaica as a model for the union. But apart from the notion of a separate treasury and to some extent the subordinate Legislature, little consideration was given to the suggestion. Indeed

---

[183] "One of the problems involved in the creation and federation of new states is essentially that of converting a system of political relations between once sovereign peoples within its boundaries, into a more comprehensive political organization." Lienhardt, Godfrey, *Social Anthropology*, Oxford: Oxford University Press, 1966, p. 63.

nowhere in the debates are the names of the Turks and Caicos and Jamaica mentioned.

In the case of the union between Trinidad and Tobago, which were both British Crown colonies, the governors of the two colonies met and agreed to the annexation. Unlike the Union of Scotland and England, there was no treaty, but the Order in Council of 1888 did spell out the conditions of the arrangement. One can speculate that if a team from both colonies had been appointed to negotiate the terms, the final decision would have been more realistic, given the contribution of Mr Fenwick to the debate. Had such a procedure been followed in the case of the union of Trinidad and Tobago, the result would most likely have been more harmonious, although the negotiations would have been decidedly more acrimonious, as indeed they were between Scotland and England. There was during the principal debates surprisingly little dissent. Mr Fenwick, an exception, accurately highlighted the difficulties of the union as proposed in 1888 and with equal accuracy foretold the outcome. Indeed, in 1898, when there was an almost universal clamour for Tobago to be fully incorporated in the united colony, Governor Jerningham did appoint a commission chaired by the commissioner for Tobago, and persons normally resident in the respective colonies were represented. The commission, whose report it is difficult to locate, reported in favour, and the rest is history.

Dr Williams rightly pointed out that the responsibility for Tobago rested principally with the imperial power. But he failed to acknowledge that by virtue of their close proximity and the growing political and commercial relations between the two colonies, Trinidad was destined to enter into a union with Tobago, as it was likely to be called to play in the wider West Indies in the twentieth century. The decisions were taken as democratically as they could have been given the state of political education in the two colonies at the time, and the resolutions of their Councils were almost unanimous in that regard. Of all the options available the decision taken was obviously the best. Indeed, the arrangement was quite acceptable to the majority of the people of Tobago, who literally voted with their feet on this matter. While the annexation was clearly of no immediate benefit to the merchants and planters, the peasants and ordinary folk of Tobago benefited from the lower costs of goods in Trinidad and from an impartial judiciary that brought swift justice to the hardship that they had suffered by judges biased in favour of the ruling merchant and planter class. They demonstrated their own confidence in the new country not by going back to the Windward Islands, as was advocated by the planters and merchants, but by migrating to Trinidad to participate in the greater opportunities created by the annexation. This optimism about the future of Tobago in the union was aptly expressed by the West India Royal Commission of 1897, which stated:

> *"The record of Tobago for the past 20 years is a gloomy one, but happiness is not synonymous with wealth, and the condition of the people is decidedly better than the figures we have given would appear to indicate. This result appears to be mainly due to the healthiness of the climate, and the fact that Trinidad provides a market close at hand for both produce and labour."[184]*

FACTORS THAT INFLUENCED THE DECISION

The two principal issues that confronted the policy makers in 1888 were the economic viability of the island community and the constitutional arrangement for its effective government. When in retrospect we judge the merits of the decision process of such historic political events, we have, in fact, to make two different judgements. Firstly we assess the decision based on the facts and opinions that went into the decision making process, and secondly we look at the outcome and results. A judgement of the second type requires a historical review of the performance of the union and is not my concern here. The union of Trinidad and Tobago is therefore to be judged here in the historical context in which the decision was made.

---

[184] *Report of the Royal West India Commission 1897*, printed as *Council Paper No. 153 of 1897* of the Legislative Council of Trinidad and Tobago.

THE ECONOMIC PROBLEM AND ITS SOLUTION

- **Physical Size**

The small physical size of Tobago, we know, need not be a crippling handicap. There are several modern examples of minuscule states that are economically viable. There is the classical example of the Greek city-states and modern examples in Vatican City (0.4 square kilometres; Monaco (1.89 square kilometres); Liechtenstein (160.01 square kilometres); Barbados (430 square kilometres); Singapore (573 square kilometres; and Hong Kong (1046 square kilometres). Tobago's small physical size, in combination with a number of other inherent shortcomings, led to its neglect by those with a proprietary interest in the colony. The challenge posed by its size is best summed up by the historian Gordon K. Lewis:[185]

> *"The general neglect of the West Indies was worse, of course, for the smaller units of the Leewards and Windwards, due to the comparative smallness of their constituent communities, the tiny scale of their economic activities and their distribution over an oceanic area large enough to make frequent communication a fairly expensive matter."*

- **Economy Based on a Monoculture of Sugar**

Adding to the shortcoming of physical size was the monoculture of sugar production. Buoyed by the success of sugar production, particularly during the French occupation, earlier production of indigo and cotton had dwindled to a trickle. The economy therefore suffered a double blow when price deflation set in throughout the sugar industry worldwide after the Napoleonic wars. Despite a sevenfold

---

[185] Lewis, Gordon K., *The Growth of the Modern West Indies*, New York, NY: he Monthly Review Press, 1968, p. 118.

increase in the production of coconuts between 1850 and 1880, the colony relied on the sugar industry, which was affected by factors such as the introduction of the sugar beet; the introduction of bounties; the introduction of new technology and management in the manufacture of sugar; the refusal of absentee landlords to reinvest in the industry after the abolition of the slave trade; and the abolition of slavery. However, there were efforts to diversify the agricultural production. In 1860, coconuts had become the second largest source of export earnings, and cocoa was conceived as an alternative to sugar cane. The Royal West India Commissioners of 1897 were clear that the failure of the sugar industry in Tobago was not due to inadequate supervision or industry but to the obsolete plant used and the antiquated technology used in the production of sugar. In recommending the complete amalgamation of the island with Trinidad, the commissioners prognosticated that there was little or no future for the sugar industry in Tobago.

- **Labour Problem**

The abolition of slavery added to the labour problems of the island. Because of the low level of wages, the island could not afford the cost of importing indentured workers (as was done in Trinidad), nor did its low wages attract surplus labour from the neighbouring territories. Compared with the other West Indian islands it had poor infrastructure. The low wages available in Tobago precluded migration as a means of attracting labour.

- **Poor Infrastructure**

Thus while we tend to emphasise the weakness of the economy as the principal reason for the decision, we tend to overlook the deficiencies in the transport and telecommunication facilities between Tobago and the outside world that severely hampered its development. Estranged from its principal administrative centre in Grenada at the time of the union,

Tobago had no telegraphic service and a mail service that left a great deal to be desired.

The roads connecting the coastal villages and the sugar estates were of poor quality; much travel around the island was done by sea; there were poor shipping arrangements with the other West Indian islands.

- **Security**

Most essential for the viability of the colony was the capacity for defending its borders. The history of the island had taught, if anything, the lesson of its vulnerability. Apart from the issue of economic viability, there are the matters of security and foreign relations. The uncertainty that surrounded the fate of Tobago late in the 1880s was similar to that experienced by a number of smaller islands in the Caribbean: the Turks and Caicos Islands, the Cayman Islands, Montserrat, St. Kitts-Nevis-Anguilla, and the British Virgin Islands.

THE SOCIAL PROBLEM AND ITS SOLUTION

With the plantocracy in Tobago in retreat because of their economic woes, their attitude towards the lower classes was hardly likely to change. The union, however, as a possible solution would embed the mass of the people of Tobago into a larger community and one where there was manifestly less hostility towards the lower classes. This was not an entirely new idea, since Tobago was in such a position for most of the time period 1763 to 1888. But the growing relationship with Trinidad, with the prospect of improved interisland transport and communications and the healthy economic prospects, was more likely to produce new opportunities for the majority of the people of Tobago as never before. Trinidad had undergone a vast social transformation over the past hundred years, beginning with the Cedula of Population and waves of immigration that involved Europeans, runaway and freed slaves from the West Indies, immigrants from India, and to some extent those from China and Portugal.

SOLUTIONS TO THE DEVELOPMENT ISSUE

The most drastic proposal for the solution to problem of Tobago came from the governor of Trinidad, Sir William Robinson. Familiar as he was with the problems of colonial administration generally, and of the administration of Tobago in particular when he was governor of the Windward Islands based in Barbados, he proposed that Tobago be depopulated, with its entire population moved to the area of Moruga in south Trinidad. His proposal mirrored a policy pursued in Trinidad since the 1780s with the grant of Crown lands to immigrants. In any event it was evident from the Tobago census of 1881 that emigration was taking labourers from Tobago to Trinidad. The notion of relocation was not a new one to the West Indies; after the riots in Barbados in the early nineteenth century, that country exiled many dissidents by sending them to the British colony of Belize in Central America and to Sierra Leone. His proposal also attempted to reduce drastically the cost of administration in Tobago.

FISHERIES

Tobago, as an island with little land area, possessed relatively large marine resources. The island had a great fishing resource which if properly exploited would have been sustainable and would have improved its economic viability. According to *Young's Journal*:

> *"Fish abound: turtle; grouper; kingfish; snappers; green cavali; snook and mackerel of the best kind and largest size."*[186]

It is somewhat surprising given the abundance of fish reported in Tobago that no attempt was made to develop the fishing industry during the trying times experienced in the colony. While the production of marine nutrients appears to be relatively low throughout the Caribbean, the situation in Trinidad and Tobago is

---

[186] Young, Sir William, *Young's Journal*, cited in Douglas Archibald, Rupert, *Tobago: Melancholy Isle, Vol. II*, 1782-1805, Port-of-Spain, Trinidad: UWI School of Continuing Studies, 1995, p. 155.

moderated by a number of factors: its geographical location in the South Equatorial current, the riverine discharges from Venezuela and Guyana, and the proximity to the continental shelf. One possible explanation for neglect of fishing as an industry may have been a question of economic viability.[187] But the Nova Scotia fisheries were exploited by Europeans not long after the voyages of Columbus and were certainly well known to the French, British, and the Basques of Spain. Indeed the staple of production from those fisheries—the salted cod—became a staple of the diet of the slaves of the West Indies. But given the dire hardship experienced in Tobago, fishing as a means of livelihood was known to the Amerindians and was a ready alternative to the floundering sugar industry. Little training and capital were required as, indeed, most of the fishing in the New Foundland fishery was done from small boats.

REARING OF FARM ANIMALS

There was further potential for economic diversity in the rearing of selected animals. The Royal West India Commission of 1897 reported of Tobago:

> *"It is better for the rearing of horses, cattle and sheep than any of the other southern islands of the West Indies."*[188]

Although the colonies of the West Indies were almost all sugar producing, the decline of the industry did not cause them all to collapse, as did the economy in Tobago. What made Tobago economically vulnerable and unviable was its lack of capital and sustainable revenue, and the lack of diversity in its economic programme.

---

[187] "The importation of large and cheap quantities of cod fish, dating from the 17th century, reduced the dependence on local maritime resources and relegated fishing to a tertiary industry." Editor's note in Kenny, J. S. and Bacon, P. R., *Aquatic Resources* in Cooper, St. G. C., and Bacon, P. R. (Eds.), *The Natural Resources of Trinidad and Tobago*, London: Edward Arnold Publishers, 1981, p. 112.

[188] *Report of the Royal West India Commission 1897*, printed as *Council Paper No. 153 of 1897* of the Legislative Council of Trinidad and Tobago.

Diversification of Agriculture

Towards the end of the nineteenth century Trinidad and Grenada between them had a virtual monopoly on cocoa in the British market, and Tobago had the potential of participating in this lucrative market. It was only in 1876 that the start was made for cocoa to replace sugar cane as the main staple. The increase in the production of coconuts after 1850 had only a marginal effect on the fortunes of the colony

Change of Financial and Economic Policy

The brief French interlude had demonstrated the benefits of state dirigisme. Both the mercantilism that protected the colony's trade in the early nineteenth century and the laissez-faire policy that followed it had failed, and a fresh approach was required with some sort of financial assistance from the imperial government. All solutions to the economic problem required substantial finance. It was clear that the resources for development could not be raised on the island, where landowners could not pay the metayers, estate owners could not pay taxes, and money was a very scarce commodity.

The Constitutional Problem and Its Solution

The Weakness in the Order in Council of 1888

The Order in Council of 1888 intended the formation of a unitary state and not a federal state, since there was one Legislature for the two former colonies. But there were weaknesses, nevertheless, inherent in the legislation that went to great lengths to specify the functions of the Legislature and of the judiciary in the new colony. Its one weakness was in specifying the role of the executive. If, indeed, a form of local government was intended for Tobago, the legislation ought to have drawn clear lines between the executive authority of the newly created central government and that of the local government in Tobago. It was true that the executive authority was vested in the governor acting with the advice of the executive council but a proper specification of that authority would have reduced the ambiguity surrounding the new executive at the same time that it placed a greater responsibility for the latter in the development of Tobago. As the law stood then, the government was responsible for everything in Tobago except that which was allocated to the Financial Board by the Order in Council of 1888. In this respect the Order in Council of 1898 went a great deal further in defining areas from which the Legislature in the central government was excluded. But the oversight of 1888 was excusable. Trinidad was so much larger and so much more resourceful than Tobago that it was tacitly assumed, as that was the natural thing to do, that the executive in Trinidad would run the show. In any event as a Crown colony the executive was dominated by the governor. This perhaps is the real reason why more consideration was not given to the matter in 1888. However, national government and local government were not new concepts, certainly not new to Trinidad, where the Cabildo of the earlier Spanish government had mutated into municipal government. Local government already existed in Trinidad: there were three municipalities, and the ward system had been established since 1840.

Although it was contemplated that the Tobago Financial Board would be responsible for some form of local government, the relationship between the national government and the local government needed to be spelt out in more detail. The powers of the Financial Board of Tobago have been largely exaggerated. The wardens of Trinidad as conceived in 1851 held similar powers and for similar purposes. This may seem pedantic in a population of less than 250,000 persons. The existence of this subordinate form of government in Trinidad should have informed those participating in the decision making process for the union as it became increasingly obvious to the legislators after 1889. When he was making the case for party politics in Trinidad and Tobago in 1955, Dr Williams took pains to point out the difference between local government and national government:

> "The programme is a national programme, too, in the sense that it deals with national issues affecting the country as a whole and not parochial issues limited to a section of it. Standpipes, drains, sidewalks, telephone

*boxes, cemeteries are parochial matters, not national
issues. They come within the jurisdiction of the County
council, and not the Legislative Council.*[189]

This definition of local government, given by Dr Williams some
seventy-seven years later, bears an uncanny resemblance to Clause
XX of the Order in Council of 1888 and supports the interpretation
that some form of local government was what was intended by that
order. The persons to whom the weakness of the Order in Council of
1888 would have been least obvious were the authorities in Tobago.
They saw the change, not so much in terms of losing their autonomy
to a central government based in Trinidad but rather as shifting the
locus of the centre of their own administration from Grenada to
Trinidad. Although it took some time to recognise this weakness it
was corrected eventually by the Order of Council of 1898.

That order placed the government in Tobago on a proper footing with
the government of Trinidad and Tobago by defining it as a specific
area for administrative purposes. That definition recognised at once
the peculiar nature of Tobago as a special area by having its name
integrated into the name of the colony.

We must in retrospect not overlook the fact that the colonial
administration in establishing the union was in relatively uncharted
waters. In none of the prior arrangements for Tobago were the
administrators in Tobago subordinate to their legislators, even after
the downgrades from governor to lieutenant governor and from
lieutenant governor to administrator.

THE DECAY OF CIVIL SOCIETY

The effect of the abolition of slavery has been viewed mainly in
economic terms, largely because of the impact of the loss of forced

---

[189] Williams, Dr. E. E., *The Case for Party Politics in Trinidad and Tobago,*
in Sutton, Dr. Paul K., Compiler, *Forged From the Love of Liberty:
Selected Speeches of Dr. Eric Williams,* Port-of-Spain, Trinidad: Longmans
Caribbean, 1981, p. 107.

labour on the sugar industries. But in some cases the impact on the functioning of the society was just as disruptive and nearly disastrous. Napoleon's attempt to reintroduce slavery in Santo Domingo produced the Haitian Revolution; when Lincoln in the United States finally announced his intention to put an end to slavery, the result was the threat of secession followed by Civil War; the aftermath of the abolition of slavery in Jamaica was the Morant Bay riots of 1868 that resulted in the imposition of Crown colony government.

In Tobago the social erosion and decay in civic life was slow but definite and reached its peak in the Belmanna riots of 1876. Signs of disaffection by the leadership in Tobago first appeared in the period before emancipation. There was strong reaction, including petitions to the Crown, against the attempts by the imperial government to ameliorate the condition of the slaves. Emancipation only made that situation worse because the rights of the slaves had been enhanced whilst those of the plantocracy were correspondingly reduced. The hostility towards the lower classes increased with the extension of the franchise so that when Crown colony government was introduced, it was a welcomed source of relief to the plantocracy, who viewed the change in terms of political power passing to the imperial government and thus curbing the power of the lower classes. By then there was an erosion of the Legislature, when the planter class became indifferent due to their personal decline and the increasing rights of the black population. Eventually the members began to absent themselves from meetings of the Legislative Council and other community meetings. The record shows that several attempts to modify the constitution between 1850 and 1888 brought no relief to the island. There is no better expression of the sense of injustice in which the majority of Tobagonians lived than in the fervour with which they welcomed the chief justice on each of his visits to Tobago. It must be noted that the attitude of the plantocracy towards the humble folk had changed only minimally since the abolition of slavery, even as we must sympathise with them over their huge financial losses. The state of justice as found by the new chief justice was so deplorable that he was moved to hear cases *in forma pauperis* in a programme of affirmative action, much to the disgust of the members of the plantocracy.

It is clear in retrospect that some sort of constitutional reform was needed in Tobago, and the union was probably the best choice of all the alternatives available at that time.

ALTERNATIVES TO UNION

In formally proposing the union with Trinidad as a solution to the Tobago problem, Lord Glanville suggested the relationship between the Turks and Caicos and Jamaica as a model for the constitutional arrangement. That was one of several options available. In studying colonialism, Osterhammel distinguished more than forty categories of overseas territories in British colonial law at the start of the twentieth century.[190] The proposal raised at once questions of the constitutional arrangements and the name of the new entity that would result. Some of these are all examined in retrospect. It will be seen that they were all challenged with economic viability. Cost was most certainly a factor that all the alternatives to the union would have had to address. The decision to form the union, therefore, was not a knee jerk reaction to the bankrupt economy of Tobago but was the considered opinion of leaders with wide knowledge and wide experience of the West Indies.

- **Complete Sovereignty**

Complete sovereignty to Tobago in 1889 would have anticipated the decolonisation movement by some sixty years. There was a precedent in Haiti, which won its independence from France in 1804. But Haiti won its independence by fighting a revolutionary war and, despite its freedom, was far from being an ideal state. If anything, it was considered a pariah of sorts; its independence was only recognised by France in 1825 in return for some crippling reparations, by Britain in 1833, and by the United States in 1862. In Tobago the Belmanna riots were put down after three days, as good

---

[190] Österhammel, Jürgen, *Colonialism*, Princeton, NJ: Markus Wiener Publishers, 1995, p.15.

an indicator as any that Tobago was in no position to fight for its independence nor was the imperial power prepared to yield. Indeed, without the advancement of huge sums for its infrastructural development in addition to substantial technical aid, it would have been perverse to grant to Tobago complete sovereignty at that time.

- **Traditional Assembly**

To grant the traditional colonial Assembly to Tobago in 1889 would have turned the clock backwards a few years. That system was rejected for a number of reasons and would have reintroduced costs without corresponding benefits, since the material condition of the people had not been altered to make democracy viable even if the pressing economic problem was disregarded.

- **Crown Colony**

Tobago could have been made a separate Crown colony like Trinidad. This was almost the status it had in 1888 but would have required the reinstatement of the post of governor with the attendant costs for security.

- **Confederation with Windward Islands**

This would have been a reversion to the Constitution of Tobago of 1888. This option was clearly not acceptable to the mass of people who were migrating to Trinidad and were establishing commercial links between the two colonies as small traders.

- **Confederation with Trinidad**

To create a viable confederation would have been very challenging given the wide disparity in resources that existed at the time from Trinidad, with its population of 200,000, and Tobago, with its population of 18,000.

- **Federal Constitution with Trinidad**

The British North America Act of 1867 had given Canada a federal constitution; in 1885, Australia had been given a federal council (although it had no executive powers). The federal Constitution of Canada did not deprive Britain of its legislative control or of its control of foreign affairs. Indeed, it was only with the passage of time, with the growth of provincial rights, and through judicial interpretation that the Constitution of Canada became truly federal. In any case such a federal structure for Trinidad and Tobago would have made the government top heavy and unduly unbalanced, given the disparity in the sizes of the islands, although it would have possessed the advantage of having its administrative functions more precisely defined.

- **Modified Unitary Statehood with Trinidad**

The union could have anticipated the form of the relationship of Northern Ireland (1920) in the United Kingdom. Northern Ireland by statute has its own cabinet and complete autonomy in domestic affairs, although its Parliament remains subordinate to the Parliament at Westminster.

- **An Archipelagic State**

The internal structure could have been like the Turks and Caicos, the Bahamas, St. Vincent and the Grenadines, and the Cayman Islands. If it were intended that Tobago be a dependency of Trinidad, that colony could have easily been renamed Trinidad and its Dependencies, with Tobago listed among the latter. A similar procedure had been followed in St. Vincent and the Grenadines. That country, for administrative purposes, is divided into six parishes, with five of them in St. Vincent and with the Grenadines making up the sixth parish. In any event, the name of the unified colony since 1889 has been Trinidad and Tobago, so that the identity of Tobago was never lost in the union, although as a neutral isle during the early eighteenth century it had no clear identity, as was agreed at the Treaty of Aix-la-Chapelle.

- **British Overseas Protected States**

As another alternative, Tobago could have been retained as a British colony, as it was during the period 1763 to 1888. This is essentially the condition of Anguilla; Bermuda; British Virgin Islands; Cayman Islands; Montserrat; and the Turks and Caicos Islands. But cognizance must be taken that in some cases the journey has been almost as tortuous as that of Tobago. The worst example is that of the Turks and Caicos. In this case the country was exploited by the Bermudans and then by the Bahamians; it opted for independence; it was linked to Jamaica; it was taken over as a colony of Jamaica; it severed links with Jamaica; it was ruled by Bahamians; finally it was a British protectorate. This appears to be the option favoured by most of the critics of the union, although it is inconsistent with the political independence that they all seem to crave.

- **Relocation of the Population**

As a last resort, the population could have been relocated. Relocation of the population was an administrative measure familiar to the people of Barbados. The idea of relocation went to the root of the problem. It sensed (correctly, in my opinion) that the political failure of Tobago was a consequence of the poor societal structure that arose from the colonisation process as a sugar producing country. Relocation, like total annexation, would have the effect of embedding the population of Tobago into a larger, more integrated group where the leaders were generally less hostile to the mass of the populace. After the riots of the 1820s in Barbados, some of the rioters were relocated to Belize and Sierra Leone. The internal structure could have been like the Turks and Caicos, the Bahamas, St. Vincent and the Grenadines, and the Cayman Islands.

Almost all of these alternatives to the constitutional arrangement, however, would have been counterintuitive. They would have imposed a more costly administration in a situation where the requirement was to reduce that cost. In particular the federal structure that would have preserved Tobago as a separate state would have necessitated a political superstructure of three legislatures, three judiciaries, and three executives. That choice would have added to the burden of administration without having any significant improvement over the system that was proposed. There was no viable option for a union in which the interests of the Tobagonians would not be subordinate to the interests of Trinidad. The flaw in the Order of Council of 1888 was that it attempted to maintain the status quo in Tobago when change was required. Any form of union, whether with Trinidad or any other island or group, would have resulted in loss of identity and of autonomy in Tobago, and the arrangements in which it stood alone were unviable. In a federation, there would still be loss of identity, autonomy, and self-determination. These losses come about simply because the uniting parties are subject to a new authority. The Legislature in Trinidad equally lost its identity. Before the union the members of that council did not have to abide the opinions of members from Tobago. The unitary option was therefore the best possible arrangement for Tobago at that time. With Trinidad its closest neighbour, its communication problems were minimised. The vibrant economy in Trinidad provided a ready market for the goods produced in Tobago; surpluses generated by the economy of Trinidad would be available for infrastructure and general development in Tobago.

The Amerindian name for the island was "Tabaco"; Columbus named the island "Assumption"; the early Europeans named the island "Tobago" "Tobago" has endured.

It is ironic, calling to mind Santayana's dictum, that the people of Tobago sought in the late 1970s to reintroduce a system that, when it was abolished, was oppressive to the majority of Tobagonians. The misplaced nostalgia over the ancient House of Assembly that existed only between 1874 and 1888 can be explained only by a perception that the circumstances had changed radically from what it was in 1888.

A major factor propelling the union was the high cost of the administration in Tobago. During the 1830s, Herman Merivale, who had served in the Colonial Office, pointed out the top heavy nature of the administrations in the West Indian colonies. The aim of reducing the cost of governance was a major consideration in the union in Canada, brought about by the British North America Act of 1867.

THE IMMEDIATE EFFECTS OF THE UNION

The most harmful effects of the union were the change of identity, and loss of autonomy, and self-determination by the people of Tobago. Change of identity is inevitable whenever two entities unite to form a larger single entity.

THE CHANGE OF IDENTITY

The very act of union creates a new identity. This was certainly the case in the unity of Sparta and Athens, in the union of England with Scotland, and in the federation that established the United States of America. The term "loss of identity" is perhaps inaccurate, for what occurs in most cases is a new identity of the smaller unit in relation to the larger unit. The identity of an object is only of significance in relation to other objects, and that relationship defines its identity. This was certainly one of the greatest fears expressed by the delegates

to the Constitution Convention to create the federal Constitution of
the United States of America. The truth about identity is that it can
have many facets. In the case of Tobago there is its identity as a
political unit together with the idyllic image created by Defoe. The
image of Tobago as a self-governing colony had to change after the
union since, as we have seen, than status was untenable. The failure
or refusal by the administrators in Tobago to accept this change in
identity as part of a unified Trinidad and Tobago hampered severely
the progress on the island in the period 1889 to 1899. But compared
with a number of other West Indian islands that had the same political
institutions as Tobago did in the eighteenth and early nineteenth
century, Tobago lost an identity that the others preserved. The loss of
identity, if acknowledged, was not unique in the evolving geopolitics
of the Americas. By 1889 Quebec had been absorbed into Canada
and East Florida and West Florida were fully integrated into the
United States of America. It will be recalled that the governments
of those countries were created at the same time the government of
Grenada, which included Tobago, was created in 1763.

Loss of Autonomy

At the union Tobago was subordinate to Grenada, which was itself
a British colony. Despite the nobility of the ideas of autonomy and
self-determination, these issues were considered at the time of the
union and rejected by the British government and by the people of
Tobago. Autonomy was, obviously, not a viable option, as Lewis
pointed out, in the face of its minuscule size; it small constituent
community; and its poor infrastructure. Those factors adversely
affected its security.

Tobago's small size engendered problems of development shared
with a number of West Indian colonies: the Turks and Caicos
Islands; the Cayman Islands; Montserrat; St. Kitts-Nevis-Anguilla;
and the British Virgin Islands. The Turks Islands, in particular, had
had a tortuous existence; they had been in turn Spanish, French
and British. In 1848 the inhabitants of the Turks Islands, while
under the jurisdiction of the Bahamas, successfully petitioned the
Crown and it was made a separate colony governed by a council

president under the supervision of the Jamaican government. The move turned out to be unsuccessful as the island was in financial ruin. Annexed by Jamaica in 1873 with its own Legislature, the suggestion that Lord Glanville made as regards the Turks Islands in 1886 was, therefore, apt and a worthwhile precedent. We know from the studies of classical Greece that physical size need not be a critical variable in the determination of the economic viability of a state. This is so despite the fact that size may be related to other critical factors such as population, natural resources, and proximity to markets. Apart from the issue of economic viability there are the matters of security and foreign relations. The uncertainty that surrounded the fate of Tobago late in the 1880s was similar to that experienced by a number of smaller islands in the Caribbean. This was the arrangement proposed by Lord Glanville.

LOSS OF SELF-DETERMINATION

Of all the options available, the one that was least likely to be adopted was independence for Tobago. The United Provinces of Holland in 1581, the United States of America in 1776, and the Haitian Revolution of 1804 had settled the right of self-determination by warfare. As early as 1651 the notion of independence had arisen in Barbados in reaction to the passage of the Navigation Act in the English Parliament.[191] The act had threatened to restrict the trade between Barbados and the North American colonies. This was essentially a problem of security and was most likely in the wake of Barbados's Declaration of Independence of 1651. The Barbados reaction came after the promulgation of the Navigation Act of 1651.

---

[191] That Act was itself a form of retaliation to a failed attempt by the English to negotiate with the Dutch over the lucrative sea trade that the latter then dominated. Despite the defeat of the Spanish Armada by the British in 1588 it was the Dutch mariners with their superior science and technology that broke the back of Spanish sea power and dominated the maritime trade by early in the seventeenth century as they became the foremost commercial nation of the world. cf., Braddick, Michael J., *The English Government, War, Trade, and Settlement, 1625-1688.* In Canny, Nicholas (Ed.), *The Oxford History of the British Empire, Vol. I,* Oxford: Oxford University Press, 1998, p.302.

The Declaratory Act of 1766, passed with the repeal of the Stamp Act that met with widespread criticism in America, asserted the authority of the British Parliament over the colonial governments.

The attitude of the British hardened after the loss of the American Colonies. Humiliated in a series of naval reverses only twenty years after the naval supremacy that was evident at the end of the Seven Years War, the British were not prepared to countenance independence movements in any of their colonies. In fact the tendency was, where politically feasible, to bring the colonies under direct control in the Crown colony system.

In an era of colonialism, the concept of self-determination by referendum did not exist. To grant independence to Tobago in 1889 would have been perverse, and the new colonial policy of Joseph Chamberlain had confirmed if not initiated a new sense of responsibility. If Palmerston was the champion of laissez-faire, then Joseph Chamberlain, was the champion of state intervention to provide the invisible guiding hand. Chamberlain stated:

"It is not enough to occupy certain great spaces of the world's surface unless you can make the best of them— unless you are willing to develop them."[192]

Indeed, Britain's loss of dominance had promoted the notion of constructive imperialism that sought to consolidate all the British colonies into a unit for the purpose of defense and economic viability. This was a rudimentary start of the British commonwealth and in that circumstance the autonomy of Tobago was not on the cards. The idea of Tobago being given independence in 1889 pre-dated by thirty years Canada's full-fledged membership of the community of nations; by forty years the Statute of Westminster; and by nearly sixty years India's independence from Britain.

---

[192] Cited in Green, E. H. H., *Political Economy of Empire.* in Porter, Andrew (Ed.), *The Oxford History of the British Empire Vol. III: The Nineteenth Century*, Oxford: Oxford University Press, 1999, p. 351.

The option of Tobago seeking autonomy, as Haiti did in the face of economic doom, was suicidal and not considered, particularly by the people of Tobago. Their antipathy to the union with Trinidad would have been resolved preferably by a reversion to the association with the Windward Islands, as the petitioners had requested when the union was falling apart in the mid-1890s, or in the extreme case, an association with Canada, as the Bajans had tried. Autonomy is seen as a virtue, but separatism is seen as a vice. The realisation of the union, therefore transcended whatever Tobago lost in its identity, autonomy, and self-determination from the union.

The faulty development policies of the colonial government may have precipitated the union with Trinidad. One way of avoiding the union was to examine the causes of the failure. A 1957 report noted:

> *"Had the necessary capital, labour and skill been available in the 19th century, when things began to decline, the island might have been one of the most prosperous territories in the Caribbean."[193]*

The report was accurate in its assessment but it does not answer the questions of why there were shortages of capital, skills, and labour in Tobago at that time. Perhaps a glance across the sea to Trinidad may yield some explanation. For while Tobago was languishing, its neighbour Trinidad was prospering. One of the differences had to do with land ownership. The Tobago estates were owned by absentee landlords.

One of the effects of the union was the heightening of political consciousness on both islands. The union added stability to the administration in Tobago at the same time it assigned the greater responsibility for the laws, standards and security to a body much larger in outlook and scope than the Tobago Legislature. In the case

---

[193] *Tobago, Planning Team Report*, Port-of-Spain, Trinidad: Colonial Development and Welfare, 1957), p.20., cited by Robinson, A. N. R., *The Mechanics of Independence*, Cambridge, MA and London: MIT Press, 1971, p. 19.

of Tobago there were public meetings and memorials about the state of the union. In the case of Trinidad there were a series of attempts to institute an elective Assembly.

The union had the following economic effects in Tobago: it immediately enlarged the market for goods produced in Tobago and brought that market closer to home; it stimulated the diversity of its agricultural produce; it increased the opportunities for its labour force to gain access a greater range of jobs and skills with higher wages through the freedom of movement; it resulted in a reduction in the cost of imported goods through the common external tariff; it provided its entrepreneurs access a larger pool of development resources and provided a marginally improved communication with the external world.

THE NEW COLONIAL POLICY

Lewis suggests that one reason why Tobago found itself in its predicament at the time of the union was because of neglect by the imperial government. To an extent Dr Williams agreed with this and went further to put the blame on colonial policy. He thought the arrangement an example of:

> *"Britain's readiness to propose or support any arrangement, however fantastic, which might reduce financial obligations to the West Indies, relieve it if the burden of administering these small colonies, and make concessions to any vested interest which Britain thought it necessary to placate, as it had throughout the 19th century placated the sugar interest in Trinidad in respect of indentured immigration at public expense."[194]*

Williams seems to have tacitly acknowledged the laissez-faire attitude of the British government towards development in Tobago.

---

[194] Williams, Dr. E. E., *History of the People of Trinidad and Tobago*, New York, NY: A & B Publishing, 1993, p. 147.

In doing so, Dr Williams was embedding the matter of the policy of the British government towards Tobago in the broader problem of the British government's position on the development of the West Indies. But it is possible that he overlooked a change that was taking root in the British colonial policy towards the end of the nineteenth century.

In Trinidad, if not in Tobago, there were glimpses of this new colonial policy one year after the Morant Bay riots took place in Jamaica. Embarrassed by the many irregularities that confronted him after he assumed the governorship, Sir Arthur Hamilton Gordon made a portentous speech at Couva in November 1869:

> *"During my administration . . . at least one important change has taken place. The new policy of England [Britain] with regard to the colonies is now better-established and better understood than heretofore . . . Five-and-twenty or thirty years ago, the conduct of England [Britain] towards her colonies was generous and liberal, but above all it was masked by a desire to Anglicize—to print her own stamp on all her subjects—to introduce her laws and institutions wherever she ruled. She now has realized the impolicy of such a course when she has to deal with an established civilization and another race. . . . The colonies shall be treated on quite another principle to that on which they have hitherto been ruled."[195]*

By the 1890s, the new position, probably implemented by Chamberlain and inspired by J. R. Seeley and W. A. S. Hewins, arose from the need to consolidate the empire then threatened by the rise of the United States, Germany, Russia and France. The urgency was seen in the demise of the sugar industry and its effects in the British West Indies. The report of the West India Royal Commission that examined the state of the sugar industry in the West Indies in 1897 hinted at this new policy. The commission recognised the role

---

[195] Wood, Donald, *Trinidad in Transition*, Oxford: Oxford University Press, 1986, pp. 292, 293.

that bounties given in Europe and elsewhere for the production of sugar led to a fall in demand for West Indian sugar. There were other factors: the Germans produced their beet sugar using less labour and modern chemical technology. But the commission was adamant that Britain held great responsibility for and had a role to play in the future development of the West Indian colonies, even if it involved pecuniary sacrifices on the part of the mother country. The pecuniary sacrifices were to be given in terms of development loans for infrastructure and education from money raised on the London market through the Crown Agents. Very noticeable was the humanitarian approach to the issue.[196]

"The black population of these Colonies was originally placed in them by force as slaves; the race was kept up and increased under artificial conditions maintained by the authority of the British government. What the people were at the time of emancipation, and their very presence in the Colonies at all, were owing to British action, or the action of other European nations for the results of whose policies the United Kingdom assumed responsibility on taking possession of the territories in question; we could not by the single act of freeing them, divest ourselves of the responsibility for their future which must necessarily be the outcome of the past and the present. For generations the great mass of the population must remain dependent upon British influence for good government, and generally for the maintenance of the progress that they have made hitherto. We cannot abandon them, and if economic conditions become such that private enterprise and the profits of trade and cultivation cease to attract white men to the Colonies, or to keep them there, this may render it more difficult for the British Government to discharge its obligations but will not in any way diminish the force of them. We have placed the labouring population where it is, and created for it the conditions moral and material,

---

[196] *Report of the West India Commission 1897*, printed as *Council Paper No. 153 of 1897* of the Legislature Council of Trinidad and Tobago.

279

*under which it exists; and we cannot divest ourselves of
responsibility for its future."*

Under the old laissez-faire policy, there was very little direct
investment by the British government in the colonies. In keeping with
the prevailing economic doctrine, there was little or no intervention
from the state in economic matters. One exception appears to have
occurred after the devastation by the hurricane of 1847. After being
petitioned by the Council and Assembly, the Crown agreed to grant
a sum of £50,000 by way of a loan to be repaid from the revenue
of the colony. The money was disbursed in minimum sums of £50
by loan commissioners to owners and others—interested in landed
property—who were affected by the hurricane. In general, charters
were granted by the king, giving exclusive rights, and Crown lands
were sold to enterprising individuals. This arrangement reached it
apotheosis in the establishment of the East India Company (British)
that held a monopoly over trade in the East Indies.

The success of the union would depend not only on the creativity
of the new Legislature but to some extent on colonial policy. We
saw already, in the recommendations of the Royal West India
Commission of 1897, a fresh acknowledgement of responsibility
for the mother country in the granting of loans for infrastructure
development. This was a marked departure from the laissez-faire
policy of the Palmerston era. But this in itself was taking place with
policy changes on a broader canvas. The time had come to act on J.
R. Seely's aphorism:

> *"We seem to have conquered and peopled half the world
> in a fit of absence of mind."*[197]

Seely's aphorism depicts the serendipitous approach of the British
to the empire. This was also noted by Elliot when comparing the

---

[197] Cited by Green, E. E., *The Political Economy of Empire, 1830-1914*, in
Porter, Andrew (Ed.), *The Oxford History of the British Empire Vol. III: The
Nineteenth Century*, Oxford: Oxford University Press, 1999, p. 346.

Spanish Empire with the British Empire in the Americas.[198] Towards the end of the nineteenth century, when the rise of the United States of America, of Germany, of Russia and of France presented a growing challenge to the empire, the outcome was a rethinking of the empire and its future. From 1886 a series of Colonial Conferences were held involving Britain and the self-governing colonies. If Palmerston was the champion of laissez-faire, then Joseph Chamberlain, who was secretary of state between 1895 and 1903, was the champion of state intervention to provide the invisible guiding hand. Chamberlain stated:

> *"It is not enough to occupy certain great spaces of the world's surface unless you can make the best of them— unless you are willing to develop them."[199]*

The new policy of political economy, although it augured well for the future of the union, promised greater intervention and supervision from the mother country, it would be some considerable time, however, before those policies took shape. In the aftermath of the union, Trinidad and Tobago had to rely on its own resources for its economic development.

THE UNION AND THE LEGACY OF THE COLONIAL SYSTEM

British colonialism left the union with a universal language, modern laws, a strong central government, and cultural ties with a large number of people scattered over the earth. The colony was underdeveloped economically, but that was something that time and

---

[198] "The relatively slow and haphazard moves towards the imposition of the empire stood in marked contrast to the speed with which Spain's American territories were formally incorporated within the effective imperial network." Elliot, J. H., *Empires of the Atlantic World: Britain and Spain in America 1492-1830*, New Haven, Conn: Yale University Press, 2006, p. 119.

[199] Cited by Green, E. H. H., in *Political Economy of the Empire*, 1830-1914, in Porter, Andrew, (Ed.), *The Oxford History of the British Empire Vol. III: The Nineteenth Century*, Oxford: Oxford University Press, 1999, p. 350.

energy would cure. The most debilitating effect of the colonialism was the effect of social stratification by colour, particularly in Trinidad and it created an atmosphere in which there was a permanent sense of tension between the ruled and their rulers. This was markedly so since there were no laws enforcing such discrimination, and secondly, unlike countries like the United States of America, where the discrimination was against minorities, here the discrimination was against the majority of people. This left the majority with a cynical view of justice and a negative attitude to authority that only time would be able to heal; it also affected the ability of the society to function as a whole. It is de rigueur in the post-colonial era for politicians to blame the social ills of the West Indies on the Crown colony system. But it is fair to say that the conventional ideas here tend to confuse two issues one legal and the other social in nature: on the one hand the constitutional issue of the powerful executive exercised by the Crown with little popular participation, and on the other the sociological issue of the exclusion of the majority of people and the stratification characterised by light coloured skins at the top and the darkest skins at the bottom of the social ladder. In the US Declaration of Independence, both ideas were roundly rejected (although a political compromise entrenched racial discrimination in that country for another two hundred years).

These two problems would have been indistinguishable if the laws explicitly discriminated against people of colour, as did some of the southern US states. In fact, in the older British colonies with established assemblies, such laws did exist and their dysfunctional nature was one of the reasons for the movement towards Crown colony government. The movement was the means by which the imperial government got rid of those corrupt Legislatures. But it is evident throughout the region that even where such discriminatory laws did not exist, the same social structures emerged. The classic case of this is Trinidad. The constitutional status of Trinidad, in an era of raging debates on the humanitarian question, was settled on that of a Crown colony. At the British conquest Picton found, much to his displeasure, black soldiers in the military, lots of free coloured people, and a substantial number of property owning coloured people. Recognising the danger in passing laws to discriminate against such people, Picton hit upon the ruse of an unofficial colour bar. Despite the objectionable nature of the proposal, Picton found a willing society. Some of the immigrants that flowed to the country from the neighbouring French colonies undoubtedly brought some of their social baggage. White immigrants from Haiti, for example, would have harboured resentment against the blacks because of the revolution and its atrocities. The consequence of the imposition by Picton was a country highly stratified by colour that eventually provoked a petition to the Colonial Secretary by a member of a prominent mulatto family. The petition has been preserved for posterity and is now published in book form.[200]

CONCLUSION

The union of Tobago with Trinidad in 1889 closed a chapter in the tortuous life experienced in Tobago after the Europeans became interested in the island. Tobago, which went from its almost pristine state to that of a British sugar producing slave colony in 1763, collapsed as a viable society after emancipation in 1834. Elements of the population had lacked the experience of resolving political problems of older slave colonies, but its difficulty was aggravated by the intransigence of the plantocracy, who largely failed to adjust to the changing times. After Tobago was recognised as a failed slave colony, the union manifestly ended the instability of the previous 250 years. In some respects Trinidad was well prepared for assuming the new responsibility for the success of the union. Chacon's vision of an integrated society of free individuals living in equality without

---

[200] Jean-Baptiste Philippe was the author in 1824 of an address to Lord Bathurst, secretary of state for the colonies concerning the civil and political rights of coloured persons in Trinidad. He used the pen name *A Free Mulatto* which is the title given to the address since published in book form. He was born and grew up at Naparima in South Trinidad and graduated from Edinburgh University at the age of nineteen as a doctor. His brother Luce was a member of the inaugural legislative council of Trinidad in 1832. Michel Maxwell Philip, born 3 years earlier in the same region of Naparima known today as Philippine, is believed to be a descendent of this family that came to Trinidad from Grenada after the Cedula of population.

regard to race or origin, admired by Abercrombie[201] and endorsed by Dr James Stephen, was beginning to take shape. In the hundred years or so before the union, Trinidad had a measure of success in integrating a large and diverse number of immigrants to the colony while developing strong executive government.

The union, however, while removing the instability of life in Tobago, generated political problems of its own. The issue of which metropolitan country had the right of sovereignty over Tobago was no longer an agenda matter for the European powers. The objects of the union for Tobago were to reduce the administrative costs *"most disproportioned to its importance"*; to retain some measure of internal control; to relocate the people in a new community where normal social relationships could be developed; to be governed by a workable constitution; to foster the welfare of the people; and to provide for adequate security for the people of the island. Having viewed the alternative measures available at the time, one must conclude that the decision taken was the best that could be done. By annexing Tobago to Trinidad, the finance required for development was available from the surplus of the Trinidad economy. The relatively huge population of Trinidad provided a close and accessible market for the producers of Tobago. The successful administration in Trinidad was thought more than capable of assuming the responsibilities of the augmented colony.

We must view the suggestion of the governor, Sir William Robinson, that the island be depopulated and its inhabitants relocated at Moruga in Trinidad,[202] not so much for its eccentricity but as the desperate initiative of someone deeply concerned about the squalor and depravity in which the majority of the people of Tobago lived.

---

201 "The inhabitants are a number of Spanish, English and French. I shall endeavour as much as possible to gain them by a mild and equal government." Abercrombie, Sir Ralph, in a letter dated 28 February 1797 cited in Dunfermline, Lord James, *Lieut. Gen. Sir Ralph Abercrombie K. B., 1793-1801: A Memoir,* Edinburgh: Edmonston and Douglas, 1861, p. 57.
202 Craig-James, Dr. Susan E., *The Changing Society of Tobago 1838-1938, Vol. I, 1838-1900,* Port-of-Spain, Trinidad: Paria Publishing, 2008, p. 292.

The situation of Tobago today (2012) is vastly different from what it was in 1888. Not only has the situation there greatly improved, but the disparities between the two islands have narrowed considerably. The constitutional arrangement, however, remains naturally asymmetrical in favour of the people of Tobago: whereas Tobago has the right to secede and, according to a former prime minister, may do so at any time, it would be perverse for Trinidad to exercise such a right. In reviewing the decision to bring about the union, the victors, if any, must be the Tobagonians. The preponderance of opinions was in favour of having Tobago completely absorbed and subordinate to Trinidad, and despite this we ended with a unitary state called Trinidad and Tobago.

While they did not achieve the equality that Mr A. N. R. Robinson unreasonably desired, the identity of the island is preserved forever in the name "Trinidad and Tobago." How could equality be achieved in a union where one island had a population of 200,000 and the other a population of 18,000? It was little wonder that Sir William Robinson suggested depopulation. But although the constitution recognises Tobago as ward of Trinidad and Tobago, as an island it must be considered as different from all other wards. Circumstances change from time to time and influence political options. The Law of the Sea has given a new impetus to the secession movement in Tobago, with secessionists viewing Tobago as the Kuwait of the Caribbean. The situation in Tobago has changed radically since 1889. The population is better educated and certainly more aware of their political rights and obligations. The objective conditions may today warrant a reversion to arrangements that were unviable and impractical in 1889, should such a move prove to be in the better interest of people of Tobago.

On the broader front, the story told by Tolstoy's deaf man is a very simple one: the events that began with the Iberian claims to undiscovered lands, and the wars and buccaneerism that followed the discoveries, indicated a need for international law and international law enforcement. The American, French, and Haitian revolutions all pointed towards the establishment of a doctrine of universal human rights; Lord Mansfield's quandary over *Somerset* points to the need for the resolution of conflicts of laws; and the failure to abolish the slave trade until the treaty between the United States and Britain after the Civil War points to the need for an international authority for law enforcement. Above all else, the principal lesson learnt from the Tobago experience is that slave colonies are unviable in an era of universal human rights. One reason why those things did not occur was:

> *"Fundamentally the British Empire was about Power."*[203]

But unfortunately no one has been listening to the story of Tolstoy's deaf man.

Perhaps the most important lesson to be learnt from the Tobago experience that forced it into to the union with Trinidad relates to the constitutional doctrine of the separation of powers. Throughout the nineteenth century, in Tobago, as in several of the British West Indian colonies, there was almost constant conflict between the legislative and the executive branches of government. The conflict is inherent in all constitutions and requires to be handled with great political dexterity. As early as the 1730s this problem was observed in Trinidad between the Cabildo and the governor.[204]

An early manifestation of the conflict arose during the seventeenth century when England was declared a commonwealth and free state in 1649:

> *"All the authority formerly exercised by the Crown in Parliament was now transferred to the remnant of the Lower House, which also appropriated to itself both executive and judicial functions, interfering by means of committees even with the courts of law. It was this which led*

---

[203] Burroughs, Peter, *Imperial Institutions and the Government of Empire*, Porter, Andrew (Ed.), *The Oxford History of the British Empire Vol. III: The Nineteenth Century*, Oxford: Oxford University Press, 1999, p. 170.

[204] Borde, Pierre Gustave Louis, *The History of the Island of Trinidad Under the Spanish Government, Second Part (1622-1797 (1876))*, Port-of-Spain, Trinidad: Paria Publishing, 1982, p. 107.

Cromwell to describe it long afterwards as **the horridest** **arbitrariness that ever was exercised in the world.**"²⁰⁵

Charles-Louis de Secondat, Baron de Montesquieu, having studied the British Constitution, which he admired greatly, formulated his doctrine of the separation of powers, which was included in his publication *L'Esprit des Lois* in 1748. The doctrine was refined by Madison, one of the founding fathers of the United States of America. He, writing in *The Federalist Papers* in 1788, pointed out that in a sovereign state there can be no true separation of powers and, quite to the contrary, stipulated that the powers must not be so far separated as to have no constitutional control over each other. If the truth must be told about this, Madison's warning that the legislative branch had the natural tendency to dominate all others played itself out fully in the fledgling assemblies of the British West Indies, to the detriment of progressive executive government.

So harmful was such a relationship that the British government had to invoke transcendental powers on the grounds of humanitarianism in order to bring about the emancipation of the slaves and to replace self-governing assemblies with Crown colony government. It was the vested interests of the merchant and planter class, entrenched in the Legislature, seeking their own interests rather than those of the population at large, that prevented Tobago from achieving its full potential during the nineteenth century.

POSTSCRIPT

THE ATTITUDE OF THE PRIME MINISTER IN 1976

At the general election in 1976, the ruling People's National Movement (PNM) government, for the first time in over twenty-five years, had no parliamentary representative in Tobago. This immediately provoked questions about the administration in Tobago, more so

---

²⁰⁵ Tanner, J. R., *English Constitutional Conflicts of the Seventeenth Century 1603-1689,* Cambridge: Cambridge University Press, 1960, pp. 155, 156.

as the leader of the Tobago representatives, Mr A. N. R. Robinson, had strained relations with the prime minister after resigning from the PNM in 1970. In a victory speech that ranged over a large number of topics, Dr Williams, the prime minister, dealt with the selections of candidates for the election, the selection of ministers, the representative of the cabinet in the Senate, the appointment of candidates defeated at the election to the Senate, and the issue of Tobago.

The following are extracts from the speech concerning Tobago:[206]

"I have one final point to make dear friends, in terms of the electorate and the wishes of the electorate and somebody has raised with me the question of Tobago."

"I don't know why the question was raised. What is there has been there all the time. Nothing new and nothing much. It is part of a general malaise all over the world, a general sickness with all sorts of people wanting to go off on their own, part of a particular Caribbean madness resulting from all the flotsam and jetsam brought to the Caribbean over a century."

"They want to go off on their own small island, and they have different ways of looking at things, OK! I am not one to bother."

"I said it in Tobago: 'If you want to go, go.' We are not holding you. I'm not going to send any Coast Guard or ship or army there to hold them back. What for? They want to go, go."

"Everybody understands today that whatever used to be said in the past, we don't live in any world of true eternal love. The greatest thing today is the divorce celebration! Let's have a divorce celebration."

---

[206] *Trinidad Guardian*, 27 September 1976.

"It's a financial matter: what terms do we agree on without bitterness, without any emotion? All they have to tell me is what it is they want and how to do it. I appoint somebody to do it. I have more important things to do. So whenever they are ready, my friends, and they have voted one way, OK."

"I shall be particularly careful not to do anything in my position as Prime Minister of the country to keep Tobago in line by force. I am against [using force] and I would advise the population not to do that."

"I told Tobago a long time ago when this came up, 'You all talk about Tobago seceding from Trinidad; no big thing. The thing that you have to worry about is when the movement starts for Trinidad to secede from Tobago—that would be serious.' I am for neither."

"I claim nothing; I propose nothing, except no force. The voters have voted, and I will not use any subterfuge."

"I don't know how the party would feel; I really don't. If only on grounds of conscience, and sound political conviction, I would take no part in any move designed to keep any part of the Caribbean to some allegiance that part does not want."

The Order in Council of 1888

WHEREAS BY THE TRINIDAD and Tobago Act, 1887, Her Majesty is empowered by the Order of the Council to declare that the Colony of Trinidad and the Colony of Tobago shall, from a date to be mentioned in such Order, be united into and form one Colony on such terms and conditions as Her Majesty should, in such Order in Council, or in any subsequent Order or Orders, think fit to appoint; Now, it is hereby ordered by Her Majesty, by and with the advice of Her Privy Council as follows:

I. From and after the first day of January 1889 (hereinafter referred as "the appointed day") the Colony of Trinidad and its Dependencies and the colony of Tobago shall be united into and constitute one Colony, which shall be called the Colony of Trinidad and Tobago, upon the terms and conditions in this Order expressed, and the powers and functions of the Governor-in-Chief of the Windward Islands in respect of the Colony of Tobago, and the Administrator of Tobago, shall thereupon cease and determine, and the Executive and Legislative Council of Tobago shall thereupon cease to exist.

II. From and after the appointed day Her Majesty's Letters Patent under the Great Seal of the United Kingdom of Great Britain and Ireland, bearing date the First day of October 1880, constituting the office of Governor and Commander in Chief in and over Trinidad and its Dependencies, and all Instructions under her Majesty's sign Manual and signet to the

Governor and Commander in Chief of Trinidad and its Dependencies shall, subject to the provisions of this Order, apply to the Colony of Trinidad and Tobago, and all the provisions thereof shall, subject as aforesaid, be considered and take effect as if the Colony of Trinidad and Tobago has been named therein respectively instead if the Island of Trinidad and its Dependencies.

III. The Governor may, from time to time, appoint a fit and proper person to be commissioner for Tobago, and may, by an instrument under his hand and his public Seal of the Colony, authorize the Commissioner to exercise in Tobago, in the absence of the governor, any of the powers and authorities vested in the Governor by virtue of his Commission and of any Letters Patent for the time being in force constituting his office and of this Order, except the powers of appointing and suspending from public offices, and of exercising the prerogative of pardon.

IV. The Commissioner shall be *ex-officio* an official Member of the Legislative Council of the Colony, and at least one Member of the Legislative Council of the Colony shall be a person ordinarily resident in Tobago.

V. There shall be in Tobago a Board which shall be called the Financial Board of Tobago, and shall consist of the Commissioner and five other Members, being persons ordinarily resident in Tobago, of whom two shall be nominated by the Governor and three shall be elected as hereinafter provided.

VI. The nominated Members of the Board shall hold their seats therein until the next dissolution of the Board after the appointment unless they shall have previously resigned their seas or have been removed by virtue of the instructions from Her Majesty through the Secretary of State, or suspended by the governor, but may be reappointed. The governor may suspend any nominated Member from the exercise of his functions and shall forthwith report every such suspension to the Secretary of State. Every such suspension shall remain in force, unless and until it shall be removed by the governor, or disallowed by Her Majesty through the Secretary of State, and such disallowance shall be published in Tobago.

VII.　The Governor may from time to time appoint any person to be provisionally a Member of the Board in place of any nominated Member who shall be suspended or absent from Tobago, or otherwise incapable of exercising his functions and such Member during such suspension, absence, or incapacity, and may revoke any such provisional appointment. If any nominated member of the Board shall be absent from Tobago for six calendar months continuously, without the leave of the Governor first obtained, the Governor shall suspend him from the exercise of his functions.

VIII.　No person shall be capable of being elected a Member of the Board who,

IX.　Is not a British subject by birth or naturalization;

X.　Has not attained the age of twenty-one years;

XI.　Is the holder of any public office under the crown or under the Government of the colony;

XII.　Is not a resident occupier of a house in Tobago;

XIII.　Does not either—

XIV.　Possess a clear yearly income of £200, either in his own right or in right of his wife; or

XV.　Pay annually direct taxes of the amount of not less than £10.

XVI.　Is disqualified for registration as a voter under clause XI, of this Order.

XVII.　If any elected Member of the Board shall by writing under his hand addressed to the Governor resign his seat, or shall without the leave of the governor previously obtained be absent from the meetings of the Board for the period of six consecutive months, or shall make any declaration or acknowledgement of allegiance to any Foreign State or Power or become a citizen or subject of any Foreign State or Power, or shall be adjudicated a bankrupt, or shall be sentenced by any Court in any part of Her majesty's dominions to death, penal servitude, or imprisonment with hard labour for any term, or without hard labour for a term exceeding twelve months, or shall for a period of one month remain a party to a contract with the Government of the Colony, or shall accept any office of emolument under the Crown or under the said Government, his seat in the said Board shall thereupon become vacant, and the Governor shall forthwith issue a writ for the election of a Member to fill the vacant seat. Any question as to the fact of the seat of an elected Member having become vacant shall be decided by the Governor.

XVIII. No Member of the Board, except for the commissioner, shall site or vote therein until he shall have taken and subscribed the following oath before the Governor, or the commissioner, or some person authorized by the Governor to administer such oath:—"I, A.B., do sincerely promise and swear that I will be faithful and bear true allegiance to Her majesty Queen Victoria, Her heirs and successors according to law. So help me God."

XIX. Every male person shall be entitled to be registered in any year as a voter, and, when registered, to vote at the election of Members of the Board, who

XX. Is a British subject by birth or naturalization; and

XXI. Has attained the age of twenty-one years; and

XXII. Is under no legal incapacity; and

XXIII. Is on the 1st day of January in such year, and has during the whole of the preceding six calendar months been, a resident-occupier of a house in Tobago; and

XXIV. Has during the preceding year paid direct taxes or rates, or direct taxes and rates, in Tobago to the amount of not less than ten shillings; and

XXV.   Has paid all taxes and rates due and payable by him in Tobago up to the first day of January in such year; and

XXVI.   Has not within six calendar months immediately preceding the first day of January in such year received any relief from public funds. But no person shall be so registered or entitled to vote who shall have been sentenced by any Court in any part of Her Majesty's dominions to death, or penal servitude, or imprisonment with hard labour for any term, or without hard labour for a term exceeding twelve months, and shall not either have suffered the punishment to which he was sentenced or such other punishment as by competent authority may have been substituted therefore, or have received a free pardon from Her Majesty.

XXVII.   The Governor by proclamation make Regulations for the registration of voters for the election of Members of the Board and for regulating the election of such Members, and for the determination of disputes and questions as to the result or validity of such elections, and may in like manner repeal or amend such Regulations. All such Regulations shall be transmitted by the Governor to the Secretary of State, and may be repealed or altered by any Ordinance to be enacted by the Legislature of the Colony, and unless and until the same shall be so disallowed or repealed, or so far as the same shall not be so altered, shall have the same effect as if they had formed part of this Order, provided that they shall not be inconsistent with anything contained in this Order, or in any such Ordinance as aforesaid.

XXVIII.   The first general election of Members of the Board shall be held at such time not more than three months after the appointed day, and a general election shall be held at such time within two months after every dissolution of the Board as the Governor shall by proclamation appoint.

XXIX. The commissioner shall be the President of the Board. The Governor shall from time to time appoint one of the nominated Members to be Vice-President, and may at any time revoke such appointment. The vice-President shall act as President in the absence of the President.

XXX. The Board shall meet only when summoned by the President, but may adjourn its meetings from time to time, whenever such adjournment shall be required for the despatch of business.

XXXI. The Board shall not be disqualified for the transaction of business by reason of any vacancy or vacancies among the nominated or elected Members, but no business except that of the adjournment shall be transacted at any meeting of the Board, unless there shall be present the President or Acting President, and at least two other Members, one of whom shall be a nominated Member.

XXXII. All questions proposed for decision at meetings of the Board shall be decided by a majority of the votes of the Members present, and in the case of an equal division of votes the President or Acting President shall have a casting vote in addition to his vote as a Member of the Board.

XXXIII. The Board may from time to time make standing rules and orders for the regulation of its proceedings, but such rules and orders shall not come into operation unless and until they have been approved by the Governor.

XXXIV. The Governor may by proclamation dissolve the Board at any time. The Board, if not sooner dissolved by the governor, shall be ipso facto dissolved on the expiration of three years from the date of the return of the first writ at the last preceding general election.

XXXV. Subject to the provisions of this Order, it shall be lawful for the Board to make Regulations respecting taxation other than duties of customs or duties affecting shipping or excise duty on rum or other spirits, and respecting the collection, receipt, custody, and expenditure of the public revenue of Tobago, and respecting the borrowing of money on the credit of the revenue of Tobago, and respecting markets, cemeteries, public works, roads, the relief of and medical attendance on the poor, the granting of licenses, and matters of a purely local character, and by any such Regulations to impose penalties by fine or imprisonment with or without hard labour, or fine and imprisonment with or without hard labour for the punishment of any breach or contravention of any Regulation of the Board.

XXXVI. No Regulation passed by the Board shall come into operation until the Governor shall have assented thereto and signed the same in token of such assent, and the fact of such assent shall have been published in Tobago.

XXXVII. The Governor shall, by the first convenient opportunity, transmit an authenticated copy of every Regulation of the Board to which he shall have assented to the Secretary of State, and it shall be lawful for Her Majesty to signify Her disallowance of any such Regulation to the governor through the Secretary of State, and every Regulation so disallowed shall become null and void as soon as the disallowance thereof shall be published in Tobago.

XXXVIII. Any Member of the Board may move any Resolution, or introduce any Regulation, or propose any question for debate, provided that no Regulation shall be passed, or Regulation adopted, or question allowed for debate, the object of which shall be to dispose of or charge any part of the revenue of Tobago, unless the same be moved, introduced, or proposed by the consent or under the instruction of the Governor.

XXXIX. All Regulations made by the Board shall be styled Regulations of the Financial Board of Tobago.

XL. All such Regulations shall be distinguished by titles, and the Regulations of each year also be distinguished by consecutive numbers, commencing in each successive year with the number one; and every such Regulation shall be divided into successive clauses or paragraphs duly numbered; and to every such clause there shall annexed in the margin a short summary of the contents.

XLI. In the making of Regulations each different matter mater shall be provided for by a different Regulation, without mixing in Regulations such things as have no proper relation to each other; an no clause shall be inserted in any Regulation which is foreign to the subject matter which the title of such Regulation imports; and no perpetual clause shall form part of a temporary Regulation.

XLII. It shall not be lawful for the Legislature of the colony to impose, increase, diminish, suspend, or abolish any tax or duty in Tobago other than Customs duties on shipping and excise duties on rum and other spirits, or to dispose of or charge any part of the revenue raised in Tobago for any other purpose than for the exclusive public service of Tobago. Save as aforesaid, the Legislature of the Colony shall have power to legislate on all matters respecting which the Board is hereby empowered to make Regulations; and any Regulation of the Board which shall in any respect be repugnant to the provisions of any Ordinance, and shall, to the extent of such repugnancy but not otherwise, be void and of no effect.

XLIII. Subject to the provisions of Clause XXVII. of this Order, every Ordinance enacted after the appointed day by the Legislature of the Colony shall extend to Tobago, unless it is thereby expressed and declared that it shall not extend to Tobago.

XLIV. Save as herein-after provided, from and after the appointed day the Laws of Trinidad in force on that day in relation to the following subjects, that is to say,—

i. The Law of real and personal property, including the devolution of the personal property, including the administration of the real and personal property of deceased persons, but not the inheritance of real property;

ii. The Mercantile Law;

iii. The Law relating to husband and wife, marriage parent and child, and guardianship of infants;

iv. The Criminal Law;

v. The Administration of Justice, including the constitution and jurisdiction of courts of Law and criminal and civil procedure;

vi. Quarantine;

vii. Weights and Measures;

viii. Lunatics and Lunatic Asylums;

ix. Prisons;

x. Education;

xi. Currency;

xii. Postal Service;

xiii. Copyright;

xiv. Patents, trademarks, and designs;

xv. Crown Lands;

xvi. Recovery of Crown debts;

xvii. Friendly societies;

xviii. Registration of Births, Deaths, and Marriages;

xix. Registration of Deeds and Wills;

xx. Probate of Wills;

xxi. Inquisitions *post mortem* and in cases of fire;

xxii. Bankruptcy;

xxiii. Merchant Shipping including wrecks and shipping casualties;

xxiv. Duties on Shipping;

xxv. Customs and Customs Duties other than Export duties;

xxvi. Excise duties on Rum and other Spirits;

xxvii. Shall be in force in Tobago, and the Laws theretofore in force in Tobago in relation to the same subjects shall thereupon cease to be in force. Provided that this Clause shall not affect the validity invalidity or effect of anything done or suffered before he appointed day, or any right, obligation or liability acquired or incurred before the appointed day; Provided also, that where by any law. Of Trinidad to which this clause applies it is provided that any act, duty, or thing shall be performed or done, and whether or not at or within the specified time or at any specified place by any officer or person in the public service in Trinidad, the Governor may from time to time, if he shall think fit so to do, by proclamation, declare by what officer or person and at or within what time and at what place any such act, duty or thing shall be performed or done in Tobago, and every such declaration shall have the same legal force and effect as if it had been contained in the law to which it applies

XLV. The revenue, expenditure and debt of the Island of Tobago shall be kept distinct from the revenue, expenditure and debt of the Island of Trinidad and its Dependencies.

XLVI. For the purposes of Customs Laws, all trade between Trinidad and Tobago shall deemed to be coastal trade, and all vessels while employed therein shall be deemed coasting vessels.

XLVII. For the purposes of Customs and Excise Laws, the transfer of any article from Trinidad to Tobago or from Tobago to Trinidad shall not be deemed to be exportation.

XLVIII. No customs duties shall be levied in Trinidad on articles imported from Tobago, and no customs duties shall be levied in Tobago on articles imported from Trinidad.

XLIX. All customs duties levied in Trinidad on articles imported into Trinidad and transferred thence to

Tobago for consumption in Tobago shall be deemed to be part of the revenue of Tobago, and all customs duties levied in Tobago on articles imported into Tobago and transferred to Trinidad for consumption in Trinidad shall be deemed to be part of the revenue of Trinidad.

L.   All excise duties on rum and other spirits manufactured in Trinidad and transferred to Tobago for consumption in Tobago shall be deemed to be part of the revenue of Tobago and all excise duties on rum and other spirits manufactured in Tobago and transferred to Trinidad for consumption in Trinidad shall be deemed to be part of the revenue of Trinidad.

LI.   The Governor may make such Rules as he may think necessary for carrying into effect the provision of Clauses, XXIX, XXX, XXXI, XXXII, and XXXIII of this Order. All such rules may be disallowed by Her Majesty through the Secretary of State, and may be repealed by any Ordinance of the Legislature of the Colony. Every such rule, until it is disallowed or repealed shall have the force of law.

LII.   From and after the appointed day the Supreme Court of Trinidad shall be styled the Supreme Court of Trinidad and Tobago.

LIII.   Sittings of the Supreme Court for the trial of criminal and civil cases and for hearing appeals from the decisions of Magistrates, shall be held in Tobago at least three times in every year, at such times and place as shall be appointed by Rules of the said Court made in pursuance of the Trinidad Judicature Ordinance of 1879, or if and whenever there shall be no such Rules of Court appointing the times and place of such sittings, then, as shall be appointed by the Governor; such sittings shall be held by a single Judge, who shall, for the purposes of the trials and appeals to be held thereat, have and exercise all the powers and authorities of the said Court. Provided that, except in the cases of appeals from the decisions of Magistrates, there shall be a right of appeal from the decisions and judgments of such single Judge sitting as aforesaid to the Full Court sitting in Trinidad, such appeals to be made, heard, and determined in the same manner as appeals from decisions and judgments of a single Judge sitting in Trinidad to the Full Court.

LIV. The Governor may from time to time appoint a fit and proper person to be a Commissioner of the Supreme Court in Tobago, and may revoke any such appointment. Every such Commissioner shall, whenever there shall be no Judge of the Supreme Court present in Tobago, have such of the powers and perform such of the duties of a Judge of the Supreme court as shall be prescribed by the rules of the said Court.

LV. Rules of the Supreme Court may be made, altered, and annulled from time to time in the manner prescribed in the Trinidad Judicature Ordinance, 1879, with the approval of the Governor and the Legislative council of the colony, subject to disallowance by Her Majesty, for regulating the practice and procedure in the Supreme Court in Tobago, and prescribing the times and place of sittings of the said Court in Tobago, and defining and prescribing the powers and duties of the Commissioners of the said court and of the Sub-Registrar and other officers of the said Court in Tobago.

LVI. There shall be a Sub-Registrar of the Supreme court in Tobago, who shall have such powers and perform such duties as prescribed by the Rules of the said Court, and subject to such Rules shall have such powers and perform such duties with respect to proceedings in the said Court in Tobago as the Registrar of the said court has and performs in respect of proceedings in the said court in Trinidad The said Sub-Registrar shall be appointed in the same manner, and shall hold his office, during Her Majesty's pleasure, on the same conditions as the Registrar of the said Court, and shall receive such salary as the governor, with the sanction of the Board shall appoint.

LVII. The Supreme Court shall have and use, as occasion requires, a Seal for writs and processes issued in Tobago. Until such seal has been provided the seal heretofore used as the seal of the Supreme Court of Tobago may be used for such writs and processes as aforesaid, and shall be taken to be the seal of the Supreme Court . . . The Sub-Registrar of the said Court in Tobago shall have the custody of the said seals.

LVIII. Whenever a Judge of the Supreme Court visits Tobago for the purpose of holding session of the said Court, and whenever any public officer who is in receipt of salary from the public revenue of Trinidad visits Tobago by order of the Governor for the purpose of performing any service for Tobago, the amount of the salary of each Judge or public officer during the period of his visit, including the voyages, shall be re-imbursed to the Treasury of Trinidad out of the revenue of Tobago, and the cost of his passages and such reasonable allowance for Board and lodging in Tobago as the Governor shall determine, shall be paid to such Judge or officer out of the revenue of Tobago.

LIX. The person or persons who shall on the appointed day hold the office of Police Magistrate in Tobago shall from that day deemed to have been appointed a Stipendiary Justice or Stipendiary Justices under the law of Trinidad, and shall have, exercise, and discharge, within the district or districts for which he or they shall have been appointed a Police Magistrate or Police Magistrates, all the powers and duties of a Stipendiary Justice under the law of Trinidad

LX. It shall be lawful for the Governor, with the approval of the Secretary of State, to grant to any person holding a permanent public office in Tobago on the appointed day, whose office shall be abolished or cease to exist by virtue of this Order, and to whom an appointment of to a public office of equivalent emoluments in Tobago or in some other part of Her majesty's dominions shall not be offered, an annual allowance by way of compensation, to be charged upon and payable out of the revenue of Tobago, of not greater amount than, and to be held subject to the same conditions as, such allowance as might have been granted to such officer if this Order had not been made and his office had been abolished.

LXI.   In this Order the expression "Governor" means the Governor or officer for the time being administering the Government of the Colony of Trinidad and Tobago. The expression "the Secretary of State" means one of Her Majesty's Principal Secretaries of State. The expression "the Board" means the Financial Board of Tobago. The expression "the Colony" means the Colony of Trinidad and Tobago. The expression "the Supreme Court" means the Supreme Court of Trinidad and Tobago.

LXII.   And one of Her Majesty's Principal Secretaries of State is to give the necessary directions herein accordingly.

The Legal Status of Tobago Before 1763

THE LEGAL STATUS OF Tobago for much of the period before 1763 remains uncertain. The uncertainty stems from historical commentaries that to an extent indicate that Tobago was considered a neutral island by the European powers. There appears to be two distinct ideas about the neutrality of Tobago before 1763: one advocated by Douglas Archibald,[207] that the neutrality stems from uncertainty as to whether the island belonged to Britain or to France, and the second on the lore or tradition that there was an agreement made in the colonies by representatives of the imperial powers to reserve a number of islands, including Tobago, for sanctuary of the Amerindians. These were known as neutral islands. The first idea is less credible, as the treaties between the rival countries would have recorded the status of the island in one of two ways: firstly, by cession from one state to the other or maintaining the status quo at the end of the hostilities (*status quo post bellum*), and secondly, by maintaining the status quo before the start of hostilities (*status quo ante bellum*).

THE EARLY FRAMEWORK

If we go back to 1498, it is clear that Spain of all the European countries had the best title to ownership of the island. This claim was well founded on the Papal Donation and on earlier treaties between

---

[207] Douglas Archibald, Rupert, *Tobago: Melancholy Isle, Vol. I, 1498-1771,* Port-of-Spain, Trinidad: Westindiana, 1987, p. 64 ff.

Spain and Portugal. Even if the authority of the pope in this matter is ignored, both England and Spain had accepted the principle in Roman law of *res nullius*,[208] whereby unoccupied land remained the common property of mankind, until put to use.[209] A cognate concept was also contained in the *Siete Partidas*:

> *"It rarely happens that new islands arise out of the sea.*
> *But if this should happen and some new island appears,*
> *we say it should belong to him who first settles it."*[210]

It is also apparent that before 1598, the Spaniards made no serious attempt to settle the island. On the reasons for this, we may speculate. But we must rule out the hostility of the Amerindians. From as early as 1511, the Spanish authorities were aware of the hostile nature of the Caribs in Tobago. In that year, Ferdinand V, king of Spain, issued a Cedula permitting persons to wage war on the Caribs of Tobago, to enslave them, and to sell them. The hostility did not prevent colonisation of other Amerindians far better organised and with far more resources. We must look, therefore, for other reasons why the island was not colonised despite the claim held on the island. Looking at Trinidad, which was claimed by Spain at the same time that it claimed Tobago in 1498, we note that this island was not settled until 1530. Spanish efforts in this region were devoted to seeking out El Dorado, the legendary city of gold. And the Amerindians of Trinidad, like those of Tobago, were viewed as a source of labour. Even after Trinidad was settled, the attacks by the Caribs of Tobago continued, and in 1596 consideration was given to colonisation of Tobago as a means of abating the attacks on Trinidad after complaints by the governor of Trinidad, Don Antonio de Berrio.

---

[208] The *res nullius* was a division of the *res extra nostrum patriae* of the Justinian Code (i.e., of things not owned privately).
[209] Eliot, J. H., *Empires of the Atlantic World*, New Haven, Conn: Yale University Press, 2000, p. 30.
[210] Ibid.

CHANGING OF THE RULES

The rules of the game changed radically in the middle of the sixteenth century. Jealous of the Spanish discoveries, in 1496 England wooed Columbus. The Catholic Kings warned that the undertaking of such an exercise by England would be prejudicial to both Spain and Portugal. England refused to heed the warning and in 1497 issued Letters Patent to Cabot. When England and France set out on their adventures in the New World the instructions to their navigators was to avoid lands occupied by a Christian prince. The monopoly was first violated in 1528 when an English ship anchored in the harbour in Santo Domingo with impunity. According to one historian, the English and French were forced to resort to armed aggression because of the monopolies claimed by the Iberian monarchies:

> *"The imperial monopolies claimed by the Iberian monarchies forced those who followed in their footsteps to adopt armed and aggressive methods, encouraging the growth of English and French piracy and privateering in Europe and across the Atlantic. Though unwilling to launch a direct challenge to Spain or Portugal, the English crown was prepared to sanction much of this activity for financial and strategic considerations."[211]*

Despite the early violation of Spanish sovereignty the British as late as 1584 deference was given to those lands occupied by Christian princes.

> *"Know ye that of our special grace, certain science and mere motion, we have given and granted, and by these presents for us, our heirs and successors, do give and grant to our trusty and well-beloved servant Sir Humphrey*

---

[211] Appleby, John C., *War, Politics and Colonization, 1558-1625* in Canny, Nicholas (Ed.), *The Oxford History of the British Empire Vol. I, (Oxford: Oxford* University Press, 1998, p. 56. This is a remarkable piece of historiography that justifies piracy and privateering as foundation stones of the British Empire.

> *Gilbert of Compton in our county of Devonshire knight,*
> *and to his heirs and assigns forever, free liberty and*
> *licence from time to time for ever hereafter, to discover,*
> *find, search out, and view such remote, heathen and*
> *barbarous lands, countries and territories not actually*
> *possessed of the Christian prince or people as to him,*
> *his heirs & assigns, and to every and any of them, shall*
> *seem good.*"[212]

Likewise despite the violation of Spain's sovereignty by French ships at Santo Domingo by the start of the seventeenth century, Cardinal Richelieu in the commission granted to Sieur d' Esnambuc in 1626 stipulated that such countries he claimed

> "*. . . do not belong to any Christian King or Prince.*"[213]

The plundering of the Spanish galleons was a consequence of their claimed monopoly. But when the conflict with Spain had escalated to war, this practice had grown into a maritime tradition:

> *"Although the war encouraged the idea of a militant*
> *Protestant imperialism that drew on widespread*
> *anti-Catholicism, it was tempered by a longstanding*
> *tradition of maritime war and plunder which favoured*
> *privateering at the expense of colonization."*[214]

Such militancy, alluded to by Appleby, was notably absent from the Letters Patent Queen Elizabeth of England issued Sir Humphrey Gilbert in 1584.

---

[212] From *Letters Patent of Elizabeth, Queen of England, to Sir Humphrey Gilbert,* cited in Williams, Dr. E. E., *Documents of West Indian History, Vol. I,* New York, NY: A & B Publishing, 1994, p. 209.

[213] Williams, Dr. E. E., *Documents of West Indian History, Vol. I,* New York, NY: A & B Publishing, 1994, p. 254.

[214] Appleby, John C., *War, Politics and Colonization, 1558-1625* in Canny, Nicholas (Ed.), *The Oxford History of the British Empire Vol. I,* p. 56.

PIRACY

As we have seen, the Treaty of Cateau-Cambrésis, signed by France and England on 2 April 1559 and by France and Spain on 3 April 1559, virtually legitimised piracy in the Caribbean. Thereafter, European countries jealous of Spain issued *letters of marque and reprisal*—a practice originating in the fourteenth century—that authorised their agents, known as privateers or sea dogs, to harass and pillage the Spaniards in the Caribbean. Thus the attack on the Spanish monopoly in the Americas began with individual rogues preying on the Spanish galleons and raiding the islands. These pirates settled in the Caribbean, where they were known as buccaneers. The metropolitan countries later denounced the Papal Donation, transformed the private attacks of the buccaneers into imperial policy, and fought formal wars. From that time onwards, Spanish possessions in the Caribbean were ceded to other European countries by treaty.

Nevertheless, after a century of lawlessness in the Caribbean, the Treaty of Ratisbon of 1684 put an end to the buccaneers, and possession of the islands would change only by warfare and treaty. The Treaty of Ratisbon of August 1684 was signed by Louis XIV of France and Holy Roman Emperor Leopold I on one part and on the other by King Carlos II of Spain. The treaty did not bring peace but was a truce for twenty years. It did stop the hostilities in the West Indies as well as in Europe. In addition it outlawed buccaneerism, treating the perpetrators as felons to be executed if found guilty. Britain, although not a party to the treaty, like the contracting countries stopped issuing letters of marque and reprisal. The period of relative calm that followed the Treaty of Ratisbon probably explains why Tobago was considered a neutral island from that date.

The Treaty of Munster in 1648 signalled the end of the Papal Donation.

Appendix II

THE CLAIMS

THE BRITISH CLAIM

In 1562, the English formally denounced the Papal Donation. Between 1595 and 1628, several English explorers visited Tobago, giving rise to the British claim. It was thought that Sir Thomas Warner claimed the island on a journey that took him to the Guianas late in the sixteenth century; Dudley (in 1595), Keymis (in 1596), and Robert Goddard (in 1626) all landed in Tobago. In 1628, Charles I of England issued Letters Patent to the Earl of Montgomery (later the Earl of Pembroke) for a number of unoccupied islands in the Caribbean, including Tobago. In 1639, the Letters Patent were acquired by the Earl of Warwick. He appointed Captain Robert Marsham as lieutenant governor, and the latter landed in Tobago on 9 October 1639. They were soon under attack from the Caribs and by August 1640 had abandoned the enterprise. In 1642, the Earl of Warwick in a second attempt to colonise the island sent Captain Marshall of Barbados, who experienced ceaseless attacks from the Caribs and abandoned the island a year later. In 1666, the English, led by Lord Willoughby, took possession of the island after expelling a group of Jamaican buccaneers, who had occupied the island after driving out the Dutch in 1665 and destroying the Dutch fort. Later that same year, the garrison defending the island was captured by the French, led by Le Sieur Vincent, and removed from the island. Early in 1672, England declared war on the Netherlands, and in December an expedition led by Sir Thomas Bridges accepted the surrender of Pieter Constant, the Dutch governor.

The Anglo/Dutch war ended in February 1674 when Charles II of England signed the Treaty of Westminster, which was ratified in March by the Netherlands, and Tobago was returned to the status quo ante bellum. Although several British historians and colonial administrators claimed the island before 1748, there appears to have been no claim by the British government. Certainly there were internal claims in the Privy Council and opinions sought but no formal claim was ever made.

THE DUTCH CLAIM

In 1627, the Dutch West India Company granted an exclusive franchise to Jan de Moor to settle the island. He landed in Tobago in 1628. However, that same year the Dutch were driven off the island by Don Luis de Monsalves, governor of Trinidad, indicating that Spain maintained its claim to the island. The Dutch, led again by Jan de Moor, made another attempt to settle the island in 1632. Four years later, they were driven off by the Spanish governor of Trinidad, Don Diego Lopez de Escobar.

In 1662, Louis XIV, king of France, granted Letters Patent to Adriaen and Cornelis Lampsius of the Netherlands. The Dutch were subdued by Jamaican buccaneers in 1665; however, after the Treaty of Breda was signed in 1667 by England, France, the Netherlands, and Denmark, the Dutch reoccupied Tobago. In December of 1672 the Dutch surrendered Tobago to an invading English expedition but reclaimed the island and rebuilt its fort after the Treaty of Westminster of March 1674.

In 1678, the Dutch ceded Tobago to France at the Treaty of Nijmegen.

THE COURLANDERS CLAIM

Early in 1639, adventurers from the Baltic state of Courland landed on the leeward side of the island. They attempted to settle the island but succumbed to illness contracted on the island during the same year. In 1642, Duke Jacobus of Courland acquired the Letters Patent of the Earl of Warwick as a means of strengthening his claim, and a second expedition followed that same year, led by Cornelius Caroon; Caroon returned to the original site but abandoned it in 1650 when the number of men was drastically reduced.

In 1658, the Courlanders lost possession to the Swedes, who captured the Duke of Courland.

In 1664, after the Treaty of Oliva, the Courlanders were granted Tobago by Charles I of England.

311

THE SWEDISH CLAIM

Under Charles X, Sweden sought to extend its gains from the Treaty of Munster by invading the Grand Duchy of Livonia and capturing Duke Jacobus of Courland in 1658. Possession of Tobago and a trading post in Gambia that belonged to the adventurous Courlanders passed to the Swedes. At the Treaty of Oliva in 1660, Courland was returned to its status ante bellum, and the duke regained his claim on Tobago.

THE FRENCH CLAIM

The French adventure began when Cardinal Richelieu created the French West India Company in 1664. In 1677, the French on a second attempt captured Tobago. By the Treaty of Nijmegen in 1678, the Dutch ceded Tobago to France.

For reasons which we can only guess, the French abandoned the island and merely paid visits twice a year to ensure that certain conditions prevailed. This could be attributed to the existence of an agreement, known to the French authorities, to keep Tobago as a neutral island.

The treaties on which the claims are based are included in Appendix III.

THE TREATY OF AIX-LA-CHAPELLE[215]

Aix-la-Chapelle, now Aachen in Germany, was the historic site of two treaties. The first, in 1668, ended the War of Devolution, and the second, in 1748, ended the War of Jenkins' Ear, fought in the West Indies, and the War of Austrian Succession, fought in Europe. The second treaty is extremely important, as it consolidates the agreements of earlier treaties.

---

[215] Douglas, David C. (General Editor), Horn, D. B., and Ransome, Mary (Eds.), *English Historical Documents Vol. X*, London: Eyre & Spottiswode, 1969, p. 922.

"[It] serve[s] as a basis as foundation of the general peace, and to the present treaty; and, for this purpose, they are renewed and confirmed in the best form, and as if they were herein inserted, word for word; so that they shall be punctually observed for the future in all their tenor, and regularly executed on the one side and the other; such points however, as have been derogated from in the present treaty, excepted."

THE INTERCOLONIAL AGREEMENT

The notion of neutral islands reserved for the Amerindians seems to have originated in St. Kitts and is supported by several historians, including Carl and Roberta Bridenbaugh, Burns, Coke, Crouse, Douglas Archibald, Ottley, and Woodcock.

In 1626 under the leadership of Sir Thomas Warner St. Kitts became the first British West Indian colony. The island was occupied briefly in 1528 by Huguenots from France but their stay was swiftly curtailed by the Spaniards based on Columbus' claim of 1493. Not long after the arrival of the British explorers Sieur Belain d'Esnambuc of France landed on the island. Recognising the Spaniards and the hostile Caribs as their common adversaries, Warner and d'Esnambuc came to an understanding about sharing the island and treating with the natives. According to Carl and Roberta Bridenbaugh:[216]

"The treaty between Sir Thomas Warner and Sieur d'Esnambuc, concluded first in 1627 and renewed several times down to 1666, rested on the assumption that the French and English had come out to the Caribbean as allies against the Spanish and the Caribs rather than as members of enemy nations. . . . In 1668 an accord was actually reached with Governor de Blenne (while Sir

---

[216] Bridenbaugh, Carl, and Bridenbaugh, Roberta, *No Peace Beyond the Line: The English in the Caribbean 1824-1890*, Oxford: Oxford University Press, 1972, p, 67.

> *William Stapleton energetically attempted to arrange*
> *a general treaty of neutrality between the two nations*
> *in the West Indies) for 'peace, union, concord, good*
> *correspondence, amity and neutrality'. in the islands*
> *under the control of the negotiators."*

The nexus between the island of St. Kitts and the intercolonial treaty is corroborated by Sir Alan Burns:[217]

> *"De Poincy died in 1660 in St. Kitts, one of his last acts*
> *being to approve the important treaty with the Caribs,*
> *by which the islands of Dominica and St. Vincent were*
> *reserved to them on condition that they abandoned their*
> *claims to the other islands."*

Thomas Coke was by far the most chauvinist of the historians, and even he while dilating on the neutrality of Dominica, St. Vincent and St. Lucia, had little to say about the neutrality of Tobago. Of the experience of the French and English in St. Kitts he wrote:

> *"The native Indians were hostile to the Europeans and*
> *there were frequent skirmishes. It appears that after*
> *one such skirmish in which very many Amerindians*
> *were massacred, the Europeans i.e. the French and the*
> *English agreed to transport the survivors to Dominica*
> *and St. Vincent and to regard those two islands as neutral*
> *islands. The understanding was the European countries*
> *would not compete for ownership of those islands. Both*
> *England and France made pretensions on the ground*
> *of right; so that on the score of expediency rather than*
> *on that of justice both nations acceded to a neutrality of*
> *which neither secretly approved."[218]*

---

[217]   Burns, Sir Alan, *History of the British West Indies (1872)*, London: George Allen and Unwin, 1966, p. 222.
[218]   Coke, Thomas, *A History of the West Indies Vol. 2*, London: Cass Library of West Indian Studies, 1971, p. 295 ff.

The account given by Thomas Coke supports the lore of an agreement between France and England to regard Dominica and St. Vincent as neutral islands and as sanctuaries for the Amerindians

Crouse wrote:[219]

> *"Some time before King Louis signed the declaration of war (the War of Devolution 24th May 1667), Governors De Sales and Watts had met to renew the old treaty of amity between the colonists of St. Christopher that had kept the peace for forty years. (Both De Sales and Watts were out of office in 1667.) This treaty first drawn up in 1627 by the original settlers, Belain d' Esnambuc of France and Sir Thomas Warner of England, provided for a division of the island and obligations which each had toward the other, and, most important of all in the present crisis, embodied an article guaranteeing that in the case of a war between the two governments the colonists would not attack each other unless specifically ordered to do so by their sovereigns, and then the attacking party would give notice of his intentions to begin hostilities. As it had been the custom to renew this treaty upon the accession of a new Governor or upon change of ownership, it was deemed appropriate to make another renewal now that the West India Company had taken over the island (Nevis, Antigua, Montserrat, St. Christopher, and Barbuda). A new treaty was actually drawn up, by which among other things, the attacking party was required to give seventy-two hours' notice. It was signed by the governors on January 24, 1686 and ratified in behalf of the Company by M. de Chambre on the same day."*

---

[219] Crouse, Nellis, *French Struggle for the West Indies (1665-1713)*, London: Frank Cass, 1966, p.17.

Douglas Archibald[220] devoted a full chapter to the issue of neutrality of Tobago. He was, however, vague about the origin of the agreement between France and England as regards the neutrality of the island. He thought that it was expedient for both to forgo development of the island since it had a relatively small population and the facilities on the other sugar producing colonies were far better suited for those purposes. Despite quoting several French sources that based the claim on the Treaty of Nijmegen, he was of the opinion that there was a dispute between Britain and France over the ownership of the island during the seventeenth century.

In his *History of Tobago,* Isles Woodcock, a former chief justice of Tobago, makes reference to the agreement to give asylum to the Amerindians and to the agreement of neutrality:[221]

> *"It will be remembered that in 1660 the French and English had assigned to the unfortunate Charaibs who had survived their slaughtered countrymen the islands of Dominica and St. Vincent as places of refuge and these islands were, as between the contracting parties, to be neutral ground. Afterwards St. Lucia was also declared a neutral isle, and at the Treaty of Aix-la-Chapelle, in 1684* [sic; probably the Treaty of Ratisbon], *Tobago was added to the list."*

CONCLUSION

From the discovery of the island by Columbus in 1498, Tobago was claimed by Spain, who did not colonise the island but was content to let the Amerindians live there. Nevertheless, between 1498 and 1648, the island was claimed by various European countries that included England, France, the States General of the United Provinces, Sweden, and Courland, and occupied by adventurers from Jamaica

---

[220] Douglas Archibald, Rupert, *Tobago: Melancholy Isle, Vol. I, 1498-1771,* Port-of-Spain, Trinidad: Westindiana, 1987, p. 64 ff.

[221] Woodcock, Henry Isles, *History of Tobago,* London: Cass Library of West Indian Studies, 1971, p. 31.

and Barbados. There were two means by which the claims were made: firstly on the basis of Letters Patent issued by the sovereign of the country that made the discovery, and secondly on the basis of occupancy and colonisation. However, after 1648, when the Papal Donation was formally denounced, possession passed legally to France and the States General of the United Provinces, as is evident from the treaties.

In the meantime, there was a less formal agreement between France and England in the West Indies that made provision for asylum for the surviving Amerindians in Dominica, St. Vincent. After the Treaty of Ratisbon in 1684, which ended piracy in the Caribbean, the French, who then had legal possession of the island and were aware of the hostility of the Amerindians to Europeans in Tobago abandoned the island and paid twice yearly visits to ensure that their rights were preserved. Any claims of possession or of neutrality before 1678 were superseded by the Treaty of Nijmegen, and this was confirmed by the Treaty of Aix-la-Chapelle in 1748. That England had no valid claim was acknowledged in 1721 by the Council of Trade and Plantations in response to an inquiry from Barbados.[222] Thus possession of Tobago remained with France from 1678 and ended after the Seven Years War, when the island was ceded to Britain.

While the treaties tell us much about the positions of the European countries, they tell us little about the status of the Amerindians and the putative neutrality of Tobago. Indeed, the intercolonial agreement at the onset was concerned with St. Vincent and Dominica alone and it remains unclear at what epoch or if ever Tobago was added to the list of neutral islands as places of asylum for the Amerindians. The notion that the island was considered neutral comes from the records that show that France with possession of the island from 1678 to 1763 did nothing to colonise the island; was prepared to defend it against all comers and from their base in Martinique and paid periodic visits to ensure that their rights and the neutrality of the island were not violated.

---

[222] Douglas Archibald, Rupert, *Tobago: Melancholy Isle, Vol. I, 1498-1771,* Port-of-Spain, Trinidad: Westindiana, 1987, p. 76 ff.

Appendix III

Lists of Treaties and Statutes

List of Treaties

Treaty of Medina del Campo of 1431
Treaty of Alcáçovas of 1479
Treaty of Tordesillas of 1494
Treaty of Cateau-Cambrésis of 1559
Treaty of Munster (Westphalia) of 1648
Treaty of Oliva of 1660
Treaty of Breda of 1667
The Treaties of Madrid between England and Spain between 1667
    and 1670
Treaty of Westminster of 1674
Treaty of Nijmegen of 1678, 1679
Treaty of Ratisbon (Regensburg) of 1684
Treaty of Ryswick of 1697
Treaty of Utrecht of 1713
Treaty of Baden of 1714
The Triple Alliance of the Hague of 1718
The Quadruple Alliance of London of 1718
Treaty of Vienna of 1738
Treaty of Aix-la-Chapelle of 1748
Treaty of Paris of 1763
Treaty of Paris of 1783
Treaty of San Ildefonso of 1796
Treaty of Amiens of 1802

Treaty of Amiens of 1804
Treaty of Paris of 1814
Congress of Vienna of 1815

LIST OF STATUTES

BRITAIN

Act of Union of 1707
Proclamation of 1763
The Stamp Act of 1765
The Townshend Duties
6 Geo. III, c. 12 (the Declaratory Act 1766)
The Mutiny Act 1797
3 and 4 Will. IV, c. 73
Imperial Act 28 Vict. 2 (the Three Chains Act)
Imperial Act 26 Vict. cap. 24
Imperial Act 50 and 51 Vict. cap 44
Imperial Act 39 and 40 Vict. cap. 47
Imperial Act 28 and 29 Vict. c. 63
Order in Council (Trinidad and Tobago) 1888
Order in Council (Trinidad and Tobago) 1898

TOBAGO[223]

Acts No.1-5 of 1769
Court Act of 1794
Court of King's Bench Act of 1829
Vagrancy Act of 1839
Three Rectories Act of 1844
Land Tax Act of 1852
Supply Act of 1852
Sanitary Regulations Act of 1853

---

[223] Most of the laws of Tobago existing in 1898 were repealed by the Order
in Council of that year and replaced by the equivalent laws prevailing in
Trinidad. The value of the list is strictly for historical purposes.

Estranged Estates Act of 1854
Act to Amend the Police Force of 1854
Estranged Estates Act of 1858
Tobago Appeal Court Act of 1858
Post Office Act of 1860
Post Office Act of 1861
Education Ordinance of 1870
Franchise Extension Act of 1871
Tobago Concurrent Endowment Act of 1873
Single Chamber Act of 1874
Constitution Act of 1876
Stamp Ordinance, No. 19 of 1879
Vaccination Ordinance of 1882
Medical Aid Ordinance of 1882
Turtle Preservation Ordinance, No. 2 of 1885
Wild Birds Protection Ordinance, No. 8 of 1885
Anglican Church, Incorporated Trustees Ordinance, No. 7 of 1887
Metairie Ordinance of 1888
License Regulation, No. 2 of 1893, as amended by the Amending
  Licenses Ordinance No. 6 of 1893
Regulation No. 5 of 1894 (amending the Three Chains Act)
Destitute Persons Relief Regulation, No. 10 of 1893
Liquor Licence Ordinance No. 2 of 1883, as amended by the
  Amending Licences Ordinances Regulation, No. 6 of 1893
Road Regulation No. 3 of 1894, as amended by the Road Amendment
  Regulation No. 6 of 1894

TRINIDAD

Cedula of Population 1783 (Madrid)
Code Noir 1789 (Madrid)
Articles of Capitulation 1797
Slave Code of 1800
Ecclesiastical Ordinance of 1844
Ordinance 11 of 1847
Ordinance 8 of 1849
Ordinance 10 of 1849
Education Ordinance of 1851

Ordinance 13 of 1852
Ordinance 19 of 1858
Ordinance 27 of 1875
Judicature Ordinance of 1879
Customs Ordinance of 1880
Ordinance 2 of 1881
Ordinance 5 of 1884

TRINIDAD AND TOBAGO

Ordinance 7 of 1889
Ordinance 6 of 1890
Ordinance 9 of 1892

SELECT BIBLIOGRAPHY

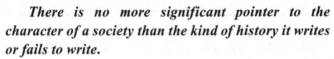

*There is no more significant pointer to the
character of a society than the kind of history it writes
or fails to write.*

E. H. Carr, *What Is History*.

Armitage, David (Ed.), *Bolingbroke: Political Writings,* Cambridge: Cambridge University Press, 1997.

Bagehot, Walter, *The British Constitution,* London: Fontana, 1968.

Bailyn, Bernard, *The Ideological Origins of the American Revolution,* Cambridge, MA: Harvard University Press, 1992.

Bailyn, Bernard (Ed.), *The Debates on the Constitution: Part II,* New York, NY: the Library of America, 1993.

Berlin, Sir Isaiah, *Against the Current—Essays in the History of Ideas,* Oxford: Oxford University Press, 1981.

Besson, Gerard, and Brereton, Bridget, *The Book of Trinidad,* Port-of-Spain, Trinidad: Paria Publishing, 1992.

Binder, Leonard et al., *Studies in Political Development 7: Crises and Sequences in Political Development,* Princeton, NJ: Princeton University Press, 1971.

Borde, Pierre-Gustave-Louis, *The History of the Island of Trinidad Under the Spanish Government, First Part (1498-1622),* Port-of-Spain, Trinidad: Paria Publishing, 1982.

Borde, Pierre-Gustave-Louis, *The History of the Island of Trinidad Under the Spanish Government, Second Part (1622-1797),* Port-of-Spain, Trinidad: Paria Publishing, 1982.

Brereton, Bridget, *A History of Modern Trinidad 1783-1962*, Port-of-Spain, Trinidad: Heinemann, 1981.

Brereton, Bridget, *Law, Justice, and Empire: The Colonial Career of Sir John Gorrie, 1829-1892*, Jamaica: University of the West Indies Press, 1997.

Bridenbaugh, Carl and Roberta, *No Peace Beyond the Line—The English in the Caribbean 1624-1690*, Oxford: Oxford: Oxford University Press, 1972.

Burns, Sir Alan, *History of the British West Indies (1873)*, London: George Allen and Unwin, 1966.

Campbell, Carl, *Cedulants and Capitulants*, Port-of-Spain, Trinidad: Paria Publishing, 1992.

Canny, Nicholas, Ed., *The Oxford History of the British Empire Vol. I*, Oxford: Oxford University Press, 1997.

Chrimes, S. B., *English Constitutional History*, Oxford: Oxford University Press, 1967.

Colonial Office Paper 295/10.

Coke, Thomas *A History of the West Indies, Vol. 2*, London: Frank Cass Library of West Indian Studies, 1971.

Cooper, St. G. C., and Bacon, P. R., *The Natural Resources of Trinidad and Tobago*, London: Edward Arnold Publishers, 1981.

Craig-James, Dr Susan E., *The Changing Society of Tobago 1838-1938*, Port-of-Spain, Trinidad: Paria Publishing, 2008.

Council Papers of the Legislative Council of Trinidad 1886-1888.

Council Papers of the Legislative Council of Trinidad and Tobago 1889-1899.

Council Papers of the Legislative Council of Tobago 1886-1888.

Crouse, Nellis, M., *French Struggle for the West Indies (1665-1715)*, London: Frank Cass Library 1966.

Cudjoe, Dr Selwyn R., *Michel Maxwell Philip*, Wellesley, MA: Calaloux Publications, 1999.

Cudjoe, Dr Selwyn R., *Beyond Boundaries*, Wellesley, MA: Calaloux Publications, 2003.

Douglas, David C. (General Ed.), Horn, D. B., and Ransome, Mary (Eds.), *English Historical Documents Vol. X*, London: Eyre & Spottiswode, 1969.

Douglas Archibald, Rupert, *Tobago: Melancholy Isle, Vol. I, 1498-1771*, Port-of-Spain, Trinidad: Westindiana, 1987.

Douglas Archibald, Rupert, *Tobago: Melancholy Isle, Vol. II, 1782-1805,* Port-of-Spain, Trinidad: UWI School of Continuing Studies, 1995.

Douglas Archibald, Rupert, *Tobago: Melancholy Isle, Vol. III, 1807-1898,* Port-of-Spain, Trinidad: Westindiana, 2003.

De Verteuil, Anthony, *Martyrs and Murderers: Trinidad, 1699,* Port-of-Spain, Port-of-Spain, Trinidad: Litho Press, 1995.

Dunfermline, Lord James, *Lieut. Gen. Sir Ralph Abercrombie K. B., 1793-1801: A Memoir,* Edinburgh: Edmonston and Douglas,1861.

Dunn, Richard S., *Slaves and Sugar: The Rise of the Planter Class in the English West Indies 1624-1713,* New York, NY: W. W. Norton, 1973.

Elliott, J. H., *Empires of the Atlantic World: Britain and Spain in America 1492-1830,* New Haven, Conn: Yale University Press, 2006.

Elton, G. R., *The Practice of History,* Glasgow: Collins Fontana, 1976.

Garcia de la Torre, Francisco (Ed., & Translator), *Spanish Trinidad, by Francisco Morales Padrón,* Ian Randle Publishers, Kingston, Jamaica, 2012

Hicks, Sir John, *A Theory of Economic History,* Oxford: Oxford University Press, 1982.

Hoetink, H., *Caribbean Race Relations,* Oxford: Oxford University Press, 1967.

John, A. Meredith, *The Plantation Slaves of Trinidad, 1783-1816,* Cambridge: Cambridge University Press, 1988.

Joseph, E. L., *History of Trinidad, (1838),* Frank Cass Library of West Indian Studies, 1970.

Jowett, B. *Plato's Republic* (translation), New York, NY: Vintage Books/ Random House, 1955.

Kingsley, Charles, *At Last: A Christmas in the West Indies,(1889),* Memphis, Tenn: General Books, LLC, 2009.

Kiralfy, A. K. R., *Potter's Historical Introduction to English Law,* London: Sweet and Maxwell, 1970.

Lienhardt, Godfrey, *Social Anthropology,* Oxford: Oxford University Press, 1966.

Lewis, Gordon K., *The Growth of the Modern West Indies,* New York, NY: The Monthly Review Press, 1968.

Maitland, F. W., *The Constitutional History of England* (1908), Cambridge University Press, 1974.

Marshall, P. J. (Ed.), *The Oxford History of the British Empire Vol. II: The Eighteenth Century,* Oxford: Oxford University Press, 1998.

Millette, James, *Society and Politics in Colonial Trinidad*, Port-of-Spain, Trinidad: Omega Bookshops Ltd., 1985.

Minutes of the Proceedings of the Financial Board of Tobago, 1889-1899

Montesquieu, Charles de Secondat, Baron de, *The Spirit of Laws, (trans.)* Amherst, NY: Prometheus Books, 2002.

Naipaul, V. S., *A Writer's People*, London: Picador, 2007.

Osterhammel, Jurgen, *Colonialism*, Princeton, NJ: Markus Wiener Publishers, 1995.

Ottley, C. R., *The Story of Tobago*, Port-of-Spain, Trinidad: Longmans Caribbean, 1973.

Palmer, Colin A., *Eric Williams & The Making of the Modern Caribbean*, Jamaica: Ian Rundle Publishers, 2006.

Philippe, Jean Baptiste, Dr, *A Free Mulatto (1824)*, Wellesley, MA: Calaloux Publications, 1996.

Porter, Andrew (Ed.), *The Oxford History of the British Empire Vol. III: The Nineteenth Century*, Oxford University Press, 1999.

Premdas, Ralph, R., *Secession and Self-Determination in the Caribbean: Nevis and Tobago*, Port-of-Spain, Trinidad: UWI School of Continuing Studies, 1998.

Report of the Royal Commission to consider and report as to the proposed Franchise and Division of the Colony into Electoral Districts, Trinidad, 1889.

Robinson, A. N. R, *The Mechanics of Independence*, Cambridge, MA: MIT Press, 1971.

Rossiter, Charles, (Ed.), *The Federalist Papers*, Signet Classic, 2003.

Rostow, W. W., *Politics and the Stages of Growth*, Cambridge University Press, 1971.

Sander, Reinhard W. (Ed.), *From Trinidad—An Anthology of Early West Indian Writing*, London: Hodder and Stoughton, 1978.

Sommervell, D. C., *An Abridgement of A Study of History Vols. I-VI, by Arnold Toynbee*, Oxford: Oxford University Press, 1987.

Stephen, James, Dr, *The Slavery of the British West India Colonies Delineated, Vols. I and II*, Cambridge: Cambridge University Press, 2010.

Sutton, Dr Paul K., Compiler, *Forged From the Love of Liberty: Selected Speeches of Dr Eric Williams*, Port-of-Spain, Trinidad: Longmans Caribbean, 1981.

The Tobago Gazette, 1886-1899.

Thomas, John Jacob, *Froudacity (1889)*, London: New Beacon, 1969.

Wheare, K. C., *Legislatures*, Oxford: Oxford University Press, 1968.

Wheare, K. C., *Modern Constitutions*, Oxford: Oxford University Press, 1968.

Williams, Dr E. E., *Capitalism and Slavery*, London: Andre Deutsch, 1987.

Williams, Dr E. E., *Documents of West Indian History, Vol. I*, New York, NY: A & B Publishing, 1994.

Williams, Dr E. E., *Britain and the West Indies, (University of Essex Noel Buxton Lecture, 1969)*, London: Longmans, 1969.

Williams, Dr E. E., *History of the People of Trinidad and Tobago*, New York, NY: A & B Publishing, 1993.

Wolf-Phillips, Leslie, *Comparative Constitutions*, London: Macmillan, 1972.

Wood, Donald, *Trinidad in Transition: The Years after Slavery*, Oxford: Oxford University Press, 1986.

Woodcock, Henry Isles, *A History of Tobago*, London: Frank Cass Library of West Indian Studies, 1971.

Index of Names

Cuyler, Maj. Gen. Cornelius · 35,
56

D

d'Esnambuc, Le Sieur · xxxi, 313
Darwin, Sir Charles · 117
de Boissiere, Dr · 83, 202
de Ridder, Rev. Francis · 147
de Verteuil, Dr L. A. A · xx-xxii,
xxvii, 83, 142, 146, 337
Defoe, Daniel · xvii, 151, 232, 252
Dessources, Georges Numa · 147
Dillon, Comte Arthur · 7
Douglas Archibald, Rupert
(historian) · xxvii, 7-9, 15-16,
22, 42, 47, 50-1, 58, 62-3,
191-2, 233-4, 247, 305, 316-17,
336-7
Drysdale, James V. · 70, 207

E

Elizabeth I, Queen of England ·
308
Elliott, J. H. · 140, 337
Escobar, Don Diego Lopez de · 62,
311
Esnambuc, Sieur d' · 308
Estrées, Jean, le 2e Comte d', · 235

F

Falquez, Don Manuel · 63
Fenwick, G. T. · 83-4, 87, 154-5,
159, 167-8, 194, 202, 256
Ferdinand II, King of Spain · 9
Ferdinand V, King of Aragon · 1,
306

Finlayson, Mr · 83
Fitt, Mr · 83
Fonseca, Bishop · 141
Fourier · 201
Fowler, Henry · 127
Froude, James Anthony · 78, 117

G

Galton, Sir Francis · 116
Garcia, Mr · 83
Gatty, Stephen H. · xxi
George III, King of Great Britain
and Ireland · 12, 15, 30, 34,
103, 212, 253
Gilbert, Sir Humphrey · 308
Glanville, Lord · xxvii, 19, 112,
124, 202, 239, 245, 267, 274
Goderich, Lord · 200
Gordon, Sir Arthur Hamilton · 77,
123, 278
Gordon-Gordon, William · xvi,
xxviii, 161, 164
Gore, Augustus Frederick · xv
Gorrie, Sir John · xxviii, 49, 137,
155-7, 168, 172, 201, 243, 336
Grey, Sir Charles · 26
Grey, Sir Edward · 173
Guiseppi, Mr · 83

H

Hamilton, John · 58
Hamilton, Mr · 127, 136
Harris, Lord · 102, 134, 139, 149
Hay, Loraine G. · 132, 154
Henderson, Ebenezer · 76-7
Henry the Navigator · 2
Henry VII, King of England · 5

Herbert, William · 147
Hewins, W.A.S. · 278
Hinde, Thomas · 147
Holland, Sir Henry T. · See Also Knutsford
Horsford, David H. · 160

I

Irving, Sir Henry Turner · 65
Isaac, J. B. · 163, 165
Isabella I, Queen of Castile · 1

J

James I, King of Great Britain · 250
James, C. L. R. · 146, 199
Jefferson, Thomas · xiii
Jerningham, Sir Hubert E. H. · xxviii, 176, 191, 241, 256
Jobity, Henry · 147
John II, King of Portugal · 1

K

Keenan, Patrick · xix-xx
Keens, Edward · 76
Kingsley, Charles · 149
Knollys, C. C. · 173
Knutsford, Lord · 88, 99, 124, 148, 157, 223, 227, 242

L

Lampsius, the brothers Adriaen and Cornelis · 311
Las Casas, Bartholomé de · 122
Leon, Ponce de · 29
Leotaud, Dr Antoine · 146

Leverton, , Rev. Nicholas · 10
Lewis, Gordon K. · 258
Llewelyn, Robert W. · 23
Louis XIV, King of France · 11, 309, 311
Low, William · 176
Lushington, Dr · 139

M

Macaulay, Zachary · 217
Macdougall, E · 171
Madison, James · 96
Maersz, Jacob · 9
Maitland, F. W. · 104, 136, 337
Mansfield, Lord · 92-4, 113, 225, 285
Mao Zedong · 210
Marsham, Capt. Robert · 10, 310
Marx · 201
Mason, George · 96
Matthews, Mickey · xxix
Maxwell Philip, Michel · xxx, 87, 146, 199, 283, 336
McCarthy, Robert H. · 177
McEarchrane, George H. · 154, 165
McGillavary, D. · 165
Melville, Gen. Robert · 15, 34, 36, 212
Merivale, Herman · 272
Mico, Lady Jane · 92
Millette, Dr James (Historian) · xxvii
Monsalves, Don Luis de · 62, 311
Montesquieu, Charles de Secondat, Baron de · 338
Montgomery, 2nd Earl of · 10, 310
Moor, Jan de · 9-10, 62, 311
More, Sir Thomas · 209

T

Todd, Rev. H. A. · 166
Toynbee, Arnold · 338
Turpin, Rev. Canon E. A. · 166

U

Ussher, H. T. · xv, 19, 120, 123, 204

V

Victoria, Queen of Great Britain
  and Ireland · 112, 131, 134,
  238, 294
Vincent, Le Sieur · 11, 310

W

Warner, Charles · 143
Warner, R. S. A. · 157
Warner, Sir Thomas · xxx, 310,
  313, 315
Warwick, Robert Rich, 2nd Earl of
  · 10, 310-11
Wheare, K. C. · 219, 249, 338
Wilberforce, William · 26, 94, 200,
  217
William III, King of Great Britain
  · 111
Williams, Dr E. E. · xxvii, xxviii,
  31, 206
Willoughby, Lord · 310
Wolf-Phillips, Leslie · 164, 235
Wood, Donald (Historian) · 98,
  112, 115, 204, 235
Woodcock, Henry Isles · 39, 208
Woodford, Sir Ralph James · viii,
  57, 111, 114, 116

Y

Yeates, Henry · 54, 69

Index of Subjects

Printed in the United States
By Bookmasters